Add your opinion to our next book

Fill out a survey

visit www.lilaguide.com

the lilaguide
by PARENTS *for* PARENTS

baby gear guide

NEW PARENT'S GUIDE TO EVERYTHING FROM STROLLERS & CAR SEATS TO TOYS & CLOTHES...

2ND EDITION

PUBLISHED BY THE LILAGUIDE/OAM SOLUTIONS, INC.
SAN FRANCISCO, CA   WWW.LILAGUIDE.COM

Published by:
OAM Solutions, Inc.
139 Saturn Street
San Francisco, CA 94114, USA
415.252.1300
orders@lilaguide.com
www.lilaguide.com

ISBN. 1-932847-34-0
First Printing: 2005
Printed in the USA
Copyright © 2005 by OAM Solutions, Inc.

All rights reserved. No part of this book may be reproduced or transmitted in any form or by any means, electronic or mechanical, including photocopying, recording or by any information storage and retrieval system, without written permission from the publisher, except for the inclusion of brief quotations in a review.

This book is designed to share parents' opinions regarding baby-related products, services and activities. It is sold with the understanding that the information contained in the book does not represent the publisher's opinion or recommendations. The reviews contained in this guide are based on public opinion surveys and are therefore subjective in nature. The publisher shall have neither liability nor responsibility to any person or entity with respect to any loss or damage caused, or alleged to have been caused, directly or indirectly, by the information contained in this book.

If you do not wish to be bound by the above, you may return this book to the publisher for a full refund.

table of contents

07	about this book
09	thank yous
10	disclaimer
11	how to use this book

15 **lila picks**

29 **checklists**

29 **active baby**
44	activity mats
48	bouncers & rockers
54	activity centers
58	jumpers
60	swings

65 **clothing & shoes**
| 67 | clothing |
| 74 | shoes |

77 **bath time & personal care**
79	infant bathtubs
83	shampoos & bubble baths
89	lotions & potions
93	sun protection
95	toothbrushes & toothpastes

99 **car seats**
101	infants
106	toddlers & convertibles
113	boosters

119 **carriers & slings**

129 **diaper bags**

143 **diapering needs**
| 145 | diaper rash ointments |
| 150 | diaper pails |

153 **for mom & dad**
| 154 | maternity clothing |
| 158 | parenting books |

167 highchairs
- 169   standard highchairs
- 175   hook-ons
- 177   booster seats

181 monitors

189 nursery furniture
- 190   bedding
- 195   standard cribs
- 201   portable cribs

205 nursing & bottle feeding
- 207   bottles & accessories
- 212   breast pumps
- 216   sippy cups

221 potty training

225 strollers & joggers
- 227   umbrella strollers
- 234   standard strollers
- 245   all terrain strollers
- 252   joggers
- 256   doubles & triples

265 indexes
- 266   by model/product
- 271   by manufacturer

about the gear guide

Now you've done it! You've gotten yourself pregnant and don't even own a mini van yet; let alone maternity clothes, a stroller, a car seat, a breast pump, a crib, baby clothing, a bouncy chair, baby bottles, sippy cups, a baby bath, a highchair, diapers, wipes, a diaper bag, diaper rash ointment, a monitor, a rocker, a baby rattle, etc.

If that sounds frightening, consider this. If you're anything like the average new parent you're about to spend anywhere from $6,000 to $11,000 on baby-related stuff during the first year of your tot's life. In fact, in aggregate we parents spend over $4 billion on our babies each year!

Fear not, helping you figure out which products to spend your hard-earned dollars on is what this nifty little guide is all about. Based on the premise that **"parents know best,"** we decided to expand on our popular city guides for new parents. Since so many purchasing decisions are influenced by **word-of-mouth feedback from our friends and families**, we thought this guide was a natural extension of our surveying efforts. Everyone we talked to had some juicy bit of advice about which baby gear they found to be the most practical. Some nugget of parenting wisdom about which stroller really does fold compactly or which car seat's straps don't constantly get twisted. It all really seemed to help. Someone, we thought, should **write this down**.

And that's when, please pardon the pun, this buyer's guide was born. The book you're now holding is literally **written by parents for parents**. It's what happens when someone does actually collect all the word-of-mouth wisdom and writes it down.

Almost 27,000 surveys have produced this edition of **the lilaguide: Baby Gear Guide**. It provides a truly unique insider's view of the many gizmos and widgets that are about to become a very big part of your life. And while this guide won't help you look as perfect and happy as the family pictured on the box the car seat comes in (keep in mind that those people are models and have had their sleep deprivation airbrushed out), it will make the process more fun and help you save a buck or two.

www.lilaguide.com

Now, take a nap and relax. Your baby is almost here and you'll have lots of decisions to make about what you're going to buy.

Enjoy!

Oli & Elysa

Oli Mittermaier & Elysa Marco, MD

thank yous

A baby guide should be more than just a bunch of facts. While it's helpful to know what features a product offers, how do you know if you need those features? How do you know if you even need the product in the first place? So much depends on where you live, how you live, what you do and who you are.

To make this Gear Guide as helpful as possible, we wanted to **find an expert** to help put it all into context for the new parent. Someone who really knows their baby products. Someone who knows what works and what doesn't. And someone who knows what new parents need.

So we turned to **Ali Wing**, a long-time consumer brand marketing expert and new mom herself who owns and operates her own baby store. As the founder and CEO of **giggle** and **egiggle.com**, Ali knows her stuff. She focuses all of her energy on **reviewing and evaluating products** so that she can give her customers the best of what's available so they don't have to slog through the rest.

Listening to customer feedback is a big part of her job, and she knows which products parents end up loving and which ones they end up having to replace with the "right" product after the fact.

That's why we thought Ali would be the perfect match to help make our Gear Guide **relevant to new parents**. At the beginning of each chapter, you'll find some of Ali's insights on the products in that category. She'll tell you what alternatives are available, what features to look for and things to consider that you might never have thought of.

about Ali Wing

Ali holds an MBA from Northwestern University's J.L. Kellogg Graduate School of Management, and a JD from Northwestern's School of Law. She now lives with her husband and son in the Bay Area, where she acts as CEO of **giggle**.

Ali founded giggle with a simple goal: to make it a whole lot easier for new parents to build a smarter nursery. giggle doesn't sell everything out there; they sell

the best of everything out there. They do the homework for you, evaluating each potential product with a list of ten lifestyle criteria based on feedback from expecting, new and experienced parents.

Their collection includes all your **must-have baby items**, pre-sorted to include only the most healthy, stylish and innovative products available - from fun, bright bedding and furniture to gear, toys, baby care, cleaning products and more.

For more information about **Ali Wing** and **giggle**, visit **www.egiggle.com**.

additional thanks

We'd like to take a moment to offer a heart-felt thank you to **all the parents** who participated in the survey and took the time to share their thoughts and opinions. Without your participation, we would never have been able to create this unique guide.

Thanks also to **Jessica Genick** and **Felicity John Odell** for leading the editorial charge, **Satoko Furuta** and **Paul D. Smith** for their beautiful sense of design, and **Lane Foard** for making the words yell.

Special thanks to **Paul D. Smith**, **Ken Miles**, and **Ali Wing** for their consistent support and overall encouragement in all things lilaguide, and of course **our parents** for their unconditional support in this and all our other endeavors.

And last, but certainly not least, thanks to **little Delilah** for inspiring us to embark on this challenging, yet incredibly fulfilling project.

disclaimer

This book is designed to share parents' opinions regarding baby-related products, services and activities. It is sold with the understanding that the information contained in the book **does not** represent the publisher's opinion or recommendations.

The reviews contained in this guide are based on **public opinion surveys** and are therefore subjective in nature. The publisher shall have neither liability nor responsibility to any person or entity with respect to any loss or damage caused, or alleged to have been caused, directly or indirectly, by the information contained in this book.

If you do not wish to be bound by the above, you **may return this book** to the publisher for a full refund.

Please remember that this guide is **not intended to be a comprehensive directory of baby products**. Rather, it is intended to provide a short-list of products that parents **deemed exciting and noteworthy**. If a specific product and/or brand is not included in the guide it simply means that nobody rated or submitted information about it to us. Please let us know of products you think **should be included** in future editions by submitting your product suggestions to us via our web site: **www.lilaguide.com**.

ratings

Most listings have stars and numbers as part of their write-up. These symbols mean the following:

★★★★★ extraordinary
★★★★☆ very good
★★★☆☆ good
★★☆☆☆ fair
★☆☆☆☆ poor

If a ✩ is listed instead of ★, it means that the rating is less reliable because a small number of parents surveyed the listing. Furthermore, if a listing has **no stars** or **criteria ratings**, it means that although the listing was rated, the number of surveys submitted was so low that we did not feel it justified an actual rating.

quotes & reviews

The quotes/reviews are taken directly from surveys submitted to us via our website (**www.lilaguide.com**). Other than spelling and minor grammatical changes, they come to you as they came to us. Quotes were selected based on how well they appeared to represent the collective opinions of the surveys submitted.

lila picks

Recommendations are great to have, but they're all relative. What's perfect for one family might not fit as well into another family's lifestyle. So to add a new dimension to our product ratings, we're adding a set of lifestyle criteria (multi-use, space, travel, value, style) to help highlight things that might be particularly appropriate for you. They don't all apply to every category, and you'll see them only where they're relevant. But when it's important how well a product fits into the way you live, you can look for our icons to guide you to the best choice.

fact checking

We have contacted all of the businesses listed to verify their address and phone number, as well as to inquire about their hours, class schedules and web site information. Since some of this information may change after this guide has been printed we appreciate you letting us know of any errors by notifying us via email at **lila@lilaguide.com**.

indexes

As an added benefit for time-starved parents, we have added **two indexes** to the back of the book. Whether you are looking for a product **alphabetically** or researching your options **by manufacturer** these lists will help you find what you are looking for quickly and easily. As always, if you have ideas or suggestions as to how else we can slice and dice the info, please don't hesitate to let us know.

lila picks

lila picks

According to the thousands of parents who participated in our survey these products represent the best of the best. They have received the greatest number of positive reviews in their category and can be considered a pretty safe bet when it comes to shopping for your baby.

active baby
- ★ ExerSaucer Mega Active Learning Center (Activity Centers & Walkers)
- ★ ExerSaucer Ultra Active Learning Center (Activity Centers & Walkers)
- ★ Learn & Groove Activity Station (Activity Centers & Walkers)
- ★ Gymni Super Deluxe Light And Music (Activity Mats)
- ★ Baby Sitter 1-2-3 (Bouncers & Rockers)
- ★ Kick and Play Bouncer (Bouncers & Rockers)
- ★ Magic Moments Learning Seat (Bouncers & Rockers)
- ★ Classic Johnny Jump Up (Jumpers)
- ★ Deluxe Jumperoo (Jumpers)
- ★ Aquarium Take-Along Swing (Swings)
- ★ Ocean Wonders Aquarium Cradle Swing (Swings)

bath time & personal care
- ★ Euro Bath Tub (Infant Bath Tubs)
- ★ Infant Bath Seat (Infant Bath Tubs)
- ★ Bebe Cold Cream (Lotions & Potions)
- ★ Daily Baby Lotion (Lotions & Potions)
- ★ Nurturing Cream for Face and Body (Lotions & Potions)
- ★ Baby Shampoo (Shampoos & Bubble Baths)
- ★ Baby Wash & Shampoo (Shampoos & Bubble Baths)
- ★ Foam Shampoo For Newborns (Shampoos & Bubble Baths)
- ★ Grins & Giggles Baby Wash (Shampoos & Bubble Baths)
- ★ Head-To-Toe (Shampoos & Bubble Baths)
- ★ Sun Busters All-In-One Swim Gear (Sun Protection)
- ★ Sunblock Lotion SPF50 (Sun Protection)
- ★ Baby Tooth And Gum Cleanser (Toothbrushes & Toothpastes)
- ★ Children's Tooth Gel (Toothbrushes & Toothpastes)
- ★ Natural Anticavity Fluoride Toothpaste for Children (Toothbrushes & Toothpastes)

car seats
- ★ Bodyguard (Car Seats: Booster)
- ★ Cricket (Car Seats: Booster)
- ★ Starriser Comfy (Car Seats: Booster)
- ★ TurboBooster (Car Seats: Booster)

www.lilaguide.com

- ★ Companion Infant Seat (Car Seats: Infant)
- ★ SnugRide (Car Seats: Infant)
- ★ Decathlon (Car Seats: Toddler)
- ★ Marathon (Car Seats: Toddler)
- ★ Roundabout (Car Seats: Toddler)

carriers & slings
- ★ Baby Carrier (Carriers & Slings)
- ★ Baby Carrier Active (Carriers & Slings)
- ★ Baby Carrier Original (Carriers & Slings)
- ★ ERGO Baby Carrier (Carriers & Slings)
- ★ Premaxx New Edition Baby Sling (Carriers & Slings)

clothing & shoes
- ★ BabyGap (Baby Clothing)
- ★ Hanna Andersson (Baby Clothing)
- ★ Old Navy (Baby Clothing)
- ★ Petit Bateau (Baby Clothing)
- ★ Teacollection (Baby Clothing)
- ★ Pedipeds (Shoes)
- ★ Robeez (Shoes)

diaper bags
- ★ Diaper Backpack (Diaper Bags)
- ★ Duo Diaper Bag (Diaper Bags)
- ★ Marsupial Diaper Bag (Diaper Bags)
- ★ Mothership (Diaper Bags)
- ★ Triple Compartment Diaper Pack (Diaper Bags)
- ★ Urban Sling (Diaper Bags)

diapering needs
- ★ Diaper Champ (Diaper Pails)
- ★ Diaper Dekor Plus Diaper Disposal System (Diaper Pails)
- ★ Baby Barrier Cream (Diaper Rash Ointments)
- ★ Baby Bee Diaper Ointment (Diaper Rash Ointments)
- ★ Baby Vitamin Barrier Cream (Diaper Rash Ointments)
- ★ Diaper Cream (Diaper Rash Ointments)

for mom & dad
- ★ A Pea in the Pod (Maternity Clothing)
- ★ Babystyle (Maternity Clothing)
- ★ Belly Basics (Maternity Clothing)
- ★ Bravado Designs (Maternity Clothing)
- ★ Japanese Weekend (Maternity Clothing)
- ★ Liz Lange (Maternity Clothing)
- ★ Old Navy (Maternity Clothing)
- ★ Brott, Armin (Parenting Books)
- ★ Cohen, Michel MD (Parenting Books)
- ★ Sears, William & Martha (Parenting Books)

highchairs
- ★ 4-Stage Feeding Seat (Highchair Booster Seats)
- ★ Baby Sitter (Highchair Booster Seats)
- ★ Cooshie Booster Seat (Highchair Booster Seats)
- ★ Caddy Table Seat (Hook-ons)

- ★ Hook On High Chair (Hook-ons)
- ★ KinderZeat (Standard Highchairs)
- ★ Prima Pappa Rocker (Standard Highchairs)
- ★ Svan Chair (Standard Highchairs)

monitors
- ★ Angelcare Movement Sensor with Sound Monitor (Monitors)
- ★ Baby's Quiet Sounds Video Monitor (Monitors)
- ★ MobiCam Baby Monitor (Monitors)
- ★ UltraClear (Monitors)

nursery & furniture
- ★ Amy Coe (Bedding)
- ★ Dwell Baby (Bedding)
- ★ Pottery Barn Kids (Bedding)
- ★ Wendy Bellissimo (Bedding)
- ★ Bellini (Cribs)
- ★ IKEA (Cribs)
- ★ Pali (Cribs)
- ★ Stokke (Cribs)
- ★ Pack N Play (Portable Cribs)

nursing & bottle feeding
- ★ Breastbottle Nurser (Bottles & Accessories)
- ★ Natural Feeding Bottle (Bottles & Accessories)
- ★ Wide Neck Bottle (Bottles & Accessories)
- ★ Isis Breast Pump (Breastfeeding: Pumps)
- ★ Pump In Style Advanced Breastpump (Breastfeeding: Pumps)
- ★ Fun Grips Soft Starter Spill-Proof Cup (Sippy Cups)
- ★ Take & Toss (Sippy Cups)

potty seats
- ★ Potty Chair (Potty Seats)
- ★ Toilet Trainer (Potty Seats)

strollers & joggers
- ★ Boogie (All Terrain Strollers)
- ★ Cameleon (All Terrain Strollers)
- ★ e3 Explorer (All Terrain Strollers)
- ★ Urban Single (All Terrain Strollers)
- ★ Duette (Doubles & Triples)
- ★ DuoGlider (Doubles & Triples)
- ★ Twin Traveller (Doubles & Triples)
- ★ Urban Double (Doubles & Triples)
- ★ Ironman Sport Utility (Joggers)
- ★ Speedster Deluxe (Joggers)
- ★ Metrolite LE (Standard Strollers)
- ★ Pliko P3 MT (Standard Strollers)
- ★ Queen B (Standard Strollers)
- ★ Snap N Go (Standard Strollers)
- ★ Swing (Standard Strollers)
- ★ Techno XT (Umbrella Strollers)
- ★ Triumph (Umbrella Strollers)

lila picks

multi-use

These products are versatile and cleverly designed. They're either fully-loaded with innovative features and/or designed to give you the most use/functionality over time. Either way, you'll get your money's worth and will be able to make do with fewer purchases in any given category.

active baby
- ★ Baby Einstein (Activity Centers & Walkers)
- ★ Learn & Groove Activity Station (Activity Centers & Walkers)
- ★ 5-in-1 Adjustable Gym (Activity Mats)
- ★ Boppy 5-in-1 (Activity Mats)
- ★ Splash Barnacle Activity Playmat (Activity Mats)
- ★ Baby Sitter 1-2-3 (Bouncers & Rockers)
- ★ Infant to Toddler Rocker (Bouncers & Rockers)
- ★ Magic Moments Learning Seat (Bouncers & Rockers)
- ★ Deluxe Jumperoo (Jumpers)

bath time & personal care
- ★ Euro Bath Tub (Infant Bath Tubs)
- ★ Facial Cleansing Cloths (Lotions & Potions)
- ★ 2 in 1 Hair and Body Wash (Shampoos & Bubble Baths)
- ★ Baby Magic Gentle Hair & Body Wash (Shampoos & Bubble Baths)
- ★ Foam Shampoo For Newborns (Shampoos & Bubble Baths)

car seats
- ★ CarGo (Car Seats: Booster)
- ★ Intera (Car Seats: Booster)
- ★ Alpha Omega Elite (Car Seats: Toddler)
- ★ Boulevard (Car Seats: Toddler)
- ★ Decathlon (Car Seats: Toddler)
- ★ Marathon (Car Seats: Toddler)
- ★ Wizard (Car Seats: Toddler)

carriers & slings
- ★ Baby Carrier (Carriers & Slings)
- ★ Baby Carrier Active (Carriers & Slings)
- ★ Baby Carry Scarf (Carriers & Slings)
- ★ ERGO Baby Carrier (Carriers & Slings)
- ★ Premaxx New Edition Baby Sling (Carriers & Slings)

diaper bags
- ★ Colorado Tote (Diaper Bags)
- ★ Diaper Backpack (Diaper Bags)
- ★ Diaper Daypack (Diaper Bags)
- ★ Duo Diaper Bag (Diaper Bags)

- ★ Lena Diaper Bag (Diaper Bags)
- ★ Parent Survival Pack (Diaper Bags)
- ★ Triple Compartment Diaper Pack (Diaper Bags)

diapering needs
- ★ Diaper Dekor Plus Diaper Disposal System (Diaper Pails)
- ★ Diaper Pail (Diaper Pails)
- ★ Baby Healing Ointment (Diaper Rash Ointments)

highchairs
- ★ 4-Stage Feeding Seat (Highchair Booster Seats)
- ★ All-in-One Reclining Booster Seat (Highchair Booster Seats)
- ★ Baby Sitter (Highchair Booster Seats)
- ★ KinderZeat (Standard Highchairs)
- ★ Svan Chair (Standard Highchairs)

monitors
- ★ Angelcare Movement Sensor with Sound Monitor (Monitors)
- ★ Baby's Quiet Sounds Video Monitor (Monitors)
- ★ In Sight (Monitors)
- ★ MobiCam Baby Monitor (Monitors)
- ★ Sweet Dreams Monitor (Monitors)

nursery & furniture
- ★ Oeuf (Cribs)
- ★ Stokke (Cribs)

nursing & bottle feeding
- ★ Elite Sensitive Response Wide Nipple Nurser (Bottles & Accessories)
- ★ Express Microwave Steam Sterilizer (Bottles & Accessories)
- ★ Natural Feeding Bottle (Bottles & Accessories)
- ★ Pump In Style Advanced Breastpump (Breastfeeding: Pumps)

potty seats
- ★ 3-In-1 Potty 'N Step Stool (Potty Seats)

strollers & joggers
- ★ Boogie (All Terrain Strollers)
- ★ Cameleon (All Terrain Strollers)
- ★ e3 Explorer (All Terrain Strollers)
- ★ Runabout (All Terrain Strollers)
- ★ Zydeco (All Terrain Strollers)
- ★ Duallie Sport Utility (Doubles & Triples)
- ★ Duette (Doubles & Triples)
- ★ DuoGlider (Doubles & Triples)
- ★ Twin Traveller (Doubles & Triples)
- ★ Urban Double (Doubles & Triples)
- ★ Deluxe Sport Utility Stroller (Joggers)
- ★ Expedition LX (Joggers)
- ★ A3 (Standard Strollers)
- ★ Escape 400 (Standard Strollers)
- ★ Metrolite LE (Standard Strollers)
- ★ Queen B (Standard Strollers)

lila picks

space

Whether you're an urban dweller, condo owner or apartment resident, these products are made with your precious living space in mind. Not everyone has walk-in closets and a big garage, so these products are made to fold, collapse, store or fit neatly into tight spaces.

---

nursing & bottle feeding
- ★ Express Microwave Steam Sterilizer (Bottles & Accessories)

strollers & joggers
- ★ Snap N Go (Standard Strollers)
- ★ Universal Car Seat Carrier (Standard Strollers)
- ★ City Savvy (Umbrella Strollers)
- ★ Techno XT (Umbrella Strollers)

lila picks

travel

These products are compact, portable and ready to go, whether you're traveling abroad or just going to Grandma's house. Plenty of products are travel appropriate, but we wanted to point out those that you'll especially appreciate when you're on the road.

active baby
- ★ Baby Playzone Take-Along Hop 'n Pop (Activity Centers & Walkers)
- ★ Travel Lite Bouncer (Bouncers & Rockers)
- ★ Aquarium Take-Along Swing (Swings)
- ★ Travel Lite Swing (Swings)

bath time & personal care
- ★ Fold-up Tub (Infant Bath Tubs)
- ★ 2 in 1 Hair and Body Wash (Shampoos & Bubble Baths)
- ★ Baby Magic Gentle Hair & Body Wash (Shampoos & Bubble Baths)

car seats
- ★ B500 Folding Booster Car Seat (Car Seats: Booster)
- ★ Cricket (Car Seats: Booster)
- ★ Starriser Comfy (Car Seats: Booster)
- ★ Discovery Infant Car Seat (Car Seats: Infant)
- ★ PortAbout Infant Car Seat (Car Seats: Infant)
- ★ SnugRide (Car Seats: Infant)
- ★ Roundabout (Car Seats: Toddler)
- ★ Sit n Stroll 5-in-1 Travel System (Car Seats: Toddler)

carriers & slings
- ★ Baby Carrier Active (Carriers & Slings)
- ★ Baby Carrier Original (Carriers & Slings)
- ★ Emi Carrier (Carriers & Slings)

diaper bags
- ★ Diaper Backpack (Diaper Bags)
- ★ Diaper Daypack (Diaper Bags)
- ★ Mini Messenger Bag (Diaper Bags)

diapering needs
- ★ Bum Bum Balm (Diaper Rash Ointments)

highchairs
- ★ Hook On High Chair (Hook-ons)

nursery & furniture
- ★ Pack N Play (Portable Cribs)

www.lilaguide.com

nursing & bottle feeding
- Isis Breast Pump (Breastfeeding: Pumps)

potty seats
- Folding Potty Seat (Potty Seats)
- Toilet Trainer (Potty Seats)

strollers & joggers
- Gecko (All Terrain Strollers)
- Aria Twin (Doubles & Triples)
- Rally Twin (Doubles & Triples)
- Twin Savvy EX (Doubles & Triples)
- Ironman Sport Utility (Joggers)
- Metrolite LE (Standard Strollers)
- Rhumba (Standard Strollers)
- Snap N Go (Standard Strollers)
- Trendsport Lite (Standard Strollers)
- Universal Car Seat Carrier (Standard Strollers)
- City Savvy (Umbrella Strollers)
- Soho DX (Umbrella Strollers)
- Soho Sport (Umbrella Strollers)
- Techno XT (Umbrella Strollers)
- Volo (Umbrella Strollers)

participate in our survey at

lila picks

value

You'll get your money's worth out of these products, regardless of price. The less expensive items are cheap enough that you don't have to agonize over your decision, and the more expensive items will give you tons of use that pays off over time.

---

active baby
- ★ Classic Johnny Jump Up (Jumpers)

clothing & shoes
- ★ Carter's (Baby Clothing)
- ★ Children's Place, The (Baby Clothing)
- ★ Gerber (Baby Clothing)
- ★ Old Navy (Baby Clothing)
- ★ Robeez (Shoes)

bath time & personal care
- ★ Euro Bath Tub (Infant Bath Tubs)
- ★ Infant Bath Seat (Infant Bath Tubs)
- ★ Bedtime Lotion (Lotions & Potions)
- ★ Daily Baby Lotion (Lotions & Potions)
- ★ Baby Wash & Shampoo (Shampoos & Bubble Baths)
- ★ Comfort Care Gum & Toothbrush Set (Toothbrushes & Toothpastes)

car seats
- ★ Cricket (Car Seats: Booster)
- ★ TurboBooster (Car Seats: Booster)
- ★ Adjustable Back Latch-Loc Car Seat (Car Seats: Infant)
- ★ SnugRide (Car Seats: Infant)
- ★ Roundabout (Car Seats: Toddler)

carriers & slings
- ★ Baby Carrier Original (Carriers & Slings)

diaper bags
- ★ Diaper DayPouch (Diaper Bags)
- ★ Do-It-All Diaper Bag (Diaper Bags)
- ★ Duo Diaper Bag (Diaper Bags)
- ★ Essentials Diaper Bag (Diaper Bags)
- ★ Little Tripper Diaper Bag (Diaper Bags)
- ★ Triple Compartment Diaper Pack (Diaper Bags)

diapering needs
- ★ Diaper Champ (Diaper Pails)
- ★ Diaper Dekor Plus Diaper Disposal System (Diaper Pails)
- ★ Baby Barrier Cream (Diaper Rash Ointments)

- Diaper Rash Cream (Diaper Rash Ointments)

highchairs
- Hook On High Chair (Hook-ons)
- IKEA Highchair (Standard Highchairs)
- Peas & Carrots Highchair (Standard Highchairs)

monitors
- On-the-Go Monitor (Monitors)

nursery & furniture
- Lands End (Bedding)
- Pottery Barn Kids (Bedding)
- Bonavita/Babi Italia (Cribs)
- IKEA (Cribs)
- OFFI & Co (Cribs)

nursing & bottle feeding
- Elite Sensitive Response Wide Nipple Nurser (Bottles & Accessories)
- Express Microwave Steam Sterilizer (Bottles & Accessories)
- Natural Feeding Bottle (Bottles & Accessories)
- Harmony Breast Pump (Breastfeeding: Pumps)
- Take & Toss (Sippy Cups)

strollers & joggers
- Boogie (All Terrain Strollers)
- Snap N Go (Standard Strollers)
- Universal Car Seat Carrier (Standard Strollers)
- Umbrella Stroller (Umbrella Strollers)

lila picks

style

Just because you've had a baby doesn't mean you have to give up your own personal style. Fashionable parents will love these stylish products that are hip, urban and thoroughly modern.

active baby
- ★ Baby Lounger (Bouncers & Rockers)
- ★ Baby Sitter 1-2-3 (Bouncers & Rockers)
- ★ Rocker (Bouncers & Rockers)

clothing & shoes
- ★ BabyGap (Baby Clothing)
- ★ Catimini (Baby Clothing)
- ★ Hanna Andersson (Baby Clothing)
- ★ Janie And Jack (Baby Clothing)
- ★ Oilily (Baby Clothing)
- ★ Petit Bateau (Baby Clothing)
- ★ Polo Ralph Lauren (Baby Clothing)
- ★ Teacollection (Baby Clothing)
- ★ Zutano (Baby Clothing)
- ★ Pedipeds (Shoes)

car seats
- ★ Bodyguard (Car Seats: Booster)
- ★ Parkway Booster (Car Seats: Booster)
- ★ Primo Viaggio (Car Seats: Infant)
- ★ Recaro (Car Seats: Toddler)

carriers & slings
- ★ Baby Carrier (Carriers & Slings)
- ★ Baby Carrier Active (Carriers & Slings)
- ★ Front & Back Pack Soft Carrier (Carriers & Slings)
- ★ Infant Carrier (Carriers & Slings)
- ★ Kangaroo (Carriers & Slings)
- ★ Peanut Shell (Carriers & Slings)
- ★ Premaxx New Edition Baby Sling (Carriers & Slings)

diaper bags
- ★ Baby Bag (Diaper Bags)
- ★ Back Pack Diaper Bag (Diaper Bags)
- ★ Bambino Diaper Bag (Diaper Bags)
- ★ Colorado Tote (Diaper Bags)
- ★ Diaper Bag (Diaper Bags)
- ★ Duo Diaper Bag (Diaper Bags)
- ★ Marsupial Diaper Bag (Diaper Bags)

- ★ Messenger Bag (Diaper Bags)
- ★ Mothership (Diaper Bags)
- ★ Shoulder Bag (Diaper Bags)
- ★ Ultimate Diaper Bag (Diaper Bags)
- ★ Un-Diaper Bag (Diaper Bags)
- ★ Urban Sling (Diaper Bags)

highchairs
- ★ KinderZeat (Standard Highchairs)
- ★ Svan Chair (Standard Highchairs)

nursery & furniture
- ★ Amy Coe (Bedding)
- ★ Dwell Baby (Bedding)
- ★ Land of Nod (Bedding)
- ★ Lulu (Bedding)
- ★ Wendy Bellissimo (Bedding)
- ★ Bellini (Cribs)
- ★ NettoCollection (Cribs)
- ★ Pali (Cribs)

nursing & bottle feeding
- ★ Hands-Free Breast Pump (Breastfeeding: Pumps)

strollers & joggers
- ★ Cameleon (All Terrain Strollers)
- ★ e3 Explorer (All Terrain Strollers)
- ★ Gecko (All Terrain Strollers)
- ★ Manhattan (All Terrain Strollers)
- ★ Rocket Stroller (All Terrain Strollers)
- ★ Deluxe Sport Utility Stroller (Joggers)
- ★ Speedster Deluxe (Joggers)
- ★ Bidwell 905 (Standard Strollers)
- ★ Culla (Standard Strollers)
- ★ Flyer (Standard Strollers)
- ★ Queen B (Standard Strollers)
- ★ Xplory (Standard Strollers)
- ★ Micro Stroller (Umbrella Strollers)
- ★ Techno Classic (Umbrella Strollers)

checklists

We came across a very telling graph once that mapped out family expenditures during a baby's first year by household income. To paraphrase, it suggested that, not including childcare, low-income families spend around $7000 per year, middle-income families around $11,000, and high-income families close to $20,000. A quick interpretation of this suggests there's **a lot of money being spent** on stuff you just don't really need. And this was confirmed by most of the parents we spoke with who agreed they were often guilty of buying baby gear that seemed necessary in the store but was nothing short of useless when they got home.

That being as it is, we've put together some checklists for you. Our hope is that these will help shed some light on what other parents feel you **must have**, **may want** (but probably could do without), and absolutely **don't need**. The checklists are intended to provide you with insight into other parent's opinions and hopefully will help you to **get what you really need**.

maternity clothing & gear

must have

- ☐ **BATHING SUIT** — *"...if you're going to be doing water aerobics or hanging poolside you'll want a new suit that supports your expanding belly..."*

- ☐ **BRAS** — *"...a nice perk – bigger boobs... your new chest will need some extra support... hit a maternity store that specializes in fitting you properly... invest in a couple good bras and you're good to go ..."*

- ☐ **EXERCISE WEAR** — *"...exercise during pregnancy is good for your body and mind... stretchy yoga pants and some comfy T-shirts are great to get you going on a brisk walk..."*

- ☐ **FORMAL/ FANCY WEAR** — *"...you'll want that little black dress even when you're pregnant... invest in one or two nice outfits for those special occasions..."*

- ☐ **MATERNITY PANTS** — *"...think neutrals and solids... find a few basics to mix and match with other items... elastic waist pants are a nice alternative to the paneled ones – can wear throughout entire pregnancy..."*

- ☐ **MATERNITY SHIRTS** — *"...show off your proud belly with a cute form fitted top... gone are the days of tent like cover-ups... jazz it up with a few solids and prints ..."*

- ☐ **SHOES** — *"...comfort, comfort, comfort... a nice pair of flats or a supportive sneaker... feet have a tendency to swell so make sure there is room for growth..."*

- ☐ **SHORTS & TANK TOPS** — *"...if you're pregnant during those hot summer months these are a must..."*

- ☐ **SWEATER/ SWEAT SHIRT** — *"...a roomy, cozy sweatshirt or sweater is always nice to throw on when it's chilly outside..."*

nice to have

- **MATERNITY PILLOW** *"...your maternity pillow is the next best thing to your bed mate or might even become your new sleeping partner... alleviates aches and pains associated with pregnancy... nice support... helps with a more restful nights sleep..."*

- **LOTIONS & POTIONS** *"...a nice lotion or scrub helps soothe stretching or itchy skin... indulge in some scented treats and pamper yourself – you definitely deserve it ..."*

- **PAJAMAS** *"...find some soft, roomy jammies and get some rest..."*

- **UNDERWEAR** *"...if thongs are your thing try the under the belly maternity variety... if you're one for more support the over the belly style works well... it's all a matter of choice when it comes to undergarments..."*

- **PREGNANCY CALENDAR** *"...a great way to track, monitor and journal your pregnancy... makes for a nice keepsake after the fact..."*

don't need

- **STRETCH MARK CREAM** *"...don't waste a penny on stretch mark creams... go ahead and moisturize your belly but don't think it's going to prevent or get rid of any marks you may get – sorry ladies they're hereditary..."*

nursery

must have

- [ ] **CRIB/ MATTRESS** — *"...probably one of the most expensive items you'll buy... make sure the gate locks quietly so you don't wake your baby when placing him in the crib... mattress should be firm and have a good plastic or rubber covering... plenty of styles, just make sure it meets all safety requirements..."*

- [ ] **BEDDING** — *"...a lot of themes or patterns to choose from, it's all a matter of preference... make sure the crib sheet fits snuggly around the mattress..."*

- [ ] **MATTRESS PADS** — *"...keeps the mattress dry during those leaky nights..."*

- [ ] **CHANGING TABLE** — *"...a sturdy one is key... a necessity for diaper changes... nice to have a table with storage for the basics – diapers, wipes, and ointments..."*

- [ ] **DRESSER** — *"...holds everything from onesies to sleepers to play clothes and keeps everything nicely organized..."*

- [ ] **DIAPER PAIL** — *"...easy to use and absolutely no odor at all... a bit of an eye sore but keeps diapers contained and odor free... we like the kind you can use regular kitchen garbage bags as opposed to the highly expensive replacement bags..."*

nice to have

- [ ] **BOUNCER/ ROCKER** — *"...a seat that vibrates will get your little one to sleep... soothes my baby and keeps him comfortable while I do things around the house... I just put baby in it and brought the seat into the bathroom so I could shower..."*

- [ ] **BABY MONITOR** — *"...they're great if you want to sit out on the porch while your baby is sleeping... most of the time I can hear my baby cry with or without the monitor..."*

participate in our survey at

- ☐ VIDEO MONITOR — *"...if you have the extra money, and like nifty gadgets... view your sleeping baby from a television-like screen even when you're doing the dishes..."*

- ☐ ROCKING CHAIR/ GLIDER — *"...gliders are safe and way more comfortable than the traditional rockers... get a good one because you'll spend hours in it and you'll want it to be comfy..."*

- ☐ FOOTREST/ OTTOMAN — *"...a great companion to the glider for added back support... nice to put my feet up while I'm nursing..."*

- ☐ NIGHT LIGHT — *"...a night-light makes it easy for you to find your way around a dark nursery... no need waking everyone in the house with bright lights..."*

- ☐ STEREO — *"...we love to play music around bed time – it soothes our baby to sleep... a fantastic way to wind down the day... a small CD player is nice to keep in the baby's room..."*

- ☐ TOY CHEST — *"... a cool looking toy chest helps make the kids room fun and organized..."*

- ☐ MOBILE — *"...helps occupy baby when you need to get things done... find a mobile with bold colors and shapes... one that plays music helps lullaby my baby to sleep..."*

- ☐ WIPE WARMER — *"... clean baby's bottom with warm wipes – especially nice during those cold winter days..."*

- ☐ HUMIDIFIER — *"... helps with congestion when baby has a cold... look for the cool water humidifier to avoid scalding..."*

- ☐ BASSINET — *"... nice to have, especially with a newborn... keeps baby safe and close to you at night... allows you to move baby from room to room, so you can carry on with your day and have baby close by..."*

baby clothing

must have

- [ ] **ONESIES** — *"...your newborn will live in these... make sure they fit easily over your baby's head... get them with long and short sleeves..."*

- [ ] **SLEEPERS** — *"...if your baby wakes easily when being changed at night, use nightgowns, makes for easy diaper changes... fleece sleepers work great for keeping baby warm at night..."*

- [ ] **RECEIVING BLANKETS** — *"...ideal for the perfect swaddle... also comes in handy for wiping up spills and as a burp cloth... can never have too many..."*

- [ ] **HATS** — *"...keeps baby's head warm and protected from the environment..."*

- [ ] **SOCKS & BOOTIES** — *"...you'll need a bunch, since they get lost easily... little rubber nubbies on the bottom help with slippery floors..."*

- [ ] **ROMPER** — *"...a little dressier than a onesie or a sleeper... nice when you're ready to venture out and dress your little one up a bit..."*

nice to have

- [ ] **SLEEP SACK** — *"...baby stays warm and cozy and gives you peace of mind – you don't have to worry about smothering... the SIDS Foundation supports sleep sacks..."*

- [ ] **SCRATCH MITS** — *"...prevents baby from scratching her face..."*

- [ ] **SNOW SUIT** — *"...ideal for bundling up baby in frigid climates..."*

don't need

- [ ] **INFANT SHOES** — *"...newborns don't walk, so they don't need shoes – save your money..."*

participate in our survey at

nursing accessories

must have

- ☐ BREAST PUMP — *"...essential for working moms who want to continue breastfeeding... allows you to pump and store your milk... gives your partner a chance to bottle feed baby your milk..."*

- ☐ MILK STORAGE BAGS — *"...useful for storing and freezing your milk..."*

- ☐ NURSING PADS — *"...absorbs leaky breast milk... protects clothing..."*

nice to have

- ☐ NURSING PILLOW — *"...makes breastfeeding more comfortable... offers baby and mommy the support they need for successful breastfeeding... they're also great support for when your baby is learning how to sit..."*

- ☐ NIPPLE OINTMENT/ CREAM — *"...soothes and heals cracked and sore nipples..."*

- ☐ NURSING BRA — *"...makes breastfeeding easier... offers proper support for nursing moms...make sure you are fitted properly..."*

- ☐ NURSING SHIRT — *"...allows you to breastfeed discreetly in public... easy, fast access can make the difference between a happy or crying baby..."*

don't need

- ☐ PRIVACY BLANKET — *"...just an extra unnecessary item to throw in the diaper bag... a jacket or a shirt to cover up works just as well..."*

feeding supplies

must have

- [ ] **BOTTLES** — *"...so many varieties out there – find one baby likes and stick with it..."*

- [ ] **BABY SPOONS** — *"...don't need them right away... check out the temperature sensitive spoons – lets you know if baby's food is too hot..."*

- [ ] **BIBS** — *"...helps protect baby's clothes against stains from breast milk, formula and food..."*

- [ ] **BOTTLE BRUSH** — *"... allows you to clean inside baby's bottle... especially handy for those without dishwashers..."*

- [ ] **BURP CLOTHS** — *"...babies often spit up a lot during the first six months - protects mommy's clothes from those little messes..."*

- [ ] **FORMULA** — *"...if you're not going to breastfeed or if you plan to supplement, choose one formula and stick with it..."*

- [ ] **HIGHCHAIR** — *"...nice to have a highchair with an easily removable tray, adjustable seat and removable padding... get something easy to hose off – no joke – it'll get messy..."*

- [ ] **SIPPY CUPS** — *"...you don't need them right away, but you might as well start getting ready... in the earlier stages, find on that isn't so wide, so it's easier for baby to grasp (even with both hands)... helps to find one with two handles... great transition between bottle and cup... ..."*

nice to have

- [ ] **PACIFIERS** — *"...buy whatever kind your baby will take... pacifier attachers are essential when baby learns how to pull the pacifier in and out of her own mouth..."*

- [ ] **BOTTLE WARMER** — *"...warms milk to the ideal temperature... perfect for thawing frozen breast milk..."*

- [ ] **PRE-MEASURED FORMULA CONTAINER** *"...handy little gizmo to keep in your diaper bag for on the go feedings... measures the perfect amount of formula..."*

don't need

- [ ] **BOTTLE STERILIZER** *"...use the dishwasher... you can boil the bottles and other accessories from time to time... if you don't have a dishwasher, hot water and antibacterial soap does the job..."*

toiletries

must have

- [ ] **INFANT BATH TUB** — *"...a sturdy tub is essential – skip the inflatable variety... make sure it will hook into your sink/tub or sit securely on a countertop so it won't topple over..."*

- [ ] **BABY SHAMPOO & BUBBLE BATH** — *"...definitely get special baby shampoo and body soap – adult products will sting their eyes... check out the head-to-toe washes to avoid product overload..."*

- [ ] **DIAPER RASH OINTMENT** — *"...get an ointment that provides a solid barrier against wetness... keep a tube at home and one in your diaper bag so you can deal with rashes as soon as they appear..."*

- [ ] **DIAPERS** — *"...of course, a must have!.. disposable or cloth, it's a matter of personal choice..."*

- [ ] **NAIL CLIPPERS** — *"...get the smallest clippers possible to avoid nicking baby's fingers... some even have a magnifying glass attached so you can see what you're doing..."*

- [ ] **WIPES** — *"...a must for wiping baby's bottom... you can choose between scented and unscented..."*

- [ ] **THERMOMETER** — *"...an absolute necessity for monitoring a sick baby's temperature... digital thermometers are accurate under the arm or rectally..."*

nice to have

- [ ] **HOODED TOWELS** — *"...cute for little ones... allows you to completely wrap them up from head-to-toe after a bath..."*

- [ ] **WASH CLOTHS** — *"...thin and soft cotton – allows you to clean all of baby's nooks and crannies..."*

- [ ] **HAIR BRUSH & COMB** — *"...self-explanatory – some babies are born with a full head of hair and some are born BALD..."*

- [ ] **BULB SYRINGE** *"...until baby can blow his nose, these are key for sucking out goop... especially helps when your little one is congested..."*

don't need

- [ ] **BABY POWDER** *"...smells nice, but absolutely not necessary... my baby smells so yummy, she doesn't need anything else..."*

- [ ] **BABY OIL** *"...see baby powder..."*

- [ ] **BABY LOTION** *"...ditto..."*

outing equipment

must have

- [ ] **CAR SEAT** *"...what can you say, how else am I going to get my tot around... if you want to make sure the seat is in properly, take it to your local fire department or police station ..."*

- [ ] **STROLLER** *"...look for an easy to maneuver, collapsible stroller and material that can be easily cleaned... make sure it has a big basket to hold excess baggage... lightweight works best – especially for traveling..."*

- [ ] **DIAPER BAG** *"...look for durable material that wont fray... nowadays there's a huge variety from your basic backpack style to the more trendy, chic diaper bag that doubles as purse ..."*

- [ ] **CHANGING PAD** *"...most diaper bags come with one... changing stations aren't always clean, or available, make sure the mat protects your baby's back..."*

- [ ] **BLANKET** *"...great for wrapping baby on cool, breezy days, or shielding her from the sun... they always come in handy, so don't leave home without one..."*

nice to have

- [ ] **BABY CARRIER/ SLING** *"...a comfortable way to carry infants... make sure it's easy to put on by yourself and easy to put baby in... great if you need both hands free... being close to mommy often helps soothe a fussy baby..."*

- [ ] **JOGGING STROLLER** *"...if you like running or off-roading with your baby, you might want to check the joggers out..."*

- [ ] **BACK PACK** *"...it's pretty much the only option if you like hiking and want to take baby with you... if you plan on using it a lot make sure it's the right size and comfortable to wear..."*

participate in our survey at

- ☐ **PORTABLE CRIB** *"...great for traveling with your baby... allows you to visit friends and not worry about rushing home for baby's bed time... make sure it's easy to assemble..."*

- ☐ **STROLLER WEATHER SHIELD** *"...protects your little one from the elements..."*

- ☐ **DISPOSABLE DIAPER SACKS** *"...a convenient way to dispose of diapers if you're not near a trashcan..."*

- ☐ **WIPE HOLDER** *"...hold a small portion of wipes and keep them moist, so you do not have to drag around a large container..."*

- ☐ **STROLLER TOYS** *"...great for distracting a fussy baby..."*

active baby

Your best bet in this category is to go slow. Start off with an activity mat and a bouncer, which can both be lifesavers for harried parents trying to enjoy a quiet mealtime. But as for other active-baby options, you might want to hold off for a while. You won't need them just yet and that will give you more of a chance to see what your baby is like. Some babies are bouncers, others will prefer a vibrating chair, and some it seems were born to jump. For quite a few babies, swings are the key to naptime and you'll find you can't live without one.

Practical Considerations: Consider the practical constraints of your house before you go shopping. How wide is the doorway you want the bouncer to fit in? How much space do you have for a swing? (Some are huge). Consider a swing that doubles as a bouncer and you'll have one less thing to store - not to mention one less product to buy.

Compatibility: Swings, jumpers and bouncers tend to stay out where they're handy to use. So consider the design and picture it in your home. Will you really want that aquarium theme on your living room floor for the next two years?

Washability: Whatever you choose, make sure it's easily washable, and remember to use gentle, toxin-free detergents. Almost every item in this category will end up in your baby's mouth at some point, so make sure it's clean and healthy!

by Ali Wing at egiggle.com

activity mats

★★★★★
"lila picks"

★ Gymni Super Deluxe Light And Music (Tiny Love)

5-in-1 Adjustable Gym ★★★★☆
Little Tykes (www.littletykes.com   800.321.0183)
Price ....$30-$35

Parent Reviews: *"...pretty basic, but entertaining... I like that we could first lay my son underneath it and then when he got older, he could stand and play... 10 different activities including a musical starfish... attractive fabric and toys—my baby loves this thing... not nearly as many things to do as some of the others out there—but then again it's a fair bit cheaper... hours of enjoyment... "*

Ali's Notes: *"...the whole point of the '5-in-1' is that the mat will grow with your baby (0-6 months as a play mat; 6-12 months as an activity center; 9-14 months to help babies stand; 12-36 months as either a play table or an easel... so, for the parent that wants more for every dollar, this one is in a class of its own for activity mats... the downside is that this one doesn't truly provide a 'mat' for floor coverage and doesn't travel well due to its design... "*

Boppy 5-in-1

★★★★☆

Boppy (www.boppy.com 888.772.6779)
Price .... $40-$45

Parent Reviews: *"...one of the best purchases we made for our baby... it's compact and we can take it everywhere... you can use it with or without the bars... just like the regular Boppy for breastfeeding, except this one works as a baby toy too..."*

Ali's Notes: *"...talk about multi-use... it's a toy, it's a breastfeeding aide, it's a pillow for mom to sit on... parents love its versatility and that it doesn't take up a ton of room in the house... lots of unobtrusive colors and patterns to choose from..."*

Discover & Play Activity Gym ★★★★☆

Baby Einstein (www.babyeinstein.com 800.793.1454)
Price .... $50-$60

Parent Reviews: *"...easy to set up and take wherever you go... baby can make lights and sounds go by pressing or kicking things... it eats up batteries pretty quickly, but my daughter has so much fun with it that I don't mind... it provides a little independence for both my baby and me... it comes with a bunch of toys that you can hang from the top... my baby especially loved the overhead star..."*

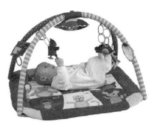

Drop & Pop Activity Gym ★★★☆☆

Lamaze (www.lamazetoys.com 800.704.8697)
Price $60

Parent Reviews: *"...nice and plush... my boy loves laying there and tries to kick and grab the toys hanging down... it folds easily and can be stored behind our couch... not too big so I don't feel like it's taking over our living room... nice carrying strap and lots of pockets to store toys..."*

Gymini 3-D Activity Gym ★★★★☆

Tiny Love (www.tinylove.com 714.898.0807)
Price .... $30-$40

Parent Reviews: *"...tried and tested—all of my friends had one of these for their babies and now that I have my daughter I understand why... very portable and helps keep my baby busy so I can get some things done around the house too... my son can stay*

on the mat for up to an hour—he loves it... half the time my baby ends up falling asleep after playing on the mat... folds easily and can be put away when you're not using it... "

Ali's Notes: "...Tiny Love's classic and most popular design... the red/white/black color scheme has been shown to have developmental benefits for infants... detachable toys can be removed and attached to car seats, cribs and strollers... portable and easy to store and launder... "

Gymni Super Deluxe Light And Music

★★★★★

Tiny Love (www.tinylove.com   714.898.0807)
Price .... $50-$60

Parent Reviews: "...a nice, soft, well-padded play area for my baby... this one has lights, sounds and even some music... lots of hidden surprises... my baby likes to crawl around on it and explore... my baby didn't seem to notice the lights until she was around 11 months old... more than just a couple of nursery rhyme songs would have been nice... the extra gizmos don't justify the price increase over the regular version... "

Ali's Notes: "...the 'deluxe' version of Tiny Love's classic Gymni... their playmats set the standard for playmats in general... many interchangeable, removable parts for use on strollers or car seats... the extra gadgets are almost overwhelming... it collapses flat and fits into pretty much any suitcase... travels well... winner of the most industry awards... "

Link-a-doos Musical Play Garden

★★★★☆

Fisher-Price (www.fisherprice.com   800.747.8697)

Price .... $25-$30

Parent Reviews: "...plush padding and toys provide plenty of entertainment... music, sound effects and crinkly things to play with... I love that you can change the toys since it is part of the Link-a-doos toy set... machine washable and very easy to stash away when not being used... "

Playnest & Activity Gym

★★★½☆

Galt Baby

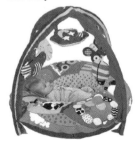

Price .... $70-$90

Parent Reviews: "...a great way to keep babies safe while they are learning to sit up on their own... our son is either sitting up and playing with the toys or lying down kicking them... if baby should fall backward he'll just land on the big plush pillow that surrounds him... the textures and activities on the fabric will keep them entertained... easy to wash... "

Splash Barnacle Activity Playmat

Mamas & Papas
Price $130

Parent Reviews: *"...it's a play mat and playpen in one... the best part is that it provides shade as well as entertainment... nice and soft with lots of dangling things to grab and pull on... rather pricey, but we've used ours a ton..."*

Ali's Notes: *"...for parents who want part playpen/part mat and don't mind the additional bulk, this is a two-in-one purchase..."*

bouncers & rockers

★★★★★

"lila picks"

★ Baby Sitter 1-2-3 (Baby Bjorn)
★ Kick And Play Bouncer (Fisher-Price)
★ Magic Moments Learning Seat (LeapFrog)

Baby Lounger
★★★★☆

Oeuf (www.oeufnyc.com 718.965.1216)
Price .... $100-$110

Parent Reviews: "...so much nicer looking than most of the other brightly colored bouncers... too bad it doesn't have the vibration feature—you'd think for the price they would be able to add that... I love the color choices..."

Ali's Notes: "...stylish and simple— it will actually look good in your living room... the ultimate minimalist bouncer (no vibrations or flashing lights), this bouncer is designed to fit into your living space along with the other 'adult' funiture..."

Baby Papasan Infant Seat
★★★★☆

Fisher-Price (www.fisherprice.com 800.747.8697)
Price .... $45-$50

Parent Reviews: "...so soft and cozy my daughter just sinks into the deep seat... love how I can throw the cover in the washer and dryer... a velour blanket attaches and is easy to detach too... light and easy to carry from room to room... a lifesaver when I need to get things done around the house... if they made them for adults, I would love to take a nap in it..."

Baby Sitter 1-2-3

★★★★★

Baby Bjorn (www.babybjorn.com 800.593.5522)
Price .... $99-$110

Parent Reviews: "...like everything else from Baby Bjorn this is a well-designed product... easy-to-wash (machine washable) cover... it collapses down very flat which is great for transporting it wherever you go... the restraint can be removed so when your baby gets bigger he can still use it as a seat... non-slip footpad keeps it steady on the floor..."

Ali's Notes: "...finally, a bouncer that you won't mind looking at as it sits on your living room floor... the bonus is that it's as functional as it is well-designed, with the ability to move it into the sleeping position without waking your dozing baby... includes a simple removable toy bar... as one of the few bouncers that can hold a bigger baby (up to 29 lbs) it's the perfect alternative to a playpen for containing a mobile toddler a few minutes for a quick shower break... not for parents who want electronic features like a vibrating seat or music..."

[multi-use] [style]

Cover N Play Bouncer

★★★★☆

Fisher-Price (www.fisherprice.com 800.747.8697)
Price .... $17-$20

Parent Reviews: "...it comes with a toy bar and cozy blanket... the blanket is attached so it can't fall off... a basic bouncer with a vibrating motor... it uses one D battery and seems to last for a while... the toys on the toy bar come off so my baby can chew on them too..."

Deluxe Activity Rocker

★★★★☆

Combi (www.combi-intl.com 800.992.6624)
Price .... $75-$85

Parent Reviews: "...a bouncy seat with some really nice features... plush, comfy seat that has three different recline positions... it vibrates and also rocks back and forth... a big canopy provides protection for when you're outside... soft toys on the toy bar are entertaining but I found my baby got bored with them pretty quickly... folds easily and relatively compactly..."

Discover And Play Bouncer ★★★★☆
Baby Einstein (www.babyeinstein.com 800.793.1454)

Price............................ $45-$50

Parent Reviews: "...a comfortable seat for playing or napping... fun for baby while mommy gets to take a shower... a fun piano for baby to bang on... the piano can also be set to be motion activated... smooth vibrations... lots of lights and music that is soothing but can also drive you a little crazy when it's constantly going off in the background... this seat was the first thing we were able to put our son into to give our arms a break..."

Flutterbye Dreams—Flutter & Chime Bouncer ★★★★⯪
Fisher-Price (www.fisherprice.com 800.747.8697)

Price.................................. $30

Parent Reviews: "...fun colors and works great—our baby loves the chair, especially when it's vibrating... the toy bar contains lots of things to look at to keep baby entertained... the music is cute, but can get a little annoying for adults... definitely worth having around to give you a break from holding your baby... fun little birdie on the tool bar that flutters his wings..."

Infant Rocker ★★★⯪☆
Hoohobbers (www.hoohobbers.com)

Price................................... $70

Parent Reviews: "...removable sun canopy is nice for when my baby's napping out on the porch... nothing fancy—no vibrations or anything... quite stable and the rocking motion seems soothing... the toy bar gets in the way of taking my baby in and out... nice looking..."

Infant to Toddler Rocker

★★★★☆

Fisher-Price (www.fisherprice.com   800.747.8697)
Price .... $30-$35

Parent Reviews: *"...I like that I can rock him or turn the vibrations on if I need to go do something else... the seat can be adjusted to a couple of different positions which is nice because now that my baby is older he likes to sit up more... fun hanging animals to play with... now that my boy is bigger, we use it as a rocking chair for him... good value for the money..."*

Ali's Notes: *"...it starts out as a solid vibrating infant seat and morphs into a cute toddler rocker... it can support a baby of up to 40 lbs... given the high weight limit, this is a great multi-stage purchase... at 8 lbs and without a lot of collapsibility, not geared to the frequent traveler..."*

(multi-use)

Kick and Play Bouncer

★★★★★

Fisher-Price (www.fisherprice.com   800.747.8697)
Price .... $30-$35

Parent Reviews: *"...a must for all parents with a newborn—it was the only way I was able to do things like take a shower or fold laundry... the vibrations calm baby and the music is actually quite nice... 10 songs and several sound effects that are activated by my baby's movements... the vibrations are great for getting my baby to sleep... I like that it has a bunch of toys attached to it—it seems more entertaining than just sitting in the seat watching me..."*

Ali's Notes: *"...this little bouncer sure can keep a baby busy... with the ever-important on/off options for sound, lights and volume control, this is one fully equipped entertainment bouncer... fun to watch little ones discover the kick-activated music and lights— at last, something they control (little do they know!)... every bouncy bell and whistle you could need—especially for the price..."*

(value)

Link-a-doos Bouncer

★★★★☆

Fisher-Price (www.fisherprice.com   800.747.8697)
Price .... $20-$25

Parent Reviews: *"...cute toys that are interchangeable with other Link-a-doos products... very soothing and calms my baby down—he loves sitting in it... the blanket is attached to the seat fabric... washable seat covers... the toy bar can be removed if you want your baby to take a nap... the blanket is attached to the seat..."*

Magic Moments Learning Seat ★★★★★
LeapFrog (www.leapfrog.com 800.701.5327)
Price $50

Parent Reviews: "...a must to keep baby occupied and entertained while you get something done around the house... my son loved grabbing the hanging toys which activate the lights and music... vibrating seat... play bar can be removed... nice and sturdy... the volume control is a lifesaver—some of the tunes will drive you batty after hearing them for the 500th time..."

Ali's Notes: "...in classic LeapFrog fashion, the Magic Moments Learning Seat is not just about fun but also about learning... equipped with three musical play modes—one for classical music, one for playful songs and one for word games... plenty of features to stimulate baby while still giving parents the highly underrated option of volume control... extra-wide base makes it super stable for no-worry playtime at home..."

Ocean Wonders Aquarium Bouncer ★★★★⯨
Fisher-Price (www.fisherprice.com 800.747.8697)
Price ....$35-$40

Parent Reviews: "...a fun, comfy little chair for my baby... my 6-month-old has practically lived in the thing for the last three months... my baby loves watching the water bubbles and fish... it looks like a real aquarium and the music is relaxing... it kept my daughter occupied while I was getting ready for work each morning... the toy bar comes off which is convenient when you want to use the chair for feeding..."

Rocker ★★★★☆
Maclaren (www.maclarenbaby.com 877.442.4622)
Price $70

Parent Reviews: "...a great neutral look, instead of the shrill bright colors that don't fit in anywhere... vibrations soothed baby when small... easy to adjust the height of the chair... it doesn't rock well on carpet... nice design... the harness straps are thin and sometimes difficult to adjust..."

Ali's Notes: "...a sophisticated and smart innovation that is true to Maclaren's style— stylish yet very functional... it easily morphs from an infant vibrating seat to baby rocker (up to 20 lbs)... no flashy neon colors—this rocker actually looks good in your living room..."

participate in our survey at

Soothing Massage Bouncer

★★★½☆

Fisher-Price (www.fisherprice.com 800.747.8697)
Price .... $30-$35

Parent Reviews: "...I liked this one because of the back massager, vibrator and music/sounds options that come with it... when my baby wasn't old enough to kick the bouncer for himself, I found that it was very easy to rock him... love how light it is—it made taking it to our grandparents' much easier... the one thing I didn't like about this is that it takes up to four D batteries... many gimmicks we never ended up using, but it worked great for naps and even feeding..."

Travel Lite Bouncer

★★★½☆

Graco (www.gracobaby.com 800.345.4109)
Price .... $50-$60

Parent Reviews: "...solid construction... it folds compactly and easily... the seat padding comes off and can be washed... two speed vibrations for napping... the toy bar comes off and the canopy provides great shade so I can take her with me out on the porch... it comes with a travel bag which makes it easy for us to take it wherever we go..."

Ali's Notes: "...true to its name this bouncer is ready for travel... packaged with its own travel bag... solidly built (it holds up to 18 lbs)... removable sun canopy and toy bar... compact and designed with easy two-step folding, this is one of few bouncers actually designed with travel in mind..."

activity centers

★★★★★
"lila picks"

★ ExerSaucer Mega Active Learning Ctr (Evenflo)
★ ExerSaucer Ultra Active Learning Ctr (Evenflo)
★ Learn & Groove Activity Station (LeapFrog)

Baby Einstein
★★★★☆

Graco (www.gracobaby.com 800.345.4109)

Price .... $75-$80

Parent Reviews: *"...chock full of things to touch, turn, push and explore... the seat turns all the way around so my baby can always see where I am... the legs extend so you can make it taller as you child grows... lots of flashing lights and sounds... a large, bulky eyesore in our living room—if it wasn't so much fun for my tot I'd get rid of it in a second... 14 toys provide hours of entertainment for my son and a few precious moments for me to get stuff done around the house..."*

Ali's Notes: *"...one of the best values around... known for its multilingual word activities... the emphasis is on music, colors and language development... another fully loaded (i.e. busy) activity saucer, but with some 'best of' features..."*

multi-use

Baby Playzone Take-Along Hop 'n Pop

★★★½☆

Fisher-Price (www.fisherprice.com 800.747.8697)
Price ....$40-$50

Parent Reviews: "...cheap, fun and very portable... balls pop, lights go on and songs and sounds abound as my baby jumps around... it bounces nicely when your baby tries to jumps up and down... it comes folded into a relatively compact unit and can be stowed away much more easily than those big round activity centers..."

Ali's Notes: "...designed to be the easy travel solution for the activity saucer category... it's definitely designed for easy collapsibility... carry handle makes it easy to lug around... realistically, it still requires dedicated cargo space in your car or suitcase..."

Baby Sit & Step 2-in-1 Activity Center

Kolcraft (www.kolcraft.com 800.453.7673)
Price ....$70-$80

Bouncin' Baby Play Place

★★★★☆

Safety 1st (www.safety1st.com 800.544.1108)
Price ....$40-$50

Parent Reviews: "...all the toys and stimulation my baby could ask for... 10 different toys and a bunch of songs and sounds that come and go depending on what he just played with... the seat spins around all the way... three height adjustments... it took my boy some time to figure out what to do with the car, but now he spends hours pushing it around the track..."

ExerSaucer Deluxe

★★★★☆

Evenflo (www.evenflo.com 800.233.5921)
Price ....$35-$40

Parent Reviews: "...plenty of activity for my baby... seven toys and three height adjustments... the seat swivels but can also be locked at six different positions if your baby wants to focus on a particular toy... sturdy and durable—my son banged on this thing for months and we were still able to pass it on to our neighbor..."

Ali's Notes: "...Evenflo's lightweight and minimalist addition to their activity center line... a 'less is more' approach, but otherwise a standard Evenflo saucer... decent collapsibility for storage..."

ExerSaucer Mega Active Learning Center

Evenflo (www.evenflo.com 800.233.5921)
Price .... $60-$65

Parent Reviews: "...durable, stable and very entertaining... colorful and offers lots of stimulation for my baby... it adjusts to three height positions so he can get used to standing on his feet... the seat swivels all the way around but can also be locked... the seat is removable and I was able to wash out all of the milk and food stains very easily... it folds flat and even has a carry handle for easy transportation to grandma's house..."

Ali's Notes: "...Evenflo dominates the activity center/exersaucer market wins accolades for 'most saucer for the money'... the 'mega' has more than enough to keep your baby busy... some think even the medium models overwhelm most babies... decent collapsibility for storage..."

ExerSaucer SmartSteps

Evenflo (www.evenflo.com 800.233.5921)
Price .... $90-$110

Parent Reviews: "...the seat swivels so your baby has 360 degrees of stuff to touch and play with... some of the toys are hard to figure out... adjusts to 3 different levels which gives it a pretty good shelf life... works nicely if you have a playroom—ours was in the living room and it sure took up a lot of room... kept my little one entertained so I could get some things done around the house..."

Ali's Notes: "...the luxury version of Evenflo's saucers... they've added electronic flip books and overhead toy bars to an already complete array of activities... the larger size requires additional space and some parents comment that babies outgrow this seat faster than similarly designed options..."

ExerSaucer Ultra Active Learning Center

Evenflo (www.evenflo.com 800.233.5921)
Price .... $75-$90

Parent Reviews: "...just like the Mega Active Learning Center but with a few extras... a buzzing, blinking, swiveling and spinning action machine—my daughter loves it... 11 toys and 22 songs... three height adjustments and a 360 degree swiveling seat... my son entertains himself for hours, which gives me a chance to take care of things around the house... my baby eats, plays and would probably sleep in this thing if he could... folds and comes apart for easy transportation..."

Ali's Notes: **"**...*Evenflo dominates the activity center/exersaucer market and they win 'most saucer for the money' accolades... think of the 'ultra' as a step up from the 'mega'—more than enough to keep your baby busy...* **"**

ExerSaucer Walk Around

★★★½☆

Evenflo (www.evenflo.com 800.233.5921)
Price ....$35-$45

Parent Reviews: **"**...*a walker that has one stable leg and two on wheels so he can walk around in circles... perfect for practicing walking since it prevents my daughter from walking into dangerous zones... eight toys and a few songs that they can activate on their own... enough activities to keep baby occupied for more than 30 minutes so I can prepare dinner... woks well even on thick carpeting... three height positions that are easily adjustable...* **"**

Learn & Groove Activity Station

★★★★★

LeapFrog (www.leapfrog.com 800.701.5327)
Price ....$75-$90

Parent Reviews: **"**...*well-made and fun for my boy... 5 positions—all with something to touch or gnaw on... 3 different positions to adjust for different heights... the seat cover is machine washable... it does fold a little, but not nearly compactly enough to fit in our closet...* **"**

Ali's Notes: **"**...*a fully-loaded activity center with the usual smart design and developmental focus that we've become accustomed to from LeapFrog... music, numbers and color based focus... it collapses but not very well for small storage areas... hard to beat for smart fun...* **"**

jumpers

★★★★★

"lila picks"

★ Classic Johnny Jump Up (Evenflo)
★ Deluxe Jumperoo (Fisher-Price)

Classic Johnny Jump Up
★★★★★

Evenflo (www.evenflo.com 800.233.5921)
Price .... $18-$20

Parent Reviews: *"...a fun little jumper with a clamp that fits doorjambs up to six inches wide... the spring has a casing so neither you nor your baby will get your fingers pinched... my baby loves hanging out in his jumper—bounces around and swings back and forth... the seat is machine-washable..."*

Ali's Notes: *"...this bouncy little thing is a classic and a consistent favorite among parents... good value—well made, easily portable and overall good value for the money..."*

Deluxe Jumperoo
★★★★★

Fisher-Price (www.fisherprice.com 800.747.8697)
Price .... $50-$60

Parent Reviews: *"...I like this jumper because I don't have to scratch up my doorway... easy to set up and take down... all the springs have soft covers so you won't get your fingers caught... since it's freestanding you can use it anywhere... attached toys and music make for hours of fun and give me a chance to catch up on things around the house..."*

Ali's Notes: *"...more than a bouncer—it's also an activity center and rocker... equipped with toys and music, this bouncer is likely to keep even the lukewarm bouncer entertained..."*

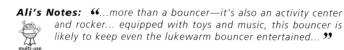

Doorway Jumpster

Graco (www.gracobaby.com 800.345.4109)
Price ....$25-$30

Parent Reviews: *"...my son finds it very comfortable... this jumper keeps my baby busy for at least a half hour—very fun to watch... the spring has just the right amount of tension... easy to adjust the height depending on the doorway or the height of the child... fits on pretty much any doorway with a ledge..."*

ExerSaucer SmartSteps Jump & Go

Evenflo (www.evenflo.com 800.233.5921)
Price ....$45-$50

Parent Reviews: *"...good idea, but didn't work the way we expected... our baby managed to grab the side of the jumper and banged his hand on the door frame... we liked the toys on the toy bar... a jumper with lights and activities... not long enough for our higher-than-normal door..."*

Twist 'n Shout Bumper Jumper

Graco (www.gracobaby.com 800.345.4109)
Price ....$30-$35

Parent Reviews: *"...the bumper helps prevent my boy from crashing into the side of the door... the tray is good for keeping toys although they don't stay on there for long and inevitably end up on the floor... both my children loved this jumper, it kept them active and entertained for 20 minutes at a time... the seat comes off and is washable..."*

swings

★★★★★

"lila picks"

★ Aquarium Take-Along Swing (Fisher-Price)
★ Ocean Wonders Aquarium Cradle Swing)

2-in-1 Smart Fold Swing

Evenflo (www.evenflo.com 800.233.5921)
Price $90

Parent Reviews: *" ...what a life saver—there were many nights when my daughter would only go to sleep in her swing... very adjustable... brightly-colored toys keep my baby busy... compact and folds easily... "*

Aquarium Take-Along Swing

Fisher-Price (www.fisherprice.com 800.747.8697)
Price ....$55-$60

Parent Reviews: *" ...it folds flat and is easy to take along when we visit friends... eight speed settings... six songs with twinkling lights... volume control is key if you get tired of hearing the same songs over and over... two hanging toys which baby can pull to activate music... quite effective at soothing our fussy baby... my son loved it and often fell asleep in it... "*

Ali's Notes: *" ...for the swing-dependent sleeper (I hear of them often!), this is our pick for traveling... compact and reasonably priced... "*

Deluxe Quick Response Swing with Remote Control

Fisher-Price (www.fisherprice.com 800.747.8697)
Price .... $80-$90

Parent Reviews: "...*high tech!.. I can adjust the swing speed and music from the kitchen... five swing speeds, five music selections... three position recline... I like the remote control idea, but I keep losing it and so I end up having to go over to the swing anyway... the toy tray is removable...*"

Flutterbye Dreams Swing

Fisher-Price (www.fisherprice.com 800.747.8697)
Price $80

Parent Reviews: "...*kind of gimmicky, but we all love the 'fluttering birdie'... lights, music and the bird flapping overhead keeps my baby entertained for quite a while... plenty to look at and pull on... 6 swing speeds and a comfy reclining seat... it folds well for storage and looks good in our living room...*"

Link-a-doos Magical Mobile Swing

Fisher-Price (www.fisherprice.com 800.747.8697)
Price .... $70-$80

Parent Reviews: "...*lots of features... six swing speeds... 10 songs including the twirling bee and butterfly... room on either side to mount Link-a-doos toys for entertainment... the seat reclines... this swing has been a lifesaver in terms of allowing us to take care of some things around the house while knowing that she is safe and happy...*"

Link-a-doos Open Top Take-Along Swing

Fisher-Price (www.fisherprice.com 800.747.8697)
Price .... $40-$50

Parent Reviews: "...*the Link-A-Doos toys are all interchangeable so it's almost like having a new swing every few weeks... five swing speeds and five songs... my daughter loves hanging out in the chair and it gives me a chance to take a shower... low to the ground and safe... easy to get baby in and out...*"

swings

Nature's Touch Baby Papasan Cradle Swing

★★★★⯪

Fisher-Price (www.fisherprice.com 800.747.8697)
Price .... $40-$50

Parent Reviews: "...it swings both ways, the birds move around and the mirror is fun for my baby to look at... my baby's favorite way to fall asleep... the music always starts back at the same tune... a side-to-side or front-to-back swing— definitely more versatile than other swings... plush and soft..."

Ocean Wonders Aquarium Cradle Swing

★★★★★

Fisher-Price (www.fisher-price.com   800.747.8697)

Price .... $70-$80

Parent Reviews: "...so many features... music, lights and ocean waves... the swing takes up a fair amount of room... it has 6 speeds and 8 songs... the seat reclines which is great for getting my baby to rock to sleep... the pads all come off and can be machine washed... not only does it swing forwards and backwards, but it also moves side-to-side like a cradle..."

Ali's Notes: "...best known for its sideways swinging capability (yes, this is in addition to a standard front-and-back swing)... this one has become the new parents' swing of choice..."

Open Top Swing Deluxe

★★★★☆

Graco (www.gracobaby.com   800.345.4109)

Price .... $50-$60

Parent Reviews: "...it comes with either 2, 3 or 6 speeds... the seat reclines to three different positions... this swing has rocked my baby to sleep so many times I can't even count them... uses 4 D batteries which are a bit of a pain to replace... quiet operation and easy to get baby in and out... plays 15 songs and comes with a detachable mobile..."

Peaceful Time Open Top Swing

Fisher-Price (www.fisherprice.com 800.747.8697)
Price .... $45-$50

★★★★☆

Parent Reviews: **"**...easy to assemble and clean... 2 swing speeds, 5 songs and 3 recline positions for the seat... it really sucks battery power—I feel like I'm constantly having to change them... the pad comes off easily and is machine-washable... **"**

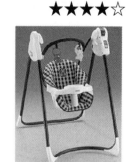

Perfect Height Swing With Mini Maestro

Kolcraft (www.kolcraft.com 800.453.7673)
Price .... $80-$90

★★★½☆

Parent Reviews: **"**...this swing has a height adjustable seat... it seems like a minor detail, but it does help in terms of me not having to hunch over the whole time... lights and music... removable snack tray... it takes up a fair amount of room but that also makes it more stable... comes with infant head support pillow... **"**

Smart Stages 3-in-1 Rocker Swing

Fisher-Price (www.fisherprice.com 800.747.8697)
Price $70

★★★★☆

Parent Reviews: **"**...2 swing speeds and 5 different lullabies... low to the ground and quite compact... the coolest part is that the seat comes off and can be used as a stand-alone rocker... smart design—at home we use it as a swing, and when we travel we just take the seat... fun toys to pull and play with... **"**

Swyngomatic Infant Swing

Graco (www.gracobaby.com 800.345.4109)
Price .... $40-$45

★★★½☆

Parent Reviews: **"**...music and 6 swing speeds... it's low to the ground which makes me feel like it's safer for my baby... it works well, really calms my baby and allows me to get some things done... pretty basic but very effective... **"**

Travel Lite Swing

Graco (www.gracobaby.com 800.345.4109)
Price ....$65-$75

★★★⯨☆

Parent Reviews: *"...designed so you can take it on the road with you... nice carry handle and it folds really easily... the seat reclines to three positions... a couple of toys hang down from the canopy and there also are flashing lights and music... feels sturdy and safe... our baby seems very happy whenever we put him in it..."*

clothing & shoes

Most first-time parents have no idea whether they prefer T-shirts to onesies, pajamas to gowns, or plain undershirts to ones that snap. The only way to find out is to try them. It also helps to get to know your baby - many of whom have their own very clear likes and dislikes. The best approach is to not buy too many of any given thing until you've explored all your options.

Comfort: Remember, comfy is more important than cute. Besides, babies look cute in just about everything! It's particularly amazing how much their tummies can change sizes throughout the day, and soft, stretchy materials will help ease the transition from play time to meal time to nap time.

Chemicals: Pay special attention to the fabrication and finish of newborn clothing. Look for formaldehyde-free finishes and avoid unnecessary chemicals that can irritate young skin - especially considering that babies, pound for pound, are more highly affected by chemicals than adults are.

Stocking Up: Remember, during the first few years, children outgrow their clothes quickly. Most sizes last about three to six months, tops. Although it's tempting to buy every cute outfit you see, a few dress-up outfits at a time will usually do. Other than that, value-priced basics you can mix and match are a smart way to go.

Shoes: Shoes should provide traction and protection for tiny feet, while not restricting them in any way with hard, tight or inflexible soles. Babies have chubby little feet that start out more rounded than flat, so look for shoes that are flexible, soft and simple. Not all shoes are made round enough for some babies' feet, even among really great brands, so be sure to try them out before you buy.

Roominess: From a practical perspective, make sure you can slip your baby's shoes off and on without feeling like you have to twist their legs off. Remember, looser is better - just so long as they don't fall off on the way to the park!

Don't Overbuy: Most parents find little ones are happiest with no shoes, and even those who wear them grow out of them quickly. So don't overbuy. One or two of each size is usually more than enough. Especially since shoes, unlike clothes, are tougher to pass on as seconds.

by Ali Wing at egiggle.com

clothing

"lila picks"

- ★ BabyGap
- ★ Hanna Andersson
- ★ Old Navy
- ★ Petit Bateau
- ★ Teacollection

Agabang ★★★★½
(www.agabang.com)
Parent Reviews: **"**...great separates—easy to mix and match... I love the whimsical, fun styles... excellent selection for newborns... the basic patterns make it easy to shop... the bold, bright colors are so much fun... their website is really easy to use... good selection for both boys and girls... their cotton-blend clothing is so soft... **"**

Anita G ★★★★★
(www.anitag.com   800.717.0789)
Parent Reviews: **"**...my kids love the bright colors... so easy to take care of and they wear really well... the simple styles make this clothing kid-friendly... reasonably priced clothes and shipping... excellent return policy... well-made clothing... fun Hawaiian-style swim wear... love this company's socially conscious approach (they donate a percentage of their sales to kid's charities)... **"**

Baby Lulu ★★★★☆
(www.babylulu.com)
Parent Reviews: **"**...pretty fabrics... lots of flowers... excellent, comfortable cotton fabrics... stylish and fun—fair value... lasts a long time—so far through three baby girls... expensive... worth the splurge every now and again for your little princess... created by a fashion designer, so the clothes are both elegant and fun... colorful prints and great patterns... **"**

Baby Wit ★★★★⯨
(www.babywit.com)
Parent Reviews: **"**...hip T-shirts with a sense of humor (everything from pop culture to political imprints)... quirky and fun styles... so many T-shirts to choose from... funky, whimsical... founded by a stay-at-home mom who has a sense of humor... the sizing chart on the website is really helpful... the only place where I can find black infant T-shirts... I love their 70's styles... I like that I can pick from a wide variety of decals... made-to-order shirts, so they do not accept returns...**"**

BabyGap ★★★★★
(www.gap.com)
Parent Reviews: **"**...I love the unisex clothing—my kids can share clothing... excellent selection for newborns... the best return policy out there... priced well enough so I can stock up... holds up after many washings... cute clothes at affordable prices... their website is great—one-stop shopping... great looking clothes that hold up to lots of scuffing and playing... as far as I'm concerned, this is the only place for basics...**"**

Ali's Notes: **"**...great for everyday wearability and basics... just like for mom and dad (except much smaller)... not always cheap, but they feature great sales regularly...**"**

Babystyle ★★★★☆
(www.babystyle.com)
Parent Reviews: **"**...basic pants and snap shirts for girls and boys are reasonably priced and great quality... 2-for-1 deals on basics are fantastic... simple, solid colors, not just blue and pink... some expensive items but they do have good sales... good basics that are all about fashion... soft and sweet... lots of good sales... the kimonos are so neat...**"**

Bon Bebe ★★★★☆
(www.bonbebeworld.com)
Parent Reviews: **"**...the highest quality layette on the market... big selection of styles... lots of ideas on the web site so I can create a wardrobe for my newborn... specialize in clothing for babies age 0 to 2 years... super soft fabrics are perfect for my baby...**"**

Carter's ★★★★⯨
(www.carters.com   888.782.9548)
Parent Reviews: **"**...great sleepers and onesies... T-shirts are always soft and keep their shape... great prices, especially at the outlet stores... very stretchy and well-placed snaps... good quality and well-designed... some of the fancy stuff for infants is overkill and hard to justify paying more for... zippers aren't the best, they seem scratchy against my child's skin...**"**

Ali's Notes: **"**...no question about it—Carter's presents a comprehensive, well-priced basic collection... we hear that many parents feel Carter's runs a bit small... not always the softest fabrics, but tough to beat their prices...**"**

Catimini ★★★★☆
(www.catimini.com)
Parent Reviews: **"**...European baby fashion at its best... this is couture for babies... I love their light, airy fabrics... such attention to detail... their exclusive fabrics are one-of-a-kind and the embroidery is really beautiful... the most luxurious garments out

there... terrible web site, too difficult to use... I like the innovative fabrics, you don't see this kind of clothing on too many kids... "
Ali's Notes: "*...big, bold European style design... all about style and fun...these classy duds require hand-washing and special care...* "

Children's Place, The ★★★☆☆
(www.childrensplace.com 877.752.2387)
Parent Reviews: "*...a great selection of everything for newborns to 10 years... amazing prices... I can get everything I need... huge inventory... great customer service... basics at wonderful prices... durable, fashionable... cute designs at great prices... terrific sales and lots of stores... the first place I shop... good return policy... you can get everything from onesies to dresses to bathing suits...* "
Ali's Notes: "*...utility pricing with most the basics covered... nothing fancy or upscale, but they are perfect for basics like socks, onesies, pants...* "

Devi Baby ★★★★☆
(www.devibaby.com)
Parent Reviews: "*...inspired by traditional ethnic wear from around the world... each item is unique and made by hand... I love the kurtas—tunics made from cotton and silk... so unique, unlike any baby clothing out there... the cotton silk pants are so cute—you certainly won't see this on every kid... the dresses are so pretty... adorable 'ethnic' ponchos... Asian-inspired silk and cotton tunics, pants and skirts...* "

Gerber ★★★★☆
(www.gerberchildrenswear.com 800.443.7237)
Parent Reviews: "*...excellent onesies that come in packs of 3... strong snaps... my newborn lives in their T-shirts, onesies, gowns, play suits and mitts... not the greatest materials... a little thin, and not quite as durable as others...* "
Ali's Notes: "*...cushiony cotton onesies just like their diapers... conventional cottons... for Gerber diaper fans, these can be great basics...* "

Gymboree ★★★★½
(www.gymboree.com 877.449.6932)
Parent Reviews: "*...lots of items with similar themes make it easy to coordinate... clothes are very durable and last through many washings and numerous siblings... lots of unisex clothing as well as gender-specific... love the accessories... competitively priced... I always find something good on their sale rack... items sell quickly, you might not be able to find an exactly matching piece... mix/match patterns and styles for easy assembly... in between contemporary everyday basics and dressy occasion wear...* "

Hanna Andersson ★★★★★
(www.hannaandersson.com 800.222.0544)
Parent Reviews: "*...fun, colorful clothing... unique styles and very soft fabrics... expensive but worth it... clothing lasts forever and doesn't seem to shrink... lots of room for growth... sweet, basic, lush—Hanna's clothes are essential treats for all babies... love*

the matching outfits for mom and child... a couple of great sales throughout the year cuts costs... "

Ali's Notes: "...simple, bright, fun separates with a fun, cheery look... made with Oeko-Tex and some organic cottons... known for their wearability and durability over time... "

Hartstrings ★★★★☆
(www.hartstrings.com   610.687.6900)
Parent Reviews: "...love the quality and styles... withstand wear and tear... I bought a lot of this brand for my oldest daughter, loaned it to my niece, and now it's looking great on my youngest daughter... reasonable prices... dresses do not come with matching bloomers for infants... sometimes styles have a bit too much glitz or embroidery going on... "

HealthTex ★★★★☆
(www.healthtex.com   800.554.7637)
Parent Reviews: "...cute, functional styles—perfect as play clothes... dependable and appropriately priced... good sizing for babies... pajamas wear extremely well in the wash and stay nice and soft... not good for hand-me-downs—clothes just don't last that long... mix and match outfits—animal tags make matching for preschoolers easy... "

Jacadi ★★½☆☆
(www.jacadiusa.com   914.697.7684)
Parent Reviews: "...all clothing is made in France... European clothing means superb quality... excellent attention to detail... upscale baby clothes with beautiful workmanship... huge selection of nursery items... the ultimate Easter dress brand... for the special photo-op (before the ice cream and messy chocolate cake are served)... fantastic quality... high-end... can be high maintenance in terms of care, and a bit pricey... "

Janie And Jack ★★★★☆
(www.janieandjack.com   877.449.8800)
Parent Reviews: "...I love the European style of the clothes... beautiful hand knit Merino wool and cashmere sweaters, hats and blankets... high-end... sale items are still pricey... nicely designed and decorated stores... adorable gift wrapping... the clothes hold up to lots of washings, the buttons stay on and colors don't run... perfect for gifts ... "

Ali's Notes: "...this is Gymboree's high-end line... perfect for special events or dressy wear... European influenced... clean and elegant designs... pricey, but worth the quality... high maintenance in terms of care... "

Kelly's Kids ★★★★½
(www.kellyskids.com)
Parent Reviews: "...clothing that definitely makes a statement... excellent customer service... a great selection of Polarfleece items... unique patterns and bold, bright colors... can be purchased by attending 'home parties' where representatives show the clothing line... "

Le Top
(www.letop-usa.com)
Parent Reviews: **"**...unique, whimsical clothing... excellent selection of clothes for preemies... very well-made... I found a great Halloween costume... their cotton feels really soft and holds up through many washes... I love the toys that match the outfits... they make everything from layette to outerwear... extra touches like bows and stitching make this clothing unique....**"**

Little Me
(www.littleme.com)
Parent Reviews: **"**...big selection and variety of styles... attention to detail is impressive... I love that the onesies have matching snaps... a good selection for premature babies... the double-needle top-stitching makes clothes look good and is durable... reasonably priced... signature lines for all styles and price points... think Macy's and Nordstrom's...**"**

Oilily
(www.oilily-world.com)
Parent Reviews: **"**...absolutely darling... the cutest clothes ever... colors are vibrant and beautiful... $158 for a cardigan, are they kidding?.. it's the type of clothing you'd find in a European boutique... very unusual... good deals to be found on eBay and other discount sites...**"**

Ali's Notes: **"**...fabulous and expensive... great for special-occasion pieces... bold, bright, almost baby couture... nice construction... fancy items that will require special care during cleaning...**"**

Old Navy
(www.oldnavy.com 800.653.6289)
Parent Reviews: **"**...high inventory turnover means you can always find something new... really fun stuff at great prices... very comfy fabrics... great styles and cheap enough that you can buy lots of stuff... fun, cute clothes and adorable seasonal items... many of the shirts I bought for my toddler faded quickly and some started coming apart at the seams... I wish they didn't put their logo on so many of their basics... not always as inexpensive as advertised... wait for the sales...**"**

Ali's Notes: **"**...great prices and good selection (especially for girls)... always fresh and almost impossible to beat their prices (and sales) for your everyday 'run around in the park' clothes... clothes wear and fade faster than other brands, but given the price you can go back to get new duds...**"**

OshKosh B'Gosh
(www.oshkoshbgosh.com 800.692.4674)
Parent Reviews: **"**...who can resist a toddler in OshKosh overalls?.. my daughter is wearing my old overalls—now that's durability... some toddler clothes are too babyish... pricey for everyday wear—wait for the sales or go to the outlets... most designs have the handy diaper snaps up the legs... durable, durable, durable...**"**

Petit Bateau ★★★★★
(www.petit-bateau.com)
Parent Reviews: *"...not many US stores but can find clothing in other retail stores... lovely soft, stretchy and slim fitting baby clothes... their onesies are especially nice for babies... clothing lasts forever... fabric feels like it will hold up to many washings... true, their clothes are expensive but, once you see your baby in their clothes you won't be able to resist..."*
Ali's Notes: *"...from the French company that makes the number 1 rated women's T-shirts, we get great quality onesies and basics... they're known for their fabrics and conservative styling..."*

Polo Ralph Lauren ★★★★☆
(www.polo.com)
Parent Reviews: *"...classic and hip baby wear... love the preppy baby look... quality is excellent and built to last... great markdowns on the sale racks and in discount stores... stylish and durable..."*
Ali's Notes: *"...think preppy baby... higher quality fabrics means more care required when washing... pricey, pricey, but nice..."*

Preemie-Yums ★★★★☆
(www.preemie-yums.com)
Parent Reviews: *"...for infants up through 6 lbs... you can customize products to create individual styles... the Velcro snaps are so helpful... their clothing allows for medical needs to be met... the web site is for wholesalers and retailers only, but their clothes can be ordered from individual retailers..."*

Sweet Potatoes ★★★★☆
(www.sweetpotatoesinc.com 800.634.2584)
Parent Reviews: *"...adorable unique clothes... one-of-a-kind designs... easy to get babies in and out of these clothes... really soft cotton that lasts long and wears well... great deals at the outlets... the quality isn't as good as it could be considering the cost..."*

Talbots ★★★★☆
(www.talbots.com)
Parent Reviews: *"...Talbots kids has the most beautiful, best quality baby and children's clothing... very well made, can wear through many kids... beautiful christening gowns are available too... great selection online... sale and clearance prices are great..."*

Teacollection ★★★★★
(www.teacollection.com)
Parent Reviews: *"...practical clothing that looks and feels wonderful... they have a really good mix of stylish yet practical... on the higher end in terms of both pricing and quality... adorable..."*
Ali's Notes: *"...one of the most popular lines on the market... smart, sophisticated and beautifully constructed... dressy yet very suitable for everyday wear... you pay for the sophistication..."*

Wry Baby

(www.wrybaby.com)

Parent Reviews: **"**...onesies and T-shirts with hilarious logos, graphics and phrases... so creative and exceptionally funny... the best web site out there, I laughed out loud as I was shopping... unique and hip baby clothing... so many people comment and ask me where I got my kid's onesie... great gift sets.... the perfect gift for any newborn with a sense of humor...**"**

Zutano

(www.zutano.com   802.223.2229)

Parent Reviews: **"**...really cute, coordinated clothing for up to 24 months... everything matches their solids so you can mix and match easily... good selection of gender-neutral clothing... costly and seems to run small... washes and wears well... my boy couldn't look cuter in these fun patterns...**"**

Ali's Notes: **"**...fun, bright, and cheery... easy to mix and match... great for everyday wear, but nice enough for somewhat formal occasions... simple and contemporary...**"**

shoes

★★★★★
"lila picks"
★ Pediped s   ★ Robeez

Bobux ★★★★☆
(www.bobux.com)
Parent Reviews: *"...super soft natural leather infant shoes... helps absorbs sweat in during the summer and keeps little feet warm in the winter... my son wore them for months and didn't wear them out... about $30..."*

Elefanten ★★★★⯪
(www.elefanten.de)
Parent Reviews: *"...a must-have for those first walkers, second best only to bare feet!... contemporary styles—your toddler will not only be comfortable, but will look just adorable... no need to break in... easy to walk and run in... flexible and offer good support... very well-made shoes..."*

Keds ★★★★⯪
(www.keds.com   800.680.0966)
Parent Reviews: *"...nice styles and lots of sizes from baby through adult... their shoes last for a long time... the cutest tennis shoes that look adorable on little ones... not cheap, but great quality..."*

Naturino ★★★★☆
(www.naturino.com)
Parent Reviews: *"...really cool shoes for crawlers and toddlers too... very comfortable and well made... they've got that wonderful Italian shoe thing going on which also applies to kids' shoes... great styles and colors—even for boys!... stylish and well-made—they last for years through several kids..."*

Payless Shoes ★★★★☆
(www.payless.com   877.474.6379)
Parent Reviews: "...excellent shoe selection for babies and toddlers... great place to get ballet shoes... cute casual styles, durable enough for rapidly-growing feet... my son loves the cartoon character sneakers... pretty sandals and general play wear... they often have sales... definitely not high-end but your kids feet grow so fast they won't wear them for long... cheap..."

Pedipeds ★★★★★
(www.pedipeds.com   800.880.1245)
Parent Reviews: "...comfy and cool looking... my baby used them as he was learning how to stand up and walk and I feel like they protected his feet and helped him find traction on the floor... more expensive than other baby shoe brands, but you totally get what you pay for..."

Ali's Notes: "...the next best thing to bare feet—not only do they have a soft leather sole (which is highly recommended by pediatricians for babies' developing feet), but they're adorably stylish... they also provide better protection than ordinary soft-sole shoes because of their two layers of durable leather and cushioned soles..."

Platy Paws
(www.platypaws.com   877.752.8979)

Preschoolians ★★★★★
(www.preschoolians.com)
Parent Reviews: "...excellent shoes for babies who are crawling and just learning how to walk... light, flexible, cute and easy to size appropriately... the best 'first shoes' money can buy... so flexible—it's almost like walking barefoot... I love the view-through sole so you can see how they fit... they come with 3 foot beds for feet of different widths... shoes for every phase from crawlers to walkers... great designs... never slip off..."

Robeez ★★★★★
(www.robeez.com   800.929.2649)
Parent Reviews: "...awesome baby shoe selection... slip-on shoes that don't slip off... the best gift we've received... perfect for hardwood floors when learning to walk... keeps those socks on... durable toddler shoes that easily last through a couple kids... cute styles for play as well as special occasions... about $25 for a good pair... the elastic can dig into chubbier feet..."

Ali's Notes: "...a popular favorite, particularly for the price... the biggest selection of styles from basics (solid colors) to bright and fun... Robeez really sets the market standard for baby slip-on shoes, with the only regular complaint that they can be tight for some chubby baby feet..."

Shoo Shoos ★★★★☆
(www.shooshoosusa.com)
Parent Reviews: "...machine-washable, breathable Napa leather moccasin style shoes... great selection for babies learning to walk... provided my baby with comfortable protection without confining her feet... sturdy, practical, and my child loves them... darling patterns and styles..."

Stride Rite Shoes

(www.striderite.com 800.650.7708)

Parent Reviews: *"...great arch support and quality construction... a great place for fittings and to find baby's first 'walking' shoe... not always easy to find... a little pricey but worth it... my daughter loves her shoes -they're the only ones she'll wear... walkers have the 'natural motion system', with flexible soles that allow baby to walk as naturally as possible..."*

bath time & personal care

This is one area where you won't lack for choices. There are tons of remarkably similar, molded-plastic baby tubs on the market. Luckily, they're generally pretty inexpensive, so you can't make a big mistake. And while you'll be glad you have a tub you love early on, you might be amazed at how quickly your baby outgrows it. There are also lots of personal care products to choose from, but really, you only need a couple of well-chosen basics. Keep bath time fun with these worry-free tips for picking a tub and bath products!

Tub Styles: Baby bathtubs come in two different styles: those for the sink and those for the tub. Sink tubs are for newborns, and tub styles can be for all ages. If you're tall (or a little less than limber) you might want to take advantage of the sink and save bending over a tub for later stages.

Tub Features: Basic features almost everyone will want are a non-slip surface and some form of recline or adjustability for growing, changing babies. Depending on your lifestyle, you might also want to explore portability.

Multi-Stage Tubs: More and more baby tubs are offering a multi-stage approach to take you from newborn to toddler tub in one purchase. If you do choose a multi-stage, make sure the tub you choose is still pretty basic and doesn't require a degree to figure out how to adjust or position. You'll be nervous enough as you begin bathing…eliminate unnecessary stress where you can!

Bath Products: When it comes to bath products, less is definitely more. When a little warm water and a washcloth aren't enough, use mild, hypoallergenic, natural or organic products. Babies are delicate, and gentle skin care softens their introduction to our chemical world.

Newborn Basics: Focus on the basics. For newborns, you'll need some gentle, foam shampoo or wash, a good diaper barrier cream and mild diaper wipes. Unless you're treating a specific problem area, that's really all you'll need.

Toddler Basics: As your newborn turns into a toddler, you'll want to upgrade to tearless shampoo and gentle bubble bath. Add in sunscreen for everyday wear and you've got the basics covered!

by Ali Wing at egiggle.com

infant bathtubs

★★★★★
"lila picks"

★ Euro Bath Tub (Primo)
★ Infant Bath Seat (Primo)

Comfort First Tub
★★★★☆
Evenflo (www.evenflo.com 800.233.5921)
Price $12
Parent Reviews: **"**...*a nice padded backrest... the 'clean water' area is pretty small and gets soapy water in it anyway, so it's kind of gimmicky... the drainage plug changes color when the water temperature is too hot... I like the hook—that way we can get it off the floor to dry...* **"**

Deluxe 4-in-1 Bath Station
★★★½☆
Safety 1st (www.safety1st.com 800.544.1108)
Price ....$17-$20
Parent Reviews: **"**...*it expands and contracts so you might get longer use out of it, compared to other tubs... good idea to put suction cups on the bottom so it doesn't slip around in the tub... best of all, it collapses so it doesn't take up a ton of room when you're storing it... the only problem is that my son ended up sliding down to the bottom because there wasn't much to hold him from sliding down—once he was able to sit on his own it wasn't a problem...* **"**

www.lilaguide.com

Euro Bath Tub

★★★★★

Primo (www.primobaby.com 973.926.5900)
Price ....$35-$40

Parent Reviews: "...simple, yet really well made with plastic inserts that prevent baby from sliding down... we use it either in the bath or even just on the floor of the bathroom... pretty big and kind of bulky to store... it's large enough that you can use it for a while—from infant to 2 years..."

Ali's Notes: "...its unique anatomical design holds infants up to 6 months in a reclining position, then allows them to graduate to a sitting position (up to 3 years)... safety posts help prevent baby's head from slipping underwater... very simple, but effective design... the downside is that this is a big tub, so you really need to plan to have it in a bathtub (or room for it in your bathroom)..."

Fold-up Tub

★★★★☆

Safety 1st (www.safety1st.com 800.544.1108)
Price ....$10-$12

Parent Reviews: "...it folds up compactly and was very cheap... my baby didn't like being only partially in the water—he was always cold... the pad is nice and plush and it looks comfortable... I found that water would leak out of the joints where the tub folds—not a huge deal, but it meant we always had to use it in the sink... just the right size to travel with..."

Ali's Notes: "...this tub that folds small enough so that you can travel with it if need be..."

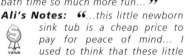

Infant Bath Seat

★★★★★

Primo (www.primobaby.com 973.926.5900)
Price ....$10-$12

Parent Reviews: "...this makes bathing my baby so much easier—at least I felt more at ease knowing he can't slip out of my hands... it's shaped like an ergonomic racing seat... the best $12 I ever spent... it fits into our kitchen sink and makes bath time so much more fun..."

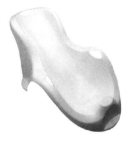

Ali's Notes: "...this little newborn sink tub is a cheap price to pay for peace of mind... I used to think that these little 'first stage' sinks were an unnecessary purchase until we heard testimonials from parents about how much this inexpensive tub eased the anxiety surrounding baby's first bath..."

Infant to Toddler Tub

★★★★☆

Evenflo (www.evenflo.com 800.233.5921)
Price ....$16-$18

Parent Reviews: **"***...nice and sturdy... the infant insert can come out so when your baby gets bigger he can sit in the main part of the tub... the plug changes color if the temperature gets too hot...* **"**

Safety Duck Tub

★★★★⯪

Munchkin (www.munchkininc.com 800.344.2229)
Price $15

Parent Reviews: **"***...inflatable and fun... it's pretty big so make sure you have a bathroom or tub that's big enough to hold it... although it's inflatable we rarely deflate it—it's too much of a hassle to store it and blow it up every time we want to bathe our baby... when it's hot out we even take it out on the porch...* **"**

Sure Comfort Newborn-to-Toddler Tub

★★★★⯪

The First Years (www.thefirstyears.com)
Price ....$15-$17

Parent Reviews: **"***...great for little kids who can't sit up yet... all the plastic molding makes sure my baby doesn't slide down... it worked great in our kitchen sink so we didn't have to bend over the bathtub... nice soft pads and a drain plug that changes color if the water is too hot... now that my boy is bigger the molded parts actually get in the way and he seems to enjoy the regular bath tub more... toddlers seated in the opposite direction are supported by a comfortable back seat...* **"**

Tub-to-Seat Bath Complete

★★★⯪☆

The First Years (www.thefirstyears.com)
Price ....$25-$30

Parent Reviews: **"***...money well spent... it worked well for us and made everyone more comfortable during bath time... it converts easily from baby tub to a seat... bar across front with toys and helps child feel secure... it was great being able to purchase only one tub and have it grow with your baby...* **"**

infant bathtubs

www.lilaguide.com

Tubside Bath Seat

Safety 1st (www.safety1st.com 800.544.1108)

Price $20

Parent Reviews: *"...less a bath tub, but more like a seat that goes into an adult tub... it hooks on to the side of the tub and is easy to use... it doesn't fit every bath tub and we had to return ours... it swivels and makes washing my baby really easy and convenient... my daughter seems really safe in this seat since she can't fall back or slide down..."*

shampoos & bubble baths

"lila picks"

★★★★★

- ★ Baby Shampoo (Erbaviva)
- ★ Baby Wash & Shampoo (Aveeno)
- ★ Foam Shampoo For Newborns (Mustela)
- ★ Grins & Giggles Baby Wash (Gerber)
- ★ Head-To-Toe (Johnson's)

2 in 1 Hair and Body Wash

★★★★½

Mustela (www.mustelausa.com 800.422.2987)
Price .... $9-$10   Features 6.8oz

Parent Reviews: "...we have used this product from day one—our daughter was born with a full head of hair and never lost any of it so it's important for me to use quality products to keep her hair and body in great condition... haven't figured out what the fuss is all about—thought this was at best an average product... it's very delicate, doesn't dry hair or skin... won't sting baby's eyes... I really trust Mustela products!.. pricey but all their products are well worth the money..."

Ali's Notes: "...Mustela's line of hypoallergenic products is a new-mom favorite, particularly for babies with sensitive skin... this gentle, soap-free formula does double duty, cleaning baby's hair and body with no stinging and no tears... parents rave about the signature Mustela scent, a great 'one product option', very convenient for travel..."

Baby Bee Shampoo Bar

★★★★☆

Burt's Bees (www.burtsbees.com 800.849.7112)

Price .... $5-$6
Features 3.5oz

Parent Reviews: *"...smells yummy, all natural ingredients... if it gets in the eyes it stings!... a bit of a splurge but lasts a long time... it comes as a bar soap so there are no drips... sweet honey and milk fragrance..."*

Baby Gentle Foaming Hair & Body Wash

★★★★☆

Kiehl's (www.kiehls.com)

Price .... $18.50-$24.50
Features ....

Parent Reviews: *"...very gentle and unobtrusive scent... this is one of the few products with a scent I like... baby's hair gets very clean without any crying—this is the only shampoo we will use... fabulous on cradle cap... incredibly expensive..."*

Ali's Notes: *"...a natural favorite, and becoming more available as a result of its popularity... known as much for their adult line as their baby line, their products inspire a loyal following..."*

Baby Magic Calming Milk Bath

★★★★½

Playtex (www.playtexbaby.com 800.222.0453)

Price .... $4-$5
Features .... 9oz & 15oz

Parent Reviews: *"...smells delicious—I just want to gobble my baby up after her bath... works as a facial wash for mom too!.. smallish bottle for the price—can't seem to find it in bulk... no need for an additional moisturizer... love the whole Baby Magic line—my baby's skin stays so soft and smells so good all day..."*

Baby Magic Gentle Hair & Body Wash

★★★★½

Playtex (www.playtexbaby.com   800.222.0453)

Price .... $4-$5
Features 15oz

Parent Reviews: *"...nice and gentle and the aloe smell is a plus... doesn't condition my daughter's hair well, I usually end up using a separate shampoo... love having the hair and body wash all in one... really no tears—our daughter has a lot of hair, and when she is squirmy it's hard to miss her eyes when rinsing... worth the money... I still use it on my older tots..."*

Ali's Notes: *"...a nice mild shampoo and body wash that parents rave about... great for travel since it's all you'll need (adults can use it too!)..."*

Baby Moose Foaming Wash

★★★★☆

Gerber (www.gerber.com   800.443.7237)
Price .... $3.50-$4
Features 10oz

Parent Reviews: *"...a pump bottle dispenses a foamy, mousse-like soap.... my daughter loves to play with it in the tub... it smells great, too... very hard to find—not many stores carry it... doesn't drip into my baby's eyes... leaves my son's hair feeling oily... very affordable..."*

Baby Shampoo

★★★★★

Erbaviva (www.erbaviva.com   877.372.2848)
Price .... $15-$16
Features 5oz

Parent Reviews: *"...wonderful smell and best of all it's all-natural... this company makes a great line of baby shampoos, ointments and oils... I received it as a present and only realized how expensive it is when I went to purchase more... the best shampoo we ever tried..."*

Ali's Notes: *"...part of their heavenly organic line, Erbaviva is known for their mommy-care and adult lines as well as for their baby products... this mild baby shampoo is gentle enough for newborns and contains organic lavender and chamomile... no dyes, artificial fragrances or synthetic chemicals... quite expensive, but worth it during those first weeks/months..."*

shampoos & bubble baths

Baby Shampoo & Body Wash ★★★★☆

Tom's Of Maine (www.tomsofmaine.com)
Price $8
Features 8oz

Parent Reviews: **"**...I use this on my son and myself... smells wonderful and is very gentle... nature-friendly company... really got rid of my baby's cradle cap... smells like honeysuckle...**"**

Baby Wash & Shampoo ★★★★★

Aveeno (www.aveeno.com 877.576.2825)
Price................................$5-$6
Features.............................. 8oz

Parent Reviews: **"**...gentle wash... great smell... I still use it on my 5-year-old as well as my 2-year-old... great for sensitive skin... my mom bought the whole Aveeno line when I was expecting my son who's now 10-months-old, he's never had a breakout of any kind... I feel good using this natural product on my newborn... a must-have for chicken pox, mosquito bites and diaper rashes...**"**

Ali's Notes: **"**...a value favorite within the 'high-end' and natural lines... increasingly available at most outlets... a reasonable price for the parent who prefers the more natural alternatives...**"**

Calming Shampoo & Bodywash ★★★★☆

California Baby (www.californiababy.com 877.576.2825)

Price.............................$9-$10
Features...........................8.5oz

Parent Reviews: **"**...smells good and it's not tested on animals... works as a body wash and shampoo—one product in the tub is a plus... uses natural essences—love the fresh scent... concentrated—one bottle has lasted me over 7 months and I still have a third left... texture seems to vary from bottle to bottle... pricey but we can't live without it...**"**

Dove Soap

★★★★½

Dove (www.dove.com)
Price .... $2-$4
Features 4.75oz

Parent Reviews: *"...it's cheaper and seems to work better than all the other fancy brands I've tried... my pediatrician says this is the best way to clean my baby's skin... I like that it doesn't have all kinds of artificial perfumes in it... it cleared up my baby's baby acne and keeps his skin so smooth... I love not having to buy separate soaps for everyone in the house... "*

Foam Shampoo For Newborns

★★★★★

Mustela (www.mustelausa.com 800.422.2987)
Price .... $10-$11   Features 5oz

Parent Reviews: *"...gentle foam for newborns... it prevents any signs of cradle cap... I always give a bottle to all pregnant friends... easy to use, easy to rinse... lovely smell... won't drip into baby's eyes... does cost quite a bit for shampoo... "*

Ali's Notes: *"...parents with babies sporting cradle cap swear by this shampoo... because it's foam instead of liquid, it's a lot easier to keep out of baby's sensitive eyes (although it's still a non-sting formula just in case)... a great full-body wash solution for the less-is-more approach for infant bathing... "*

multi-use

Grins & Giggles Baby Wash

★★★★★

Gerber (www.gerber.com 800.443.7237)
Price .... $3.50-$4
Features 15oz

Parent Reviews: *"...truly no tears... it's the only baby wash that doesn't make my son's skin break out in a rash... great scents (lavender & oatmeal)... lots of suds... easy to use bottle... non-drying for baby's skin... aromatherapy wash is soothing... get good deals at Toys R Us and discount stores... "*

Ali's Notes: *"...along with Johnson & Johnson, this is one of the 2 American classics with a loyal, multi-generational following "*

Head-To-Toe

★★★★★

Johnson's (www.johnsonsbaby.com 866.565.2229)
Price .... $3-$4   Features 15oz

Parent Reviews: *"...great scent, nice long lasting bubbles, no tears... head to toe—washes body and hair with one product... trusted brand... makes bath time quick and easy... seems to dry out my child's skin—I always use an additional moisturizer once she's out of the tub... can't beat the price—even better in bulk... saw my daughter through her first three years... "*

Ali's Notes: *"...along with Gerber, one of the 2 American classics with a loyal, multi-generational following... "*

shampoos & bubble baths

www.lilaguide.com

SoftWash

Johnson's (www.johnsonsbaby.com   866.565.2229)

Price ....$5-$6
Features 8.4oz/13.5oz/20.3oz

Parent Reviews: "*...these were great before baby's umbilical cord stump fell off when he couldn't be immersed... very soft and creamy against my daughter's skin... difficult to create a good lather... definitely no more tears...* "

Soothing Vapor Baby Bath

Johnson's (www.johnsonsbaby.com)

Price................................$5-$6
Features................... 9oz & 15oz

Parent Reviews: "*...thank goodness for Johnson & Johnson!... the worst thing about having an infant with a cold is they can only breathe through their nose—I don't like putting Vicks on their skin so this is a great alternative, it works like a charm!... helps my child sleep a lot better when he's feeling under the weather... the vapors aren't overpowering... I still use it on my older kids when they're sick...* "

Super Sensitive Shampoo & Bodywash

California Baby Products (www.californiababy.com   877.576.2825)

Price .... $9-$10
Features 8.5oz

Parent Reviews: "*...natural and hypoallergenic, developed by a mother... the honeysuckle scent is yummy... stinky—could do without the smell... I've used the whole line for over a year and my son and I love them!... my daughter goes nuts over the bubble wand in each bottle... great for allergic kids and sensitive skin types... not cheap...* "

lotions & potions

★★★★★ "lila picks"

- ★ Bebe Cold Cream (Mustela)
- ★ Daily Baby Lotion (Aveeno)
- ★ Nurturing Cream For Face And Body (Kiehl's)

Baby Bee Buttermilk Lotion for Sensitive Skin

★★★★½

Burt's Bees (www.burtsbees.com)
Price .... $8-$9
Features .... 7 oz

Parent Reviews: "...this product smells wonderful, and is all-natural, which is a huge plus... sometimes hard to find... left my daughter silky soft... great for pregnant bellies too... kind of expensive but a nice treat for mom and baby... it solved my child's dry skin and 'eczema' issues..."

Bebe Cold Cream

★★★★★

Mustela (www.mustelausa.com 800.422.2987)
Price $12
Features .... 1.4 oz

Parent Reviews: "...it smells so sweet and provides a nice layer of protection on my baby's hands and cheeks... we've tried other brands but this one seems to work best... pricey, but it's not like you use tons and tons—a little goes a long way..."

Ali's Notes: "...an intensive solution for chapped skin or babies prone to eczema... Mustela's hypoallergenic line is a favorite, particularly for tots with extra-sensitive skin... cold-weather climate families say this is a winter must-have..."

Bedtime Lotion ★★★★½
Johnson's (www.johnsonsbaby.com 866.565.2229)

Price .... $3-$6
Features .... 9oz & 15oz

Parent Reviews: "...their whole line is fabulous... soothing lavender scent... baby smells awesome after I smooth on this rich and creamy lotion... love putting it on my son right after bath time, it's become a sweet ritual... my daughter loves it and so do I... doesn't seem to soothe the baby any more or less than other lotions..."

Ali's Notes: "...super-sized - this classic is a value pick for the most product for the least price... did I mention that it works well too?..."

Daily Baby Lotion ★★★★★
Aveeno (www.aveeno.com 877.298.2525)
Price ....$4-$5
Features ....8 oz

Parent Reviews: "...I use it on myself as well as baby... non-greasy and non-smelly... faint and pleasant smell, isn't overbearing... hypoallergenic and can be trusted!... Aveeno makes wonderful products... good for sensitive skin and mild eczema... no harsh ingredients... love to put it on my daughter after her bath... a bit more expensive compared to other brands..."

Ali's Notes: "...a great choice if you're looking to stick to natural alternatives at a reasonable price point... Aveeno is increasingly available at most outlets so it's getting easier to stock than a few years ago..."

Eczema Baby Cream ★★★½☆
Gentle Naturals (www.gentlenaturals.com)

Price ....$7-$8.50
Features ....4 oz

Parent Reviews: "...really moisturizes my son's eczema and seems to last all day.... leaves an oily residue on my baby and on me... scent can be a little overpowering—kinda flowery for boys... my daughter's skin became smooth to the touch after using this product... price seems fair..."

Facial Cleansing Cloths ★★★★☆
Mustela (www.mustelausa.com 800.422.2987)

Price $6
Features ....

Parent Reviews: "...love these hypoallergenic no-rinse cloths... helps clean baby's nooks and crannies when a full bath isn't necessary... we continue to use them on our 3-year-old who can be fussy when her face is washed... usually sell out quickly... packaging could be *better—I had to keep them in a Ziploc, since the sticker that was supposed to keep the bag shut didn't want to stay sealed after a couple of uses... my baby smells delicious after I wipe him down...* **"**

Ali's Notes: **"***...gentle and convenient cloths that leave baby's face clean, moisturized and soothed... disposable, one-step and cleansing... very mild and won't sting sensitive eyes... parents rave about these as the go-to diaper bag product for quick/unexpected cleanups for newborns to preschoolers...* **"**

Gentle Baby Lotion

Playtex Baby Magic (www.playtex.com)
Price $4
Features 15oz

Parent Reviews: **"***...it smells good and is very affordable... we've been using this almost every day since our baby was an infant... it smells heavenly—I use it on myself at work to remind me of my baby... it's a nice creamy lotion that absorbs quickly...* **"**

Moisturizing Lotion

Cetaphil (www.cetaphil.com)
Price .... $6-$7
Features .... 8 oz

Parent Reviews: **"***...only thing that really helped my son's eczema... awesome!... I used it one night on my daughter, and the next morning it was as if she had brand new skin!.. love it for babies...* **"**

Nurturing Cream for Face and Body

Kiehl's (www.kiehls.com)
Price .... $17-$19
Features .... 6.8 oz

Parent Reviews: **"***...all natural... I've always dealt with the best sales staff when purchasing Kiehl's products... smells delightful on my baby and it's not too thick... price is a little high, but don't let that be a deterrent— it's worth it... available online or at specialty stores... I'll never use anything else on my baby's precious skin...* **"**

Ali's Notes: **"***...a natural favorite, and becoming more available as a result of its popularity... known as much for their adult line as for their baby line, their products inspire a loyal consumer following...* **"**

lotions & potions

www.lilaguide.com   91

Unscented Moisture

Lubriderm (www.pfizer.com)
Price .... $10-$14
Features .... 10oz & 16oz

Parent Reviews: *"...very smooth... helps take the itch out of dry skin... my son has dry patches and his doctor actually recommended this product... really thick lotion... it can get clumpy and stick to the dispenser..."*

sun protection

★★★★★
"lila picks"

- Sun Busters All-In-One Swim Gear (DaRiMi Kidz)
- Sunblock Lotion SPF50 (Mustela)

Children's Sun Screen
★★★★☆

Erbaviva (www.erbaviva.com 877.372.2848)
Price ....$30   Features.................................. 4oz

Parent Reviews: "...okay for everyday use, but not nearly strong enough to protect on a really sunny day... it's the first barrier of protection that I put on my baby first thing in the morning... it smells great and feels good too... it's crazy expensive..."

Ali's Notes: "...part of Erbaviva's heavenly organic baby care line, this sun protection lotion is perfect for everyday application... gentle on baby's skin and easy and light to apply... not a strong enough SPF (highest is 15) to protect baby at the park... sold in specialty stores only..."

www.lilaguide.com

SPF 30 Sunscreen

California Baby (www.californiababy.com 877.576.2825)
Price $18
Features 2.9oz

★★★★½

Parent Reviews: "...it smells good and works fabulously... water resistant and high SPF—I just keep lathering it on and my baby never burns... it works great but happens to be on the expensive side... surprisingly non-greasy even though I can feel the protective film when I apply it..."

Sun Busters All-In-One Swim Gear

DaRiMi Kidz (www.darimikidz.com 415.389.8538)
Price ....   Features..

★★★★★

Parent Reviews: "...lightweight, sun-proof swimsuit that's easy to put on and quick-drying... the best sun protection money can buy... fun colors and stylish looking—I never have trouble getting my boy to put his Sun Buster on... I wish the sleeves and legs were a little longer... this makes going to the beach or pool fun rather than a constant worry about my baby getting burned..."

Ali's Notes: "...if you're planning on spending time at the beach then this is by far the best sun protection you can get... tots can wear them in the water and you'll never have to worry about whether or not the sun block is washing off..."

Sunblock Lotion SPF50

Mustela (www.mustelausa.com 800.422.2987)
Price ....$15   Features................................ 1.6oz

★★★★★

Parent Reviews: "...super effective and not greasy... we always have a tube of this sun block in our diaper bag... pricey, but it works so well (and smells good) that I wouldn't think of trading it in for anything else... the next best thing to wearing clothes to protect you from the sun..."

Ali's Notes: "...Mustela makes a fabulous sunscreen (the sunscreen stick version for nose, ears and hard to cover areas is great too!)... a hypoallergenic, solution that offers great UV protection—so much so that I know many adults who buy this line for themselves... a note of caution, make sure that you're buying their 50 SPF rather than 25 SPF (which is packaged identically) when you're relying on it for a day at the beach..."

toothbrushes & toothpastes

"lila picks"

- Baby Tooth And Gum Cleanser (Orajel)
- Children's Tooth Gel (Weleda)
- Natural Anticavity Fluroide Toothpaste (Tom's of Maine)

Baby Tooth And Gum Cleanser ★★★★★

Orajel (www.orajel.com)
Price ....$3.50-$4   Features................................ 0.7oz

Parent Reviews: "...the no-fluoride toothpaste that my dentist recommended... a great, safe product that helps form the tooth brushing habit... my boy actually looks forward to brushing his teeth... mixed fruit and apple banana flavors... my baby really seems to like the little nubby parts on the brush and the taste of the gel... coupon offers are frequently available... I also like that they don't make you buy a new toothbrush with every new tube of paste..."

Children's Tooth Gel

Weleda (www.weleda.com)

Price............................ $3.50-$4
Features...........................2.1oz

Parent Reviews: "...tastes and smells great... fluoride free and not sweet at all... pricier than other brands, but you use so little when brushing that it last for a long time... "

Ali's Notes: "...a popular German brand that touts it's all natural approach... no fluoride, detergents, foaming agents, synthetic colors and flavors, or preservatives... "

Comfort Care Gum & Toothbrush Set

The First Years (www.thefirstyears.com)
Price ....$6-$7

Parent Reviews: "...it's nice to get the toothbrush and toothpaste in one kit... my baby likes brushing (chewing) on the toothbrush and it seems like she really enjoys it... it comes with 4 different toothbrushes—one finger brush, and three other, regular brushes... we've used the finger brush every morning and night since she was 4 months old—it has become a ritual... "

Ali's Notes: "...a nice kit that will get you started teaching good oral hygiene skills... parents say that their kids like seeing the progression of brushes and get excited when they 'graduate' from one to the next... "

Natural Anticavity Fluoride Toothpaste for Children

Tom's Of Maine (www.tomsofmaine.com)
Price .... $3   Features............................. 3.5oz

Parent Reviews: "...less sweet than other 'commercial' toothpaste and as far as I know, not tested on animals... several different fruit flavors... "

Ali's Notes: "...an American branded alternative to the all natural approach... unlike the Weleda alternative, Tom's includes fluoride for those parents living in areas with non-fluoridated water... it's nice that Tom's of Maine is no longer relegated to specialty stores only—many mass merchants now carrying it as a basic as well... "

Tooth and Gum Cleanser

Gerber (www.gerber.com)
Price $6

Features................................1.4 oz

Parent Reviews: *"...a good starter for babies and they seem to like the taste... it comes with instructions to guide parents toward appropriate usage... the soft finger brush is great for my baby's gums... my baby loves to chew on the brush and loves it when I brush her tooth..."*

car seats

infant car seats

Buying your baby's very first car seat is a big decision. You'll want to get one you can trust to keep your baby safe, while also considering price range, style and brand. And while those are all good basic things to keep in mind, here are some other things to look for to make sure you end up with a car seat you'll really love:

Portability/Stroller Compatibility: The primary feature of infant car seats is that they're portable, which means you can get sleeping babies in and out of the car without waking them. But something else that could make your life a whole lot easier is a car seat that's compatible with your stroller, allowing you to take your baby shopping or to dinner without having to remove them from their car seat to take them along with ease (and still sleeping!).

Weight: One of the big advantages of most infant car seats is that they're smaller and more portable. Take advantage of their portability and make sure they're a weight you can carry.

Separate Car Seat Base: There are two reasons a separate base for your car seat is essential. First, you can install it once, have your local fire or police department review your installation, then never have to worry about it again. A "click-in" system keeps everyday installation simple and worry-free. The second reason you'll love it is that you can get extra bases. Then you can install one in each car your baby rides in (think grandparents!) and always feel confident your baby is secure.

Harness Adjustments: For the sake of convenience, make sure the harness adjustments are located in front. A harness adjustment in the back is like adjusting with your eyes closed. It's just that simple.

Overall Cushioning: In the beginning, your newborn will seem tiny and fragile in their car seat. Whether you buy a seat with lots of padding or a more minimalist one where you'll need to buy inserts, rest assured you'll want the padding and factor it into your pricing upfront.

boosters & convertible car seats

You've already gone through the buying process once with your infant car seat; now that it's time to pick out a next-stage seat, you're an old pro, right? Well, almost. While the first car seat is the hardest to choose, there are a few more things to consider for a bigger car seat after settling on price, brand and color.

Size: Some second-stage car seats are HUGE. After considering your options - but before you purchase - be sure to test your favorites in your car to make sure they fit, especially if you have multiple car seats.

Safety Rating: Safety standards in next-stage car seats have a lot more variation, so keep your particular car in mind when making your choice. If you drive an economy car, it might make sense to spend more on your car seat than if you drive a top-of-the-line, safety-rated vehicle. Consider your car's rollover rating and side-air impact and discuss these factors with your retailer.

Seat-belt Adjusters: Make sure your car seat includes the top seat-belt adjusters - particularly with boosters or convertible car seats. This will help you avoid the unnecessary frustration of twisted/tangled seatbelts, which will make you crazy.

Convertibility: Once you're past the infant stage, particularly if you have or plan on having more than one child, you may want to consider multi-stage seats to avoid buying two more when you can buy just one. There are a lot of great options, and it will help minimize your parenthood product accumulation problem.

by Ali Wing at egiggle.com

infants

★★★★★
"lila picks"

★ Companion Infant Seat (Britax)
★ SnugRide (Graco)

Adjustable Back LATCH-Loc Car Seat

★★★★☆

Baby Trend (www.babytrend.com   800.328.7363)
Price .... $85-$100
Features .... 5 pt harness
Type .... rear
Weight Limit .... 5-20 lbs; 29"

Parent Reviews: "...tight installation given the rigid base... getting the rigid locks to clip into the latch attachments in my car can be difficult—I try not to take the base in and out... triangle shaped carry handle makes it easy to carry... easy release at the front of the seat... level indicator for the car seat base... can be used with just the seat belt so if you need to jump a cab—no problem... nice deep seat... straps tighten easily with a tug... fits into our Baby Trend stroller for easy transportation... heavy and very sturdy... good price for an excellent product..."

Ali's Notes: "...listed as a 'Quick Pick' in the May 2005 Consumer Reports review, this is seat is a great option for many parents... parents love how easily the seat adjusts for small or long babies... it's a bit heavier than many other car seats and gets good marks for safety... with the handle down, the deep seat can be a tight fit for smaller cars..."

Companion Infant Seat ★★★★★

Britax (www.britaxusa.com 704.409.1700)
Price .... $175-$200   Type .... rear
Features .... 5 pt harness   Weight Limit .... 4-22 lbs; 30"

Parent Reviews: "...wonderful quality—a good example of why Britax has such an excellent reputation... more expensive than some of the other models but well worth it... infant head support can be adjusted to exactly fit my baby's head... the tilt of the base can be easily adjusted... sun canopy provides total coverage so my baby never has the sun in her eyes... padded strap covers look much more comfortable than some of the other models out there... extra safety with the rebound bar at the foot of the base... they've thought of everything..."

Ali's Notes: "...like all Britax products, really well-constructed and safe... Britax sets the standard for car seat safety in the United States... safety features (like anti-rebound bar) make it a little heavier (10 lbs) than some other models... also it's a little larger car seat, which is good for bigger babies (holds babies up to 30" long!) but makes things tight in smaller cars..."

Connection Infant Seat ★★★★☆

Combi (www.combi-intl.com 800.992.6624)
Price .... $150-$160   Type .... rear
Features .... 5 pt harness   Weight Limit .... 5-22 lbs; 29"

Parent Reviews: "...a nice snug fit—my baby looks so comfortable in it... lots of protective layers including EPS foam around the head... the sun canopy covers my baby's face adequately... I always hear a nice 'click' so I know when the seat has locked into the base securely... the level indicator on the base helps me know when the seat is installed properly... the seat cover is machine washable and the infant body pillow can be removed quite easily..."

Ali's Notes: "...all in all a good seat with nice materials and lots of protection... the biggest gripe is that it's compatible primarily with Combi strollers—so unless you're ready to go Combi all the way, I'd stop and think before purchasing..."

participate in our survey at

Designer 22 Infant Seat

★★★★☆

Safety 1st (www.safety1st.com   800.544.1108)
Price .... $75-$80
Type.................................. rear
Features .... 5 pt harness
Weight Limit .... 5-22 lbs; 29"

Parent Reviews: **"***...standard features for a pretty standard infant car seat... the best thing about this seat is the sun canopy which can almost completely cover my sleeping baby... hard to adjust straps... it seems bulkier and heavier than the infant seats my friends have...* **"**

Discovery Infant Car Seat

★★★★☆

Evenflo (www.evenflo.com   800.233.5921)
Price .... $45-$55   Type .... rear
Features .... 5 pt harness   Weight Limit .... 5-20 lbs; 26"

Parent Reviews: **"***...a comfy seat that works seamlessly with Evenflo's travel system... you definitely can't beat the price... it has an easily recognizable click when the seat locks into the base so I feel confident that it is snapped in correctly... the z-shaped handle makes it much easier to carry than other models... the straps don't have padding... the harness height can be adjusted by rethreading through the back of the seat... extra base $20-$25...* **"**

Ali's Notes: **"***...designed to be super lightweight (5.5 lbs)... parents who like the z-shaped handle rave about this Evenflo seat... the price is hard to beat, but matches its otherwise bare bones styling...* **"**

PortAbout Infant Car Seat

★★★★½

Evenflo (www.evenflo.com   800.233.5921)
Price .... $60-$90   Type .... rear
Features .... 5 pt harness   Weight Limit .... 5-22 lbs; 26"

Parent Reviews: **"***...the whole setup is easy and intuitive... it comes in three versions which are all pretty much the same except for a few bells and whistles... lightweight and well made with great materials... the Z-shaped handle is comfortable for lugging baby around... the harness can be set at three different heights... nice, subtle color options... you have to buy the sun canopy separately... optional infant head support and rubber handle... holds up really well given how much we've used it with our two kids...* **"**

Ali's Notes: **"***...Evenflo car seats are known to last a bit longer than most other infant seats (fits babies up to 26 inches)... fits two side-by-side (snap-and-go), an easier option for parents of multiples... front seat adjustability...* **"**

Primo Viaggio ★★★★☆

Peg Perego (www.pegperego.com 800.671.1701)
Price .... $140-$150   Type .... rear
Features .... 5 pt harness   Weight Limit .... 20 lbs; 26"

Parent Reviews: "...stylish Italian design and materials... very easy to install and lock into the base... comes with an infant head rest... generous cushioning and fantastic styling... the straps tighten easily by tugging from the front... getting the padding off to clean is a bit of a pain... it can't be used without the base since it doesn't have any seat belt loops... small and compact... compatible with all major stroller manufacturers... "

Ali's Notes: "...those Italians sure know how to make things look good—the Primo Viaggio is no exception... great colors and beautifully finished... easy-to-use front seat adjustability... unfortunately an increasing number of parents are complaining that their babies are outgrowing this model too quickly (are American babies really that much bigger?)... the biggest limitation, however, is that even in an emergency this car seat cannot be used without a base (keep in mind, all infant car seats are safest with their bases and should be used that way except in emergencies)... rumor has it that Peg's working on some great 2006 innovations—stay tuned!... "

SnugRide ★★★★★

Graco (www.gracobaby.com 800.345.4109)
Price .... $100-$140   Type .... rear
Features .... 5 pt harness   Weight Limit .... 5-20 lbs; 26"

Parent Reviews: "...don't bother looking for anything else—this is the infant car seat you want... they have updated it to add additional cushioning and padding... safe and easy to use... works with all Graco and most other stroller brands... the stay-in-the-car base has a level indicator so you can adjust it properly... the seat clicks in and out easily... you can also use the seat with just a seat belt, without the base... tons of padding and a head support... everything comes apart to clean... if you buy a Graco travel system you'll likely get this great infant seat as part of the package... truly a safe and 'snug' ride... extra base $30-$35... "

Ali's Notes: "...there's a reason that most stroller manufacturers make sure that the one car seat they're compatible with is the SnugRide... it's a well-made and well-designed (all the bells and whistles you can think of) and it actually looks good... super lightweight (7 lbs) makes it an obvious choice for parents on the go... great safety rating and nicely padded seat (memory foam)... by far the biggest bang for the buck... "

Tyro II Infant Car Seat

Combi (www.combi-intl.com 800.992.6624)
Price .... $120-$160   Type ....rear
Features .... 5 pt harness   Weight Limit .... 5-22 lbs; 29"

Parent Reviews: *"...very light (8 lbs) and easy to take in and out of the base... creates a travel system with Combi strollers (Savona, Urban Savvy)... the harness is easy to adjust... it snaps right into the base with a nice loud click... you can also use this seat without its base—just feed the seat belt through the loops and tighten... level indicator on the base for easy installation... large sunshade provides decent cover...*  *machine washable padding... super padded—looks like a very comfortable ride... plenty of colors to choose from... extra base costs $45-$50..."*

toddlers & convertibles

★★★★★

"lila picks"

★ Decathlon (Britax)   ★ Roundabout (Britax)
★ Marathon (Britax)

Alpha Omega Elite

★★★★½

Cosco (www.coscojuvenile.com 800.544.1108)
Price .... $140-$150   Type ..... rear/forward/belt positioning
Features .... 5 pt harness
Weight Limit.......................... 5-35 lbs/22-40 lbs/40-100 lbs

Parent Reviews: "...the only car seat you will ever need—it works as a rear facing infant seat, as well as forward facing and even as a booster... the only convertible car seat that also works as a belt-positioning booster—you can use it for kids up to 100 pounds... the shoulder straps can be adjusted without rethreading which is great if you're shuttling different kids around... comes with infant head pad... has three recline positions when facing forward... machine-washable fabric that holds up well to the abuse and slobber it receives on a daily basis... amazing value given its utility and price..."

Ali's Notes: "...a really good all-in-one solution—it can be used as an infant, toddler and booster seat... it's on the larger side (and certainly not nearly as portable as an infant seat)... although it is rated up to 100 lbs, your tot is likely to outgrow it length-wise well before reaching that weight limit..."

Avatar

★★★★☆

Combi (www.combi-intl.com   800.992.6624)
Price .... $220-$230   Type .... rear/forward
Features ....   5 pt harness; washable cover
Weight Limit 5-30 lbs/20-50 lbs

Parent Reviews: "...a nice looking, comfy convertible seat... the pivoting base is convenient and allows you to adjust the seat just right whether it's in rear or forward facing mode... extra infant padding seems comfortable and can be removed for bigger kids... secure five point harness that gets tightened by pulling at the strap in front... height adjusting the harness requires rethreading... three position recline on the seat... heavy so probably not for you if you have to change cars a lot... it has several recline positions for both forward and backward facing positions..."

Comfort Sport

★★★★☆

Graco (www.gracobaby.com 800.345.4109)
Price .... $120-$140   Type .... rear/forward
Features .... 5 pt harness
Weight Limit 0-30 lbs/20-40 lbs

Parent Reviews: "...this seat comes in a variety of styles, some more plush than others... we got the faux leather and love the look... pretty basic, sturdy and easy to use seat... not fancy or too over-the-top, which is what we liked about it... works with LATCH... love the head rests and side cups... my parents thought we paid a lot for this car seat but it was on the less expensive side... the straps tend to twist quite a bit and we find ourselves having to straighten them out every other day... the seat belt adjustment tab is so far down in front that when you have the seat rear-facing, you can't reach it to loosen the belt... a good basic seat with just the features we were looking for..."

Decathlon

★★★★★

Britax (www.britaxusa.com)
Price .... $250-$270   Type .... forward
Features .... 5 pt harness   Weight Limit .... 5-33 lbs/20-65 lbs

Ali's Notes: "...wow, more bells and whistles than the Marathon... slightly bigger, to make room for the features that make it the ultimate in luxury and comfort for your baby... renowned for their focus on safety and ease, Britax is also the cushiest ride in town... another newborn (but not portable) to booster seat solution from Britax... better than standard car seat cover options for your own style... don't forget to make sure it fits in your car..."

Husky

★★★★☆

Britax (www.britaxusa.com 704.409.1700)
Price .... $220-$250   Type ....forward
Features .... 5 pt harness   Weight Limit ....22-80 lbs

Parent Reviews: **"**...great Britax quality with a weight limit of up to 80 pounds—that means I won't be buying a new car seat anytime soon... a huge seat for my big boy... snug fitting five point harness that has up to four height slots—you have to rethread the straps to adjust the height, but it's not like I'm constantly fiddling with them... works with LATCH as well as seat belt for heavier kids... one tug on the harness makes for a snug fit... the biggest bummer is that it's so heavy and too large to be approved for airline use...**"**

Ali's Notes: **"**...this car seat is big—really big... definitely make sure it can fit in your car!.. standard Britax safety features, but given its size, consider this a special needs solution...**"**

Intera

★★★★☆

Safety 1st (www.safety1st.com   800.544.1108)
Price .... $140-$150   Type rear/forward/backless/beltpositioning
Features .... 5 pt harness
Weight Limit 5-35 lbs/22-40 lbs/40-100 lbs

Parent Reviews: **"**...comfortable, and well-padded—it comes

with all the infant padding... it's a smart looking seat with cup holder and good padding... we got it because they say it will work from infant all the way through booster—we're not there yet so we'll see... I love the idea of getting one seat that will work for all the different stages... the headrest is height adjustable which allows me to adjust it for my napping tot... nice big seat, but it takes up a lot of room which makes it hard to install another seat next to it...**"**

Ali's Notes: **"**...very multi-stage in that it works for newborns to 100 pounds!... yet another large seat to double check that it will fit in your car—especially if it needs to sit next to another car seat...**"**

Marathon ★★★★★

Britax (www.britaxusa.com 704.409.1700)
Price .... $230-$250   Type .... rear/forward
Features .... 5 pt harness   Weight Limit .... 5-33 lbs/20-65 lbs

Parent Reviews: "...the Britax Roundabout's big brother... for a little extra money you get longer life out of your car seat—this one goes up to 65 pounds or 50 inches... it's very wide and takes up a lot of seat room... reclines when facing forward which is great for naps... secure five point harness which is easily tightened from the front... harness height adjustment requires rethreading... a nice wide seat which worked great for my baby boy... approved for airline use... LATCH system makes safe installation a breeze... like all Britax products the quality is excellent..."

Ali's Notes: "...a little bigger than the ever-reliable Roundabout... you need the right car to fit this seat (I can't have anyone in my front seat when we install this in our little Audi)... it also works as infant car seat (as small as 5 lbs) but remember that there's no detachable base... it's the perfect second seat since it equips you with your stage-two solution right away... another Britax car seat that will make you jealous of your baby's ride—it looks so comfortable... Britax is best-of-class for all-around safety..."

Roundabout ★★★★★

Britax (www.britaxusa.com 704.409.1700)
Price .... $200-$220   Type .... rear/forward
Features .... 5 pt harness   Weight Limit .... 5-33 lbs/20-40 lbs

Parent Reviews: "...simply the best convertible car seat money can buy!.. easy to install—fits snugly into our car... safety, safety, safety—it was recommended by our local police station... easily adjustable five point harness... straps don't twist, well padded and looks very comfortable... straps are height adjustable but have to be rethreaded if you want to move them up... cover comes off for the occasional washing... works for tots up to 40 inches... like all Britax products, this is a really well-designed car seat that will last you for a while..."

Ali's Notes: "...the ever-popular, 'best buy' by Britax... they are in a class of their own when it comes to safety and workmanship... the Roundabout has the smallest footprint of all the Britax seats which makes it a good choice if you're planning on taking it on an airplane... the best second-stage seat—great value for the money... you can't go wrong with this one..."

Sit N Stroll 5-in-1 Travel System

Strolex (www.strolex.com 905.794.9359)
Price .... $185-$200
Features .... 5 pt harness
Type .... rear/forward
Weight Limit .... 0-22 lbs/20-40 lbs

Parent Reviews: **"**...a nifty contraption... the greatest car seat/stroller ever invented... immensely practical if you plan on taking your baby on plane trips... it converts from car seat to stroller in seconds... people stop me all the time to ask about it... although they say the wheels contract completely, they do end up getting your car's seat pretty dirty... rather heavy and since you're using it as a stroller and car seat you're doing a fair amount of lifting, but wonderful idea that actually works... a must for travel—it gets you through the airport and into the rental car without much hassle... I don't use it at home, just for travel... **"**

Ali's Notes: **"**...designed specifically for frequent travelers... I wouldn't recommend it for everyday use, but jet setters swear by this clever solution... an overdue innovation to merge a car seat and stroller for easy travel... the biggest complaint is that it doesn't roll well on anything but totally smooth surfaces... **"**

Titan

Evenflo (www.evenflo.com 800.233.5921)
Price .... $60-$80
Features .... 3 pt harness
Type .... rear/forward
Weight Limit .... 5-30 lbs/20-40 lbs

Parent Reviews: **"**...comes in two versions—basic and with the overhead shield... three point harness with chest clip... shoulder straps can be adjusted to four different positions... adjusting the shoulder straps is annoying since you have to reinsert them from the back of the seat... the seat angle can be adjusted to two different positions... the cover got a little deformed after washing it... **"**

Ali's Notes: **"**...Evenflo gets good safety ratings from Consumer Reports and has been a longtime car seat player... parents report mixed reviews on the ease of use of their seat and leg straps... **"**

Touriva

★★★½☆

Cosco (www.coscojuvenile.com 800.544.1108)
Price .... $40-$50   Type .... rear/forward
Features 5 pt harness; wash cover   Weight Limit .... 5-35 lbs/22-40 lbs

Parent Reviews: "...a good car seat for a second car... it's cheap enough that you can buy it as an extra for another car, but I wouldn't use it as my main car seat... five point harness that can be adjusted to three different heights... I washed the cover and it ended up being all stretched out and has never really fit properly since... significantly less expensive than the higher-end ones but you kind of get what you pay for..."

Triumph 5

★★★★☆

Evenflo (www.evenflo.com 800.233.5921)
Price .... $110-$120   Type .... rear/forward
Features .... 5 pt harness   Weight Limit .... 5-30 lbs/20-40 lbs

Parent Reviews: "...a well-built seat with some cool features... the harness automatically remembers how tight it was so after you put baby in the seat you're not tugging at the straps to adjust them... the buckle changes color when it is properly locked... reclines to five different position when forward facing... wide body design... removable cover that I just throw into the washing machine... pretty big at the top which makes it hard to fit other car seats next to it... the straps can be adjusted to three different heights, but have to be reinserted through the back... the DLX version comes with extras like an infant body pillow and head support..."

Vanguard

★★★★☆

Evenflo (www.evenflo.com 800.233.5921)
Price .... $80-$100   Type .... rear/forward
Features .... 5 pt harness   Weight Limit .... 5-30 lbs/20-40 lbs

Parent Reviews: "...comes in two versions— basic and DLX... get the DLX since it has 5 harness height adjustment slots instead of just 4—it will give your seat a longer life... the DLX also comes with extras like head pillow and cup holders... I like the way the buckle changes colors when I've snapped it in properly... the strap tightening mechanism is difficult to use when the seat is facing backwards since it is mashed into the seat... the front harness adjustment is positioned too low and can be difficult to reach... the buckle strap can be moved to a second position to give your baby more room as he grows... great price for what you get..."

Wizard

Britax (www.britaxusa.com 704.409.1700)
Price .... $250-$270   Type .... rear/forward
Features .... 5 pt harness   Weight Limit .... 5-33 lbs/20-65 lbs

Parent Reviews: "...what makes this seat stand out is its nifty strap height adjustment mechanism... perfect for shuttling kids of different sizes around—simply use the knobs on the sides to allow the harness to shift up or down... nicely padded harness covers... adjustable head restraint prevents my son's head from flopping to the side, although he still manages to flop forwards... I've noticed that my boy sits in awkward positions to see around the protectors... the head pad also provides added side impact protection... slightly more expensive than the Marathon, but the convenient harness adjustment mechanism is worth it..."

Ali's Notes: "...the wings around the face are a double-edged sword—they're intended for more safety, and have a side bonus of less 'head flopping' for the sleepy baby... we hear many stories of tots hating the wings around their face and constantly craning their necks to see around them... in terms of safety, Britax is best-of-class all around..."

boosters

★★★★★ "lila picks"

- ★ Bodyguard (Britax)
- ★ Starriser Comfy (Britax)
- ★ Cricket (Graco)
- ★ TurboBooster (Graco)

Ambassador Booster

★★★☆☆

Cosco (www.coscojuvenile.com   800.544.1108)
Price ....$14-$17
Type..........................backless
Weight Limit............30-100 lbs

Parent Reviews: "...*pretty basic stuff, but it works just fine... built-in cup holder and armrests make for a comfortable ride... nicely padded seat...*"

B500 Folding Booster Car Seat ★★★★½

Compass (www.compassbaby.com   888.899.2229)
Price ....$85-$100   Type .... highback/belt positioning
Features .... no harness   Weight Limit ....30-100 lbs

Parent Reviews: "...*a nice looking booster... all the features you could want and then some... adjusts to six different positions as your tot grows—that way you always know it's properly sized... plush padding and durable material... nice wide seat... armrests that flip up and down... head protection on the headrests for added protection but also good for naps... no built in harness... it even folds into a compact package if you need to transfer it from one car to another...*"

www.lilaguide.com

Ali's Notes: *"...for the parent who wants the full booster seat (with back) but who needs to travel and/or move it between cars often, the B500 is a top choice... known to be lightweight and compact when folded (despite full, comfortable seat)... winner of past JPMA Innovation Award..."*

Big Kid
★★★★☆

Evenflo (www.evenflo.com 800.233.5921)

Price .... $45-$50
Type.........high/no-back/ belt positioning
Features .... no harness
Weight Limit...............30-100 lbs

Parent Reviews: *"...futuristic looking racing seat—my boys love sitting in it... it converts into a backless booster easily... pivoting arms make getting in and out easy... belt guides make sure the seat belt is positioned correctly... two drink and snack holders contain all the gadgets my son needs to stay busy while riding in the car... good side head supports make napping more comfortable... you can also buy this seat as a no back booster for about $20 less..."*

Bodyguard
★★★★★

Britax (www.britaxusa.com   704.409.1700)
Price .... $120-$130

Type....high back/belt positioning
Features ....full back
Weight Limit.............. 40-100 lbs

Ali's Notes: *"...Britax safety and comfort... the innovative and clever width-adjustable base helps with space planning... the denim fabric provides necessary durability given the long life span of this seat (40-100 lbs)... side impact head support doubles as good head support for naps, but can also be an irritant for older kids who want to be able to see out the side..."*

CarGo
★★★★☆

Graco (www.gracobaby.com 800.345.4109)
Price .... $100-$115   Type .... highback/belt positioning
Features .... 5 pt harness   Weight Limit ....20-40 lbs/40-100 lbs

Parent Reviews: *"...comes with five point harness but can evolve into a belt-positioning booster... snug, supportive baby head pillow that is removable... easily adjustable harness... 3 belt positioning slots for use with shoulder seat belts... plenty of padding makes for a comfortable ride—my boy seems happy... seat cover comes off and can be machine washed although I found the fabric stretches out... cup and snack holders on either side... my son loves it because he has his own cup holder and holder for his toys... good value for the money..."*

Ali's Notes: *"...toddler seat and booster in one... typically Graco— good value and overall reliability..."*

Cricket

★★★★★

Graco (www.gracobaby.com 800.345.4109)
Price .... $20-$25
Type......................... backless
Features .... no harness
Weight Limit............40-100 lbs

Parent Reviews: "...pretty basic but it works just fine... just set your tot on it and the seat belt fits better... very portable and easy to move from one car to the other... can't beat the price..."

Ali's Notes: "...simple, space conscious and comfortable... easy to take with you wherever you go... Graco good value and overall reliability..."

Komfort Kruiser

★★★★⯪

Jupiter (www.jupiterindustries.com 800.465.5795 ext.24)
Price .... $100-$120
Type.. highback/belt positioning
Features .... no harness
Weight Limit............33-100 lbs

Parent Reviews: "...a very intelligently designed booster... weight limit is 100 pounds so you'll be able to use it for a while... a nice deep seat that grows well with the child... the seat can be angled back to adjust to your car's recline... although it doesn't have a built-in harness, the seat belt guides securely hold my son in the seat... the head rest can be adjusted to match your child's height... it even comes with a cloth flap that you can fold under the seat in order to protect your car seats from any chafing..."

Protek Belt Positioning Booster

★★⯪☆☆

Cosco (www.coscojuvenile.com 800.544.1108)
Price .... $20-$35   Type ....high/no-back/belt positioning
Features .... no harness   Weight Limit ....30-100 lbs

Parent Reviews: "...belt positioning booster that goes up to 100 pounds and also converts to a backless booster... no built-in harness, but it's intended for bigger kids anyway... the head rest can adjust to 7 different heights... padded armrests and easily accessible cup holder... the seat looks kind of like a race car driver's seat which my son loves... nice material and color... cheap price for a decent product..."

Roadster

★★★★⯪

Britax (www.britaxusa.com 704.409.1700)

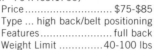

Price .... $75-$85
Type ... high back/belt positioning
Features .... full back
Weight Limit .... 40-100 lbs

Parent Reviews: "...huge and comfy... very easy to use since you just slide the back up and down until the seat belt is correctly positioned... it goes up to 100 lbs... you can also remove the backrest... "

Starriser Comfy

★★★★★

Britax (www.britaxusa.com 704.409.1700)
Price .... $80-$100   Type .... high back/belt positioning
Features .... full back   Weight Limit .... 30-80 lbs

Parent Reviews: "...wonderful Britax quality... tall back with head support and protection... you can remove the back quite easily if you need to make it more mobile... height and width adjustable... folds up nicely which makes moving it around a lot easier... pricey, but the best money can buy... "

Ali's Notes: "...you get longer use compared with most other boosters (30—100 lbs)... not a toddler seat since it doesn't have a 5 pt harness... the side impact head support doubles as good head support for naps, but can also be an irritant for older kids... best of Britax for mobility and travel given easy folding and removable back... a very popular choice... "

Summit High Back

★★★★⯪

Cosco (www.coscojuvenile.com 800.544.1108)
Price .... $90-$100   Type .... highback/belt positioning
Features .... 5 pt harness   Weight Limit .... 22-40 lbs/40-100 lbs

Parent Reviews: "...better looking that most car seats... it has all the features you could want... weight limit goes up to 100 pounds so it has a longer life than most other boosters... 3 recline positions makes snug and proper installation easy... armrests fold up for easy entry and exit for my boy... well-placed cushions support my baby's head so it doesn't flop over when he's sleeping... cup holder slides in and out... you can use it without the built-in harness too—just slide the seat belt through the belt guides... well-built and lasts forever... "

TurboBooster ★★★★★

Graco (www.gracobaby.com 800.345.4109)
Price .... $50-$80   Type ....high/no-back/belt positioning
Features .... no harness   Weight Limit .... 30-100 lbs

Parent Reviews: "...one of the best deals around... looks almost like the other fancy name-brand boosters but at a fraction of the cost... EPS foam and side impact protection... the head support is adjustable... everything is nicely padded and my son loves it... reversible seat cover that is also machine washable... cup holders on either side that slide in and out of the base... converts into a backless booster when your tot gets big enough...

Ali's Notes: "...it comes in short and tall versions ($20 more for the tall one)... good Graco safety with EPS foam and side impact protection... very affordable and good value... "

Vantage Point High Back Booster ★★★½☆

Safety 1st (www.safety1st.com 800.544.1108)
Price .... $75-$80
Type.. highback/belt positioning
Features .... 5 pt harness
Weight Limit.. 22-40/40-100 lbs

Parent Reviews: "...works as a belt positioning booster up to 100 pounds but also has a built in 5 point harness... 3 height adjustments for the harness... nicely padded and not goofy looking... adjustable belt guides ensure that I can set the seat belt to the right height... good rear head padding but nothing for my son to lean his head against on the sides... comes with a cup holder and mesh side pockets for books and other stuff... "

Ventura High Back ★★★½☆

Cosco (www.coscojuvenile.com 800.544.1108)
Price .... $50-$60
Type.. highback/belt positioning
Features .... 5 pt harness
Weight Limit 22-40 lbs/ 40-80 lbs

Parent Reviews: "...a nice booster with lots of padding... secure 5 point harness or seat belt positioners once your baby gets bigger... cup holder... decent value given the cheap price... "

Vision

Evenflo (www.evenflo.com 800.233.5921)
Price .... $55-$60
Type .. highback/belt positioning
Features .... 5 pt harness
Weight Limit 20-40 lbs/30-80 lbs

Parent Reviews: *"...pretty basic features... great value given the price... adjustable armrests on both sides... built-in 5 point harness with 3 height adjustment slots... works with the 5 point harness up to 40 pounds, after that we switched to using the seat belt and looping it through the guides on the seat... the cover comes off and can be machine washed... I'm not crazy about the color choices, but given the price I'm not complaining..."*

carriers & slings

Most developmental experts say nothing is more important to an infant's development than touch. That's why it's good to have a carrier or sling to keep baby close to you during your day. But the decision whether to use a carrier or a sling largely boils down to personal preference. Slings are more popular in Europe, though they're gaining popularity in the U.S. Here are some things to think about when choosing between the two:

Carrier Benefits: Carriers like the Baby Bjorn are truly hands-free. A good carrier will allow you to keep your baby close while you clean the house, shop, walk or make dinner, and it can turn anytime into together time.

Back Support: A good carrier should always include back support. It should also be easy to adjust for different-sized moms and dads. The more foolproof the baby harness, the less stress this gadget will cause.

Sling Benefits: Slings require a little more awareness, but are far superior for the breastfeeding mom who wants to be able to keep baby bundled while she nurses. In addition, slings often have a longer useful life by being a great hip support for a toddler when a carrier is out of the question.

Sling Styles: Slings come in two styles: the more natural kind, made of a single piece of fabric in sizes made to fit the parent, or a one-size-fits-all- sling with adjustable straps. How to know which style is right for you? Try a couple, and see which works and feels best.

by Ali Wing at egiggle.com

carriers & slings

★★★★★

"lila picks"

- ★ Baby Carrier (New Native Baby)
- ★ Baby Carrier Active (Baby Bjorn)
- ★ Baby Carrier Original (Baby Bjorn)
- ★ ERGO Baby Carrier (ERGO)
- ★ Premaxx New Edition Baby Sling (JJ Cole)

Adjustable Fleece Pouch

★★★★☆

Kangaroo Korner (www.kangarookorner.com)
Price ....$50-$55
Features ....0-35 lbs; sling/wrap

Parent Reviews: "...*fleece fabric keeps baby warm and comfy... the snap closures seem scary at first, but actually are very strong and safe... too warm in hot weather, but they also make them out of cotton... super easy to use and you can use it with a baby that's only a few days old or even a toddler... it washes and wears well... the adjustable snaps make it so that you get the perfect fit...*"

Baby Carrier ★★★★★

New Native Baby (www.newnativebaby.com 800.646.1682)

Price........................... $40-$48
Features........ 0-35 lbs; sling/wrap

Parent Reviews: "...so easy and simple and the baby is right up against you... I also like that I can nurse my baby in it without anyone knowing... thick, yet breathable cotton... easy to use since there aren't any straps to tangle with—it's just one piece... it's a simple cloth sling—when it's not in use, just stuff it in the pocket of your bag... make sure you get the right size so that you can adjust it properly or it might start straining your back... In the beginning I was worried my baby could fall out, but now that I know how to use it he feels safe and cozy..."

Ali's Notes: "...the ultimate in simplicity... if you find conventional carriers too bulky, you'll love this simple, cotton sling that can be worn on the front, back or side... it not only leaves your hands free when needed, but it's gentle on your back and shoulders and provides an ideal support for newborns... also a mom favorite for discreet nursing... a side note—they tend to run slightly small... not a practical option for moms and dads to share (one-size doesn't fit all!)..."

Baby Carrier Active ★★★★★

Baby Bjorn (www.babybjorn.com 800.593.5522)
Price .... $110-$120
Features .... 8-26lbs; carrier

Parent Reviews: "...just like the original carrier but with a little more padding... it's also a little bigger than the original one... I like the lumbar support on this model... I can wear my baby facing in or out... light weight and easy to clean (machine washable)... padded shoulder straps... the new head support buckle makes it easier-to-use than ever... great back and neck support for babies at every stage..."

Ali's Notes: "...although it costs a lot more than the original Baby Bjorn, the Active Carrier's built-in back support adds months of usability... most carrier-loving parents (as opposed to sling-lovers), end up with an awkward time when their baby is too big for them to carry comfortably but still too small for a backpack—this is where the Active Carrier works wonders... it also fits bustier/bigger moms a little more comfortably than the Original..."

Baby Carrier Original

★★★★★

Baby Bjorn (www.babybjorn.com 800.593.5522)
Price .... $80   Features .... 8-25lbs; carrier

Parent Reviews: **"**...the most comfortable front pack out there... I couldn't have gotten through the first nine months without it—I carried my daughter in it everywhere I went... I even managed to breastfeed with it on... ours lasted through three kids and I've passed it on to a friend... great for urban babies—easy to travel on buses and subways... allows you to carry your baby but still have both hands free... it can cause back strain if worn for extended periods of time or distances... the Active version is a little bigger than the Original and comes with extra lumbar support...**"**

Ali's Notes: **"**...known for its smart design that makes getting the baby in and out super easy (even allowing baby to sleep through it all!), this is a classic handsfree carrier solution... it easily adjusts to fit different sized parents making it a welcomed one-per-household purchase... if you live in a super humid climate you might want to consider the 'Air' model for better breathability (not available yet in the Active Carrier style)...**"**

Baby Sling

★★★★☆

Maya Wrap (www.mayawrap.com 888.629.2972)
Price .... $40-$50   Features .... 0-35 lbs; sling/wrap

Parent Reviews: **"**...babies are snuggled close and happy... no bulky, padded straps makes it easy to adjust... you can use it to carry your baby in the front, side or back... pocket in the tail is convenient to hold your wallet or spare diaper... made from quality materials—I feel very confident using this sling... love their designs and color choices... a little hard to learn to use at first, but once you get the hang of it, it's like second nature... I didn't have it set right the first time around and it was hard on my back...**"**

Cotton Sling

★★★★½

Zolowear (www.zolowear.com 800.609.7792)

Price $80
Features ...... 0-35 lbs; sling/wrap

Parent Reviews: **"**...cozy and well designed... we used this constantly when my boy was very young... I actually like the fact that it doesn't have all the padding like some of the other brands—it feels more comfortable than some of the other bigger, bulkier ones... love the zipper pocket for keys and wallet... lots of colors to choose from...**"**

Double Layer Slings

Mamma's Milk (www.mammasmilk.com)
Price ....$55-$75
Features ....0-35 lbs; sling/wrap

Parent Reviews: **"**...love the choice of fabrics and patterns—makes mom stylish and baby comfy... not only reversible but this sling also offers a build-in diaper pouch for diapers... wonderful selection of fabrics... no buckles, rings, snaps, or zippers... expertly sewn and beautifully designed...**"**

Emi Carrier

Sherpani (www.sherpani.us   720.214.2194)
Price ....$75-$90
Features ....8-26lbs; carrier

Parent Reviews: **"**...absolutely the best for hiking with a baby... you can store all your stuff in the backpack and keep your baby in the front... they've thought of everything with this pack/carrier—plenty of pockets, fleece lining in the carrier and lots of ways to adjust the tightness...**"**

Ali's Notes: **"**...innovative and smartly designed... they use sturdy, strong materials (backpack construction) and create a great baby carrier... it even comes with a sleeve for a camel pack... available at REI and other 'camping/hiking' outlets...**"**

ERGO Baby Carrier

★★★★★

ERGO Baby Carrier (www.ergobabycarrier.com   888.416.4888)
Price ....$90-$95
Features ....0-60 lbs; carrier

Parent Reviews: **"**...made like a backpack, but super versatile—it can be worn in front or on the back... it has a built-in pocket for storing small items—wallet, keys, sunglasses... all the straps adjust so both my husband and I can carry my daughter... most of the weight seems to rest on my hips rather than my shoulders... it even has a head support for when my baby is napping... machine washable and fully adjustable...**"**

Ali's Notes: **"**...in the front position the baby may only face inward/toward the parent... Ergo claims this is an intentional design difference to address what some experts say is a better spine position for the baby... it has most of the features of other well-known brands... a great carrier and backpack for everyday use that is designed for newborns to kids up to 60 pounds—talk about multi-stage...**"**

EuroRider

Infantino (www.infantino.com 800.365.8182)
Price ....$30-$35
Features ....8-26 lbs; carrier

Parent Reviews: "...comfortable to wear and the snaps can be released easily without waking my baby... it washes well... I feel safe when wearing my daughter in it... the cell phone holder is nice for all kind of things like change, phone, etc..."

HipHugger Baby Sling

HipHugger (www.thehiphugger.com)
Price $75
Features ....machine washable

Parent Reviews: "...lightweight and attractive... plenty of different patterns to choose from... very simple design but it works very well... this carrier was much more comfortable on my back than the front carriers..."

Ali's Notes: "...fans say this is an easy-to-use, no-fuss sling... skeptics argue that despite the good, washable fabrics it's a little tricky to use (adjustability)... no matter your take, all parents should know that this is a sling for comfortably sitting babies only—not newborns..."

Infant Carrier

Allo Baby (www.livingincomfort.com)
Price ....$70   Features ....8-26lbs; carrier

Parent Reviews: "...a comfy front carrier that lets you carry your baby either inward or outward facing... adjustable leg openings and larger padded carrier allows the Allo Baby to be used for larger/older babies than other baby carriers... the straps are nicely padded and the waist strap distributes the weight better... convenient zippered pockets to store keys and money... machine washable..."

Ali's Notes: "...known for its narrow leg opening for the baby which is considered by many to be more comfortable for the baby... nicely padded shoulder and waist straps make it a comfort pick among many parents... sleek European styling... definitely worth considering if you're in the market for a front-carrier..."

Kangaroo

★★★★☆

Kelty (www.kelty.com 866.349.7225)
Price .... $65-$80   Features .... 0-28 lbs; carrier

Parent Reviews: *"...very well padded and made out of backpack material... adjustable straps allow me to fit get a snug, tight fit... comes with a hood to protect against sun and rain... I love the pockets into which I can put my keys, wallet and stuff for baby... the pouch comes off... works both inward and outward facing... love that you can just throw this backpack in your trunk..."*

Ali's Notes: *"...for the REI style parent, no one makes quality packs like Kelty... this front-and-back carrier screams Kelty quality and style... for parents who like to take their tots on hikes or non-stroller walks..."*

Moby Wrap

★★★★☆

Moby Wrap (www.mobywrap.com 888.879.1153)
Price .... $25-$35
Features ....0-35 lbs; sling/wrap

Parent Reviews: *"...soft and easy to tie on without help... it's like wearing your baby in a T-shirt right up against you... it distributes the load over a much wider area than regular carriers with straps... much more comfortable than standard front carriers... since you tie it around you it's totally adjustable to various-sized parents... wonderful, soft cotton—I love the way it feels... you need to be a sailor to figure out how to wrap it around you and tie the knots... I never got totally comfortable with knowing whether or not I had tied it right..."*

Original Babysling

★★★☆☆

NoJo (www.nojo.com 714.895.9200)
Price .... $30-$40   Features .... 0-30 lbs; sling/wrap

Parent Reviews: *"...good for parents with fussy babies who need to snuggle close... it provides several positions in which to carry your baby... discreet nursing is very easy to do with this sling... cozy, cuddly and warm—my baby loves his spacious, padded sling and so do I... washable and easy to use... the denim fabric is sturdy and doesn't look too 'babyish'... if you're in a warm climate both you and the baby will get warm really quickly—I wish they made it out of lighter, more breathable material... if you're short you may have difficulty adjusting the straps because the padding gets in the way..."*

Ali's Notes: *"...this sling gets extra ratings by folks looking for a generous sized sling—for a larger parent or larger baby... adjustability is a little tough when on (you'll have to take it off to adjust it)... it's most famous for having been developed by Dr. Sears..."*

Pack Baby Carrier

★★★★☆

Sutemi Gear (www.sutemigear.com 206.329.0932)
Price .... $75-$80
Features .... 8-26lbs; carrier

Parent Reviews: *"...we love the wide straps on this carrier... totally adjustable and comfortable—even my husband can wear it comfortably... easy to clean... you can wear it in the front, side or back... it distributes the weight evenly to both the shoulders and hips making it more comfortable to wear for long periods of time... well-constructed with strong fabric, lots of pockets... machine washable..."*

Peanut Shell

★★★★½

Goo-Ga (www.goo-ga.com 650.400.0069)
Price .... $38-$42
Features .... sling/wrap

Parent Reviews: *"...we have a small car and I rely on this sling instead of a stroller when I go shopping... small enough that when I'm not using it I keep it folded in my purse... it comes in many patterns to match any wardrobe... easy to put on and it's machine washable... great price and very well made..."*

Ali's Notes: *"...known for its stretchable, bright, fun fabrics and tube style construction... this peanut shell sling is a relatively new entrant into the baby sling market... if you need a cold-weather sling you might want to try one of their fleece versions..."*

Premaxx New Edition Baby Sling

★★★★★

JJ Cole (www.jjcoleusa.com 800.987.6828)
Price .... $50-$60
Features 0-35 lbs; sling/hip carrier

Parent Reviews: *"...very functional and cool looking... nicely padded for both parent and baby... plenty of pockets for all the extras you're carrying with you... it doesn't provide as much support as a complete sling, but it does work well for babies who can support themselves well..."*

Ali's Notes: *"...sporty, ergonomic and adjustable...a nice unisex approach to slings that make sharing with your (different-sized) partner easy... one of the few slings Dads seem to like... sort of a backpack approach to slings, which doesn't make it as snug for nursing..."*

Ultra EZ Baby Carrier

One Step Ahead (www.onestepahead.com)
Price ....$22-$25
Features .... 5-40lbs; hip carrier

★★★★★

Parent Reviews: *"...compact and distributes the weight quite nicely... comfortable for both of us... it holds the baby off to the side on your hip, just as you would carry him without a sling... only suitable for older babies who can sit up by themselves—no neck support... my baby was much calmer in it—he would even fall asleep while we walked..."*

Wallaby

Kelty (www.kelty.com 866.349.7225)
Price ....$60-$65
Features ....0-25 lbs; carrier

★★★½☆

Parent Reviews: *"...a basic, comfortable front carrier... padded shoulder straps and pretty much everything can be adjusted... the carrier itself is padded and my baby seems to enjoy sitting in it... good value for the money..."*

Wraparound Baby Carrier

EllaRoo (www.ellaroo.com)
Price ....$70-$90
Features ....

★★★★☆

Parent Reviews: *"...incredibly versatile... you can use it from newborn to toddler... carry your baby in the front, on your hip or even back... wonderfully breathable hand-woven fabric... it takes a while to figure out how to wrap it, but once you get it, it's easy... 100% cotton hand-woven Guatemalan fabric... it requires time, training and finesse to figure out how to tie it just right so it's comfortable and secure..."*

diaper bags

These days, there are lots of different diaper bags to choose from, and it's easy to find grown-up options that match your sense of style and not just your baby's. Since your diaper bag is one of the most prominent expressions of your new parenthood - outside of the way you dress your bulging belly or little one - here are a few tips to keep in mind:

Size: If you're a pack rat and want everything with you all the time, you'll want a sturdy, high-capacity diaper bag. If you're a minimalist who wants to carry just the necessities, you'll want light, airy and efficient. Many first-time parents who want to be prepared for anything think they need a huge diaper bag during the first few months, but will later opt for the less-is-more route.

Styles: There are basically three different styles of diaper bags to choose from: backpacks, totes and fashion-accessory bags. Backpacks can be just a traditional backpack with two shoulder straps or a sling style that goes over one shoulder. Totes range from simple, canvas totes like you might take to the beach to high-end, diaper bag-style totes. Fashion-driven bags tend to look less like a baby accessory and more like a regular, stylish bag. They're the perfect complement to business attire and dressier clothes (no bunny rabbits here!).

Variety: Some people like to have one good, basic diaper bag, while others like to accessorize with a choice of diaper bags, just like they would with handbags. If you're looking for one good, basic bag, start with a basic tote and then figure out your style as you go. If you want several to choose from, cover the bases from practical to fun and from light load to heavy load.

Color: Will you be sharing this bag with your mate? Stay away from bubble-gum pink! Either find a nice, neutral bag that you both can live with or look for a special "Daddy" option.

Basics: Make sure you have at least one good everyday bag that works with your stroller, either as an accessory to it or one that easily fits in its storage bin.

Features You'll Want: Other must-haves are a changing pad, easy-access pockets, a bottle holder and comfortable carrying support (no matter how much you load it down!).

by Ali Wing at egiggle.com

diaper bags

★★★★★
"lila picks"

- ★ Diaper Backpack (Baby Bjorn)
- ★ Duo Diaper Bag (Skip Hop)
- ★ Little Tripper (Land's End)
- ★ Marsupial Diaper Bag (Loom)
- ★ Mothership (Fleurville)
- ★ Triple Compartment Diaper Pack (Lands' End)
- ★ Urban Sling (Combi)

Baby Bag

★★★★½

Sally Spicer (www.sallyspicer.com)
Price ....$90   Size ....12"x15"x6.5"

Parent Reviews: "...I can wear this as my purse... a beautiful bag that is also my diaper bag... I wish it were a bit bigger... I like that there are two bottle pockets on the outside of the bag... beautiful fabric, and durable design..."

Ali's Notes: "...Sally Spicer bags are known for their fashionable, contemporary style... their nice fabrics present a bit more of a maintenance issue than other more 'everyday' canvas, vinyl or cotton alternatives... very trendy and chic..."

Baby Bag
Vera Bradley (www.verabradley.com)

★★★★☆

Price ....$75-$85
Size........................17"x13"x6.5"

Parent Reviews: "...attractive fabric that is soft yet durable... it includes terry cloth lined changing pad, lots of pockets and plastic lined drawstring bag for wet clothing... no cooler pocket for bottles... the bag also features a full-length outer pocket that is great for holding paperwork, such as doctor's records or prescriptions... a truly nice bag, not too cutesy looking..."

Back Pack Diaper Bag
Oi Oi (www.oioi.com)

★★★★½

Price $100
Size.........................15"x11"x6"

Parent Reviews: "...this bag is very versatile- the flap is insulated and can hold 2 bottles and a sippy cup or 2 sippy cups and a bottle, so I can use it for my baby and toddler... I love the plastic pocket for dirty diapers and wipes... the padded changing mat is really comfortable for my baby... the hidden pocket holds my valuables... pricey, but well worth it..."

Ali's Notes: "...nicely designed and innovative construction... quilted nylon micro fiber and PVC lining means it's reasonably stain-proof... it comes with a changing pad and insulated bottle holder... straps are adjustable..."

Bambino Diaper Bag
Dobre Goods (www.dobregoods.com)

★★★★½

Price ....$80   Size ....12"x13"x6"

Parent Reviews: "...so many patterns to choose from... stylish... I can wear this as a purse... vintage prints... durable... so cute, but so functional... the water-resistant fabric is so smart because it also doesn't get dirty so quickly... retro styling... expensive, but worth it... small, but holds a lot... attention to detail... a beautiful, elegant bag..."

Ali's Notes: "...cute vintage prints make this diaper bag trendy and chic... simple water-resistant fabric makes it easy to wipe clean (no, you can't throw it in the washing machine)... it's a pretty basic, no-frills bag which will help you feel trendy and chic and less like the crazed mom you really are..."

Boxy Backpack ★★★½☆
Petunia Pickle Bottom (www.petuniapicklebottom.com)
Price .... $155-$165   Size .... 12.5" x 13.5"

Parent Reviews: "...great different patterns to choose from... the water resistant lining is great for spills... I really like the detachable dirty diaper bag- I just pull it out and dump in the washer... so versatile- I can wear this as backpack or on the shoulder... cons: dry clean only, and it's a bit pricey..."

Ali's Notes: "...Petunia Pickel Bottom bags are known for their fashionable Asian brocade finishes... moms tell us they're difficult to clean and without padded shoulder straps they're not for heavy, extended use... they do last well beyond the diaper changing days and most people would never know that you're walking around with a diaper bag..."

Camellia ★★★★☆
Amy Michelle
Price .... $225   Size .... 16"x7"x11"

Parent Reviews: "...created by a mom who knows about diapers... stylish, yet practical... elegant.... well made... plush changing pad is soft for my baby... lots of compartments for diapers, wipes and formula... love the insulated bottle holder... stylish, but pricey..."

Ali's Notes: "...a luxury leather (yes, leather!) diaper bag reflective of the trend toward sophisticated styling for modern moms...

equipped with just about every bell and whistle you can think of (insulated bottle holders, parent and baby sections)... the biggest drawback (after price) is that it's heavier than most diaper bags... also available in a smaller, toddler version..."

Colorado Tote ★★★★½
Catini Bags (www.catinibags.com)
Price .... $25-$30

Parent Reviews: "...so non-diaper-bag-looking... nice canvas material and designed with lots of zipper pockets... my hubby actually likes to carry this bag... a hip looking bag—great for dads... modest colors and cool outdoorsy look... one of the best deals out there when you consider style, functionality and price..."

Diaper Backpack

★★★★★

Baby Bjorn (www.babybjorn.com 800.593 5522)
Price .... $50-$55   Size .... 15"x16"x6"

Parent Reviews: "...it stays open when you put it on the ground... easy to get things in and out... well constructed, washes easily and holds up to wear and tear... insulated bottle holders... the inside is quite large and things get lost in there pretty easily, sometimes you have to rummage through everything to find one thing... like everything else from Baby Bjorn the quality is great and they obviously did their homework when designing this bag..."

Ali's Notes: "...a favorite among the backpack crowd... built with quality, loaded with compartments, and designed for the busy parent... a great everyday diaper bag solution... the bonus is that parents (moms and dads both!) love it as much as a backpack after they graduate from diaper duty as they did before... a side note—it is also a slightly lighter backpack than most diaper packs which makes it a good choice for everyday use..."

Diaper Bag

★★★★☆

Baby Bjorn (www.babybjorn.com 800.593 5522)
Price .... $75-$80   Size .... 13"x7.5"x11"

Parent Reviews: "...it feels like a little suitcase... I love that it stays open when you put it on the ground... easy to get things in and out... well designed with all of the compartments... it washes easily (wipes down) and holds up to wear and tear... insulated bottle holders... the top pops open too easily since it is made of hard material... changing pad included... adjustable shoulder straps..."

Ali's Notes: "...with its contemporary European styling, this classy Baby Bjorn diaper bag is loaded with compartments... designed for easy, one-handed accessibility, the formed construction does add weight to an otherwise smaller diaper bag..."

Diaper Bag

Timi & Leslie (www.timiandleslie.com)
Price .... $90-$100
Size .... 12"x10.5"x3.5"

Parent Reviews: "...I love the vintage fabrics... the magnetic closure is a great—no noisy Velcro... the outside zipper is very handy... what unusual patterns and fabrics... not cheap, but worth it if you want a unique bag... the matching changing pad is really cute..."

Ali's Notes: "...known for trendy, chic vintage fabrics, Timi & Leslie has developed a celebrity following... vinyl coating, water-resistant lining, 1 bottle holder, and magnetic closure..."

Diaper Case Bag

★★★½☆

Eddie Bauer (www.djgusa.com/eddiebauer 800.544.1108)
Price .... $40-$50
Size .... 8"x11"x17"

Parent Reviews: "...this is a big bag... strap is really comfortable... lots of pockets... looks too much like luggage... good for dads... this bag is too big—I feel like I'm going to the airport all day long... the removable wet/dry pouch is really handy... inside zip pocket holds a lot... holds 3 bottles... perfect for when we're on the road... "

Diaper Daypack

★★★☆☆

Kelty (www.kelty.com)
Price .... $60-$65   Size .... 12"x13"x15"

Parent Reviews: "...a solid backpack-style bag... made from sturdy backpack material so everything holds up really well... it comes with a changing pad... double zipper top entry makes it easy to get at your things anywhere in the bag... two outside pockets allow you to keep your keys and wallet within easy reach... "

Ali's Notes: "...Kelty is world-renowned for their quality and construction and this little bag is no different... it's a little small and not particularly unique as a diaper bag other than that it has a changing pad included... the best part is that this bag zips into most Kelty backpacks as an accessory... you'll be use this as a day pack well beyond your diapering days... "

Diaper DayPouch

★★★★☆

Eddie Bauer (www.djgusa.com/eddiebauer 800.544.1108)
Price .... $25-$35   Size .... 3.5"x8"x9"

Parent Reviews: "...comfortable to wear... nylon washes well... the cell phone holder on the shoulder strap is ingenious... adjustable shoulder straps allow my husband to wear it, too... great for dad because it doesn't have the 'froufy' look that many of the other bags have... only one pocket for bottles...very handy front flap pocket, and holds lots of stuff... "

Ali's Notes: "...a great 'day at the zoo with Dad' bag... it doesn't look like a girlie diaper bag and has all the essentials built in—bottle holders, cell phone holder, adjustable shoulder straps, etc... not the largest bag so you'll have to plan what to take with you... one of the best deals around... "

Do-It-All Diaper Bag ★★★★☆

Lands' End (www.landsend.com 800.963.4816)
Price .... $25-$30   Size .... 15"x11.5"x10.25"

Parent Reviews: *"...you get a lot of bag for the money... different compartments for everything... well priced and very utilitarian... looks great and comes in several fun colors... doesn't look like a baby bag... I wish the diaper compartments were bigger... it becomes very bulky and square when you fill it up... the light-colored interior makes it easy to find things quickly... good for longer trips, but a little too much for everyday use..."*

Ali's Notes: *"...simple style with reliable quality makes Lands' End bags a super value every time... cheap in price, yet rich in quality—Lands' End bags are a no-brainer—if you like the way this specific bag looks, then get it..."*

Duo Diaper Bag ★★★★★

Skip Hop (www.skiphop.com)
Price .... $55-$60   Size .... 13"x14"x3"

Parent Reviews: *"...it looks cool and works great... I love the way it attaches to my stroller—why don't all diaper bags have straps for hooking your bag to the stroller?.. it comes with a changing pad and has a couple of pockets for bottles... plenty of room on the inside to organize your things... comfortable to carry over your shoulder and doesn't look like a diaper bag—now that our boy is out of diapers my husband uses it as a gym bag..."*

Ali's Notes: *"...boy, once these bags hit the market they really took over as the favorite diaper bag hanging from most mom's strollers... truly 'stroller agnostic', it's built with a smart handle that morphs from shoulder strap to stroller clasps... a chic, simple, durable diaper bag solution... the only 2 complaints were that it's a little tight on cargo room and that the top doesn't close... so Skip Hop has solved that problem with the Expo (that looks just like the Duo but doubles the cargo room) and the Dash (a more traditional look to a diaper bag that offers a closed top)..."*

Essentials Diaper Bag ★★★★☆

JJ Cole (www.jjcoleusa.com 800.987.6828)
Price .... $30   Size .... 45"x6"x4"

Parent Reviews: *"...the most comfortable diaper bag I've tried... so well-designed—everything has its place... it has a really stylish look to it, unlike the flowery handbags that seem so impractical... it doesn't work so well if you're wearing a sling or carrier... very durable and well-made..."*

Ali's Notes: *"...an innovative approach to the modern diaper bag... it's like a long sling that holds everything you'll need for your baby—zippered compartments, insulated bottle holder... great value for the money..."*

Jasmine

Amy Michelle
Price $225
Size .... 16"x7"x11"

★★★½☆

Parent Reviews: *"...easy to find key ring... pocket for day planner and cell phone is helpful... matching purse available for purchase... nice pattern design, and free shipping..."*

Ali's Notes: *"...a luxury leather (yes, leather!) diaper bag reflective of the trend toward sophisticated styling for modern moms... equipped with just about every bell and whistle you can think of (insulated bottle holders, parent and baby sections)... the biggest drawback (after price) is that it's heavier than most diaper bags..."*

Lena Diaper Bag

★★★★½

Sherpani (www.sherpani.us)
Price .... $70   Size .... 13"x8"x7"

Parent Reviews: *"...the large opening lets me get what I need quickly... the reflective stripe on the shoulder strap is so smart- I can wear this bag when I ride my bike... the floral diaper-changing pad is so cute... the soft handle is very comfortable... great for athletic people... the magnetic closure is very helpful... I love that this bag has adjustable yoga mat straps for any size mat I use... the internal wet pocket is great for dirty diapers..."*

value

Ali's Notes: *"...an 'urban' styled bag for the active woman (and mom!)... part diaper bag, part yoga gym bag, this is a fun and functional mom-on-the go bag... changing pad included and bottle holders too... it even comes with straps for your yoga mat—talk about practical..."*

Little Tripper Diaper Bag

★★★★★

Lands' End (www.landsend.com 800.963.4816)
Price .... $15-$20   Size .... 13"x10.5"x4.75"

Parent Reviews: *"...holds tons of stuff without getting bulky... comes with a changing pad... lots of pockets for easy organization and access... a more than reasonable price given what you get... nice enough to use every day... good color choices... smaller than most diaper bags... the changing pad that comes with the bag is very stiff... a great bag for small outings..."*

multi-use

Ali's Notes: *"...simple style with reliable quality makes Lands' End bags a super value every time... cheap in price, yet rich in quality—Lands' End bags are a no-brainer—always good value for the money..."*

www.lilaguide.com

Marsupial Diaper Bag

★★★★★

Loom (www.loomlife.com)
Price .... $125-$130   Size .... 16.5"x11"x6"

Parent Reviews: **"**...an attractive messenger bag... it comes in stain resistant durable fabric in stylish color combinations... plenty of pockets, both internal and external make organizing all of your stuff easy—it makes it easy to find what you are looking for without taking the bag off your shoulder by feel... magnetic clasps make the bag not only easy to open with one hand, but also avoids that annoying Velcro sound...**"**

Ali's Notes: **"**...designed by the woman behind the now well-known Fleurville bags, Loom is trendy and chic... an elegant approach to the classic diaper tote... beautifully constructed (and no vinyl!)... rightfully a big-time new-parent favorite... always coming out with the best colors and fun patterns...**"**

Messenger Bag

★★★⯪☆

Oi Oi (www.oioi.com)
Price .... $110   Size .... 13"x16"x5"

Parent Reviews: **"**...the 2 insulated pockets hold my Avent bottles perfectly, plus the Velcro cover helps me to get to the bottles easily... the padded changing mat is very comfortable for my baby's use... the bag for the dirty diapers is so handy... the water-resistant lining makes clean-up easy... I love the color of this bag... the metal feet on the bottom of the bag protect the bag, and mine has lasted a long time... the extra long strap makes it easy for anyone to wear... I really like the magnetic closing...**"**

Ali's Notes: **"**...well-designed, comfortable to carry and spacious... magnetic closures that work... insulated bottle holder and changing mat included...**"**

Messenger Diaper Bag

★★★★⯪

Haiku (www.haikubags.com)
Price .... $160-$170   Size .... 12"x11.5"x6.5"

Parent Reviews: **"**...suede finish, streamlined look adds a stylish class... magnetic closure lets me get in and out quickly... huge front pocket is really helpful... wide, comfortable strap, doesn't hurt my back... colorful 3-dimensional lining is fun... 2 elastic mesh pockets hold a lot...**"**

Ali's Notes: **"**...Haiku is another creative player in the 'diaper bags that don't look like diaper bags' movement... stylish suede finish with Japanese-inspired graphics... trendy, chic and pricey...**"**

Messenger Diaper Bag

★★★½☆

Mum
Price .... $90-$115
Size .... 14"x12"

Parent Reviews: **"**...a spacious bag that is comfortable to wear... comes with a changing pad and lots of pockets... no thermal bottle pockets... a nice looking bag that will let you use it beyond the few months that you'll be toting diapers everywhere you go...**"**

Metro Back Pack

★★★★☆

Combi (www.combi-intl.com 800.992.6624)
Price .... $40-$50   Size .... 15"x13"x17"

Parent Reviews: **"**...a great price for a great bag... so many pockets—it holds everything... nylon exterior makes it easy to clean... two bottle pockets fit different types of bottles... my husband would carry this bag without feeling self-conscous... lightweight... I recommend this bag to my friends because it enables you to carry all your diapering products at all times...**"**

Ali's Notes: **"**...a good, solid backpack... comfortable and lightweight... the best part is that unlike the fancy leather bags, you won't mind spills and dirt with this bag—just pop it into the washer and line dry...**"**

Mini Messenger Bag

★★★★☆

California Innovations
Price .... $20-$25   Size ....

Parent Reviews: **"**...big front zippered pocket holds all my stuff... the removable changing pad and bag for dirty diapers is so helpful... special holder for pacifiers is a life-saver... a nice bag that holds everything... the insulated side pocket is really helpful...**"**

Ali's Notes: **"**...simple, black and basic... medium size but surprisingly spacious on the inside... great for moms on the move—not too big, but just big enough that you won't be left without any of your diapering essentials... check out the price—no wonder it's a favorite among so many parents...**"**

Mothership

Fleurville (www.fleurville.com)
Price .... $140-$150   Size .... 14"x13"x5"

★★★★★

Parent Reviews: "...all of their bags have such a distinctive look and I love this particular one the most... it has pockets for everything... I love the bottle pocket and the changing mat it comes with... easily accessible outer pockets for your wallet, phone, lipstick and more... it is rather expensive, but when you consider that it also acts as your purse it's definitely worth it..."

Ali's Notes: "...Fleurville is known for their trendy, chic yet very practical designs... changing pad and built-in insulated bottle holder included... the vinyl construction makes them easy to keep clean, but gets sticky when it's hot... great colors and prints make them one of the most popular choices around..."

Parent Survival Pack

★★★★½

Eagle Creek (www.eaglecreek.com   800.874.1048)
Price .... $65-$75   Size .... 14"x16.5"x8.5"

Parent Reviews: "...lots of exterior pockets... it comes with a large changing pad... it looks like a regular backpack and is perfect for airplane flights—passes as a carry-on for baby's stuff and yours as well... good color choices... built for rough handling... way too big for everyday use unless you have twins... the fabric is stiff and it feels like you're lugging a backpack around rather than a diaper bag..."

Ali's Notes: "...talk about functional... dads love this rugged diaper pack because because it looks nothing like a diaper bag... it's huge and might be overkill for everyday use... perfect for hikes, picnics and general outdoor activities... great value for the money..."

Shoulder Bag

Petunia Pickle Bottom
(www.petuniapicklebottom.com)
Price .... $165-$175
Size...................... 15"x6"x13"

Parent Reviews: "...I like the messenger style... the zip-out changing station is so smart, and so easy to use... so many great colors to choose from... the shoulder strap is really comfortable... the extra wide back pockets allow easy access to the interior, however, a bit pricey..."

Ali's Notes: "...well-known for their fashionable Asian brocade finishes—a style you either love or don't like at all... some complain that these bags aren't made for everyday use (they show their wear!)..."

Triple Compartment Diaper Pack

★★★★★

Lands' End (www.landsend.com 800.963.4816)
Price .... $35-$40   Size .... 12"x18"x7.25"

Parent Reviews: "...a great quality backpack that will never wear out... we used it even after we were done with diapers... the bottle cooler is handy... it has a changing pad and several zippered compartments to store various baby and mommy items... I wish it had more divided compartments on the inside... with all the baby gear in it, the bag can be big and cumbersome... I found it to be too much for day-to-day use but it's perfect for weekend or overnight trips..."

Ali's Notes: "...simple style with reliable quality makes Lands' End bags a super value every time... cheap in price, yet rich in quality—Lands' End bags are a no-brainer—if you like the way this specific bag looks, then get it... this particular model is quite large and has a life span well beyond your diapering days..."

Ultimate Diaper Bag

★★★★☆

Ella Bags (www.ella-bags.com)
Price .... $120   Size .... 13"x12"x6"

Parent Reviews: "...this really is the ultimate diaper bag... the most stylish bag out there... beautifully crafted... you can choose from hundreds of fabrics... I love the silver strap hook... vinyl-lined interior good for spills... it can be upgraded to a backpack... great attention to detail... very expensive, but worth it if you want to look good... lots of storage..."

Ali's Notes: "...hundreds of designer fabrics to choose from (and monogramming)... Ella Bags are a traditional style diaper bag with designer flare... well made—designer fabric inside and out, silver clasp and adjustable shoulder strap... exclusively for Mom—Dad most likely won't be heading out with this one..."

Un-Diaper Bag

★★★★☆

Babystyle (www.babystyle.com)
Price .... $65   Size .... 16.5"x12"x6"

Parent Reviews: "...microfiber material cleans up easily... stylish buckles are very trendy and hip... versatile, I can wear this anywhere... not too big, but fits the essentials... faux leather trim makes this look like a purse, not just a diaper bag... great price... I love the big pockets... cute lining and matching changing pad..."

Ali's Notes: "...it doesn't even look like a diaper bag... all the extras (changing pad, insulated bottle packs, etc) are all neatly tucked away inside... given how stylish it looks, it can be used well after you're done schlepping diapers and wipes around with you..."

Urban Sling

Combi (www.combi-intl.com 800.992.6624)
Price ....$45-$50   Size .... 20"x13"x12"

Parent Reviews: *"...it doesn't look like a diaper bag—it looks more like a cool bike messenger bag... it seems small, but carries tons of stuff... an insulated cooler big enough to store one baby's bottle or a couple of jars of food... reasonably affordable and quite comfortable to carry... a little pricey given that it's a pretty basic bag... the over-the-shoulder thing can make my shoulder ache after a while..."*

Ali's Notes: *"...parents love that this urban sling doesn't give them away at the office—it's hip and stylish... packed with all the essentials—a changing pad, smart compartments and a great insulated bottle holder... after you're done with diapering you (or your husband) can use this bag for everyday activities..."*

diapering needs

When it comes to diapers, your first big question is disposable or cloth. The jury's still out on which is actually better for the environment, and most moms will argue over which is better for baby. Really, it comes down to personal preference. The bottom line is, don't invest in a lifetime supply of either until you've tried them out and know which one you prefer. In the meantime, here are some things to consider regarding cloth diapers, disposable diapers and diaper accessories:

Disposables: Disposable diapers are more convenient and cut down on laundry, and if you're a working mom trying to coordinate daycare, they may be your only practical option. Some moms also argue that they keep babies dryer because of wicking materials and more frequent changing.

Cloth: Cloth diapers mean one less thing for the landfills. Plus, they're a lot easier to use than they were in our parents' day, thanks to washable, cloth diaper covers that don't require pins and diaper delivery services (although services are often criticized for their negative environmental effect on water).

Monitoring: If your newborn is having trouble eating, monitoring urine output is key. And most doctors will tell you that using cloth diapers makes monitoring a lot more accurate.

Other Uses: If you want to try cloth diapers, you don't have to worry about them going to waste if you don't end up using them in the long run. They also make excellent burp clothes, which means you'll be happy to have several around regardless of your diapering decisions.

Variety: Disposable diaper brands can fit differently on different kids. Try several before your pick your favorite. Many parents swear by whatever brand they use, but there's no real consensus. In other words, don't stock up until you've tested a few.

Diaper Products: As with other personal care products, less is more when it comes to caring for your baby's bottom. Daily use of a nontoxic barrier cream for sensitive skin is a great way to keep a diapered bottom rash-free. If a rash should occur, there are a lot of wonderful diaper creams available - even some with Echinacea!

Diaper Pails: Get something airtight to keep your dirty diapers in - particularly after six months when your baby is on solid foods. If you decide to invest in a true diaper pail, just make sure the required liner refills are easy to find and affordable to buy.

by Ali Wing at egiggle.com

diaper rash ointments

★★★★★

"lila picks"

- ★ Baby Barrier Cream (Little Forest)
- ★ Baby Bee Diaper Ointment (Burt's Bees)
- ★ Baby Vitamin Barrier Cream (Mustela)
- ★ Diaper Cream (Erbaviva)

Baby Barrier Cream ★★★★★

Little Forest (www.littleforest.com 888.329.2229)
Price ....$7-$9   Features 2oz

Parent Reviews: "*...pleasant smell and goes on easily... I love the all-natural ingredients they use... it cured my baby's diaper rash in a flash... it feels rich and creamy... contains zinc oxide and tea tree oil... excellent quality—like all Little Forest products...*"

Ali's Notes: "*...an all-natural favorite... Little Forest makes a great barrier cream suitable for everyday use and highly effective against diaper rashes...*"

Baby Bee Diaper Ointment ★★★★★
Burt's Bees (www.burtsbees.com 800.849.7112)
Price ....$5.50-$7
Features 1.75oz

Parent Reviews: **"**...a delightful natural alternative to chemical-based creams... clears redness quickly... I got a tube from a friend and I'm a convert... it's not horribly sticky, doesn't have a strong odor and is easy to apply... natural, gentle and smells good... can be tough to find—not necessarily available in the bigger chain stores... **"**

Ali's Notes: **"**...can be hard to find but check out a Whole Foods near you... better for rashes than everyday use (as a barrier cream)... **"**

Baby Healing Ointment ★★★★☆
Aquaphor (www.aquaphorhealing.com 203.854.8000)

Price .... $7-$13
Features ....3 & 14oz

Parent Reviews: **"**...you can feel the great quality... they gave me some in the hospital and the pediatrician recommended it for those really bad rashes... it seems to soothe my baby immediately... it also works great on infant face rashes, eczema and for healing any small cuts or scratches your baby might get... a little tube goes a long way... it helped my son's goose egg heal... comes in portable tubes that you should keep in your bag... **"**

Ali's Notes: **"**...a popular, pediatrician-recommended product for sore bottoms... best for treating skin irritations (not limited to diaper rash)... **"**

multi-use

Baby Vitamin Barrier Cream ★★★★★
Mustela (www.mustelausa.com 800.422.2987)
Price ....$7-$9   Features............................... 1.9oz

Parent Reviews: **"**...non-greasy and not sticky... very creamy and spreads very easily... we use it once a day and our son has never had a diaper rash... unlike many other brands this cream actually smells good too... soothing and very effective... **"**

Ali's Notes: **"**...parents universally rave about this cream that protects baby's delicate skin from diaper rash... zinc oxide provides an actual barrier between the baby's skin and outside irritants... shea butter soothes irritation and softens the skin... best used as it was named—as a daily "barrier" cream, rather than to remedy a rash... **"**

participate in our survey at

Bum Bum Balm

Munchskins Skin Care (www.munchskins.com 604.759.0049)
Price ....$11 Features...

Parent Reviews: "...all-natural diaper rash treatment made by a Canadian company... it comes in this great little tin that is easy to tuck into your diaper bag and won't explode or leak... not too oily or greasy and it smells pretty good too... not available in too many stores in the US, but it's relatively easy to find online... they also make several other balms that are good for baby (and adult) skin..."

Butt Paste

Boudreaux's (www.buttpaste.com 800.368.7274)
Price ....$8-$15 Features.................................... 4oz

Parent Reviews: "...you'll have some explaining to do when your friends find it in your bag... gotta love the name... smells great, feels great and really works... soothing and works on contact... the lidded container is small and easy to carry in your diaper bag... easy to spread and seems less greasy than other brands... comes in portable tubes or 1 pound jars..."

Calendula Baby Cream

Weleda (www.usa.weleda.com 800.241.1030)
Price ....$6-$9 Features............................... 2.7oz

Parent Reviews: "...nothing I've tried works nearly as well... definitely worth the price, especially if you reserve it for those really bad rashes... pleasant scent... it stays on where it's need but wipes off easily from your fingers... it seems very effective on rashes..."

Desitin Original

Desitin (www.desitin.com 800.723.7529)
Price ....$5-$13 Features........................... 4 & 16oz

Parent Reviews: "...it's hard to know which creams truly heal diaper rash, but this one always seems to do the trick... by far the best I've tried— it is easy to spread and stays on... I always have at least 2 tubes in the house... sticks and protects even through a couple of diaper changes... it gets really hard when cold— hard to get out of the tube... the original doesn't smell so hot—get their new creamy type... hard to get off your fingers after applying..."

Diaper Cream

★★★★★

Erbaviva (www.erbaviva.com 877.372.2848)
Price ....$19   Features.................... 4oz

Parent Reviews: "...wonderful smell and highly effective... very creamy but easy to apply and wipe off when changing diapers... we've been using this since the beginning and have never had much of a rash... "

Ali's Notes: "...we call this 'liquid gold'... although jaws drop when they first see the price tag, parents seem to love this soothing diaper cream... it contains Echinacea to help heal and protect baby's sensitive skin... lightly scented with organic lavender and chamomile essential oils... this cream works like magic for sore bottoms... "

Diaper Rash Cream

★★★★☆

Aveeno (www.aveeno.com 877.298.2525)
Price ....$5   Features.................... 4oz

Parent Reviews: "...not greasy or smelly... it works wonders on really bad bottoms... hypoallergenic and can be trusted—Aveeno makes wonderful products... good for sensitive skin

and mild eczema... no harsh ingredients... love to put it on my daughter after her bath... after a while it seems to separate—a watery substance drips out of the tube... "

Ali's Notes: "...simple, sensitive, effective and inexpensive compared to many other alternatives... great day-to-day product... "

Diaper Rash Ointment

★★★★☆

Balmex (www.balmex.com 866.844.2798)
Price ....$5-$11   Features......................... 4 & 16oz

Parent Reviews: "...it soothed my rash when I was a baby and still does a stellar job for my baby... it cleared my daughter's rash in no time... this works for us every time... the smell reminds me of the hospital... quick and easy to apply... creamy, but not too thick... worth every penny... "

Diaper Rash Spray

★★★★☆

RashMist (www.petkin.com 310.577.7775)
Price .... $3-$5
Features 2.5oz

Parent Reviews: "...I love it—no mess, just spray it on... it beats those pasty creams and lotions any day... so much easier to use than the creams that come in those annoying tubes... it sounds too good to be true, but it really does work... be careful not to spray toward your baby's face... it doesn't seem to provide as much coverage as some of the thicker creams but it's so much more convenient that I usually try the spray first... "

Triple Paste Medicated Ointment For Diaper Rash

Summers Lab (www.sumlab.com 800.533.7546)
Price ....$7-$8
Features 2oz; 8oz; 16oz

Parent Reviews: *"...it works quickly and effectively... excellent for that 'very-hard-to-get-rid-of' diaper rash... it protects and treats without any offensive odor... expensive, but I wouldn't buy anything else..."*

diaper rash ointments

diaper pails

★★★★★

"lila picks"

★ Diaper Champ (Baby Trend)
★ Diaper Dekor (Regal Lager)

Diaper Champ ★★★★★
Baby Trend (www.babytrend.com 800.328.7363)
Price .... $25-$30

Parent Reviews: *"...I love the fact that you don't need to keep buying special bags—we just use plastic bags from the grocery store... I can toss the diaper and seal in the stench with one hand while holding my baby... so far the nursery has stayed odor-free... it works great with cloth diapers too, when it's full we just hand it off to the diaper delivery guy... because it's so easy to use, my daughter knows how to use it and flips it back and forth on her own..."*

Ali's Notes: *"...a good basic design that just plain works... great value since you're not stuck buying proprietary bags, but rather can use regular kitchen bags... the extremely low price point makes this a no-brainer (especially as a second at grandma's house)..."*

Diaper Dekor Plus Diaper Disposal System

★★★★★

Regal Lager (www.regallager.com 800.593.5522)
Price .... $35-$40

Parent Reviews: "...easy to use—foot press opens lid... changing bags is super easy too... holds a ton of diapers and really manages to keep the smell in even when it gets really full... converts to a trash can once you've made it through the diaper stage... stock up on extra bags—it's a pain when you run out... refill bags are expensive... keeps the room odor free and looks nice too..."

Ali's Notes: "...a big step up in the category of plastic diaper pails... slightly more stylish than it's counterparts and it doesn't require you to use expensive, proprietary bags... it also holds a ton of diapers (although you'll probably want to empty it well before it's actually full)... the best part is that it converts nicely into a regular trash can when you're done with diapers... by far my favorite plastic diaper pail..."

Diaper Genie

★★★½☆

Playtex (www.playtexbaby.com 800.222.0453)
Price .... $30-$35

Parent Reviews: "...so easy to use—just stick the stinky diaper in and twist... it separates each diaper in the odor resistant plastic bag by creating a big long sausage-like tube of individually wrapped diapers... it helps keeps the nursery odor free... we even use it for our dog waste... the refill bags are expensive and actually kind of difficult to put into the genie... it holds about 30 diapers, but I recommend emptying it before you reach that capacity because things do start to smell..."

Diaper Pail

★★★½☆

Safety 1st (www.safety1st.com 800.544.1108)
Price .... $35-$40

Parent Reviews: "...foot pedal opens lid which is great when I'm also holding my baby... it uses standard size plastic trash bags... it has a special compartment to hold a deodorizing agent... works quite well and our nursery is relatively odor-free... basically works like an expensive trash can... holds up to 30 dirty diapers..."

Diaper Pail

★★★★⯪

VIPP (www.vipp.dk)
Price .... $230-$240

Parent Reviews: *"...by far the most effective 'odor-prevention' bin I've used... they come in various sizes and unfortunately all cost a small fortune... who in their right mind is going to spend this kind of money on a diaper pail?.. the bin looks good and is the only one I've found that really works... I especially like that it doesn't look like a diaper pail—it looks more like a modern garbage can..."*

Ali's Notes: *"...alone in its category for style, but also unparalleled in its efficacy... with its air tight system (originally designed for medical applications) this is the only truly smell-proof diaper pail (and that matters a lot once babies are eating solids!)... the catch is that you pay for it—almost 5 times the cost of most alternatives... proprietary bags aren't required, and this pail does live on well after baby as a beautiful trash can..."*

Neat Diaper Disposal System

★★★★☆

Safety 1st (www.safety1st.com   800.544.1108)
Price ....$20-$25

Parent Reviews: *"...it really works—no smell!.. it's so easy to use that my 4 year-old can throw away diapers and feel like he's helping... you pull up on the handle, put the diaper in and then push the lid back down... you have to buy the special Neat System bags which is a pain, but they do hold in the smell extremely well... it holds about 30 diapers..."*

Odorless Diaper Pail

★★★⯪☆

Safety 1st (www.safety1st.com   800.544.1108)
Price $15

Parent Reviews: *"...basic but good—I love the simple design... it's great that I can use regular trash bags instead of having to buy special ones... it served us well through our first baby and is ready for the new baby... sometimes the lid does not close all the way allowing odor to escape... I originally liked the idea of not needing to buy special bags, but found this pail doesn't always keep the stink in... it holds about 25 diapers..."*

for mom & dad

It's exciting being a new parent, and the tendency is to want to go buy the whole store. But wait! Once the word is out, you'll get lots of advice from your friends, family and doctor. Get used to the idea of being a parent, weigh your options carefully and consult guides to find out what you *really* need and want. There are lots of informative and well-written books out there from which you can get the answers or at least begin to formulate your questions.

As far as maternity clothes for the expecting mom, relax. It's not the 1970s anymore. There are so many options for great-looking, value-priced, functional maternity clothes today. Grandmothers everywhere are jealous. Our only advice: as with baby clothes, invest in some everyday, mix-and-match basics, and after that, have some fun.

by Ali Wing at egiggle.com

maternity clothing

"lila picks"

- ★ A Pea In The Pod
- ★ Babystyle
- ★ Belly Basics
- ★ Japanese Weekend
- ★ Liz Lange
- ● Old Navy

A Pea in the Pod ★★★★★
(www.apeainthepod.com 877.273.2763)
Parent Reviews: "...wonderful styles... excellent quality—I passed along most of my items to other expecting moms... great designers... from basics to special occasions they are bound to have something you'll like... nice looking clothes for the professional mother-to-be... nice materials and styles... clothes seem to run on the small side—I wasn't able to wear a lot of the items well into my pregnancy... good selection of outerwear... helpful and friendly staff... excellent collection of maternity bras and nursing bras... can't return online orders to retail stores... "

Babystyle ★★★★★
(www.babystyle.com)
Parent Reviews: "...they pioneered the comeback of chic and fashionable maternity clothing... their basics are cute, fun and also made of very comfortable fabrics... styles complement the equally chic children's line... going to those stores gets me more excited about having a baby... love the markdowns and email specials... "

Belly Basics ★★★★★
(www.bellybasics.com)
Parent Reviews: "...love the boxed set called the 'Pregnancy Survival kit' that include a top, pants, a skirt and a kneelength dress... you'll want to wear these every day of your pregnancy... they now have kits for everything—work essentials, yoga, warm weather, transitioning to your former body, etc... terrific new designs for work, home and going out in style ... "

Cadeau Maternity
(www.cadeaumaternity.com)
Parent Reviews: **"**...can't believe maternity clothes can be this fabulous... love their designs that make you feel good about how you look... might want to try on the pants first as some of them run very slim... made in Italy (need we say more?)...**"**

Charlotte Bloom
Parent Reviews: **"**...the jeans are so awesome and super comfy... hip shirts come in nice, bright colors that will make you smile even on not-so-great preggy days... limited line—wish there were more to choose from... lots available at Nordstrom...**"**

Childish Maternity
Parent Reviews: **"**...hip maternity line popular with the celebrity set—so much so that their products are named after celeb moms to be... designs are very sporty and 'very LA' but they are all really comfy and casual... readily available online...**"**

Duo Maternity
Parent Reviews: **"**...very popular brand available at JC Penney and other major retailers... simple, dependable styles that are not too flashy and trendy... comfortable work outfits that will last through your whole pregnancy... easy mix and match pieces...**"**

GapMaternity
(www.gap.com   800.427.78953)
Parent Reviews: **"**...trendy styles that mesh with your pre-pregnancy style... great basics... great price, especially when on sale... very stylish... love the panels in their pants for different belly sizes... pretty intimates... clothes that I would wear if I weren't pregnant... great return policy even for online purchases... some of the paneled pants didn't stay up well... love the Gap maternity jeans—I could even wear them at nine months...**"**

H&M Mama
(www.hm.com)
Parent Reviews: **"**...love that H&M carries clothes for pregnant women... they have hip styles at very reasonable prices... not available in all the stores but a lot of them do carry some... it's fun to buy anything at H&M and good to know that you can still buy there while your body is expanding leaps and bounds...**"**

IMaternity
(www.imaternity.com)
Parent Reviews: **"**...sister to Motherhood and Mimi Maternity and Pea in the Pod, this is the company's online only line... clothes are very similar to those offered by Motherhood Maternity... lots of basics and everyday wear... check online for sales—they are pretty decent...**"**

Japanese Weekend ★★★★★
(www.japaneseweekend.com   800.808.0555)
Parent Reviews: **"**...tres chic... great pants, tops and underwear... gorgeous clothing for the small-framed expectant mother... trendy, fun clothes to make pregnant women feel hip and not frumpy... the pants will last through your whole pregnancy and won't stretch or fade... you won't find jeans as comfy as these... their nursing bras did not offer me enough support... expensive, but worth every penny...**"**

maternity clothing

www.lilaguide.com

Juicy Couture ★★★★☆
(www.juicycouture.com)
Parent Reviews: "...if you're into velour, this is the brand for you... definitely overpriced but loyal followers swear by the style and comfort of this brand... I am happy that they finally came up with a maternity line—it makes a lot of sense..."

Lands End ★★★★☆
(www.landsend.com   800.963.4816)
Parent Reviews: "...I am so happy you offer maternity clothes in the same Lands End quality... stylish, classic, functional pieces made with comfort in mind... don't stop making them until after I've had my children... besides the catalog and online, you will also find this line at Sears..."

Liz Lange ★★★★★
(www.lizlange.com   888.616.5777)
Parent Reviews: "...the most stylish, well-made maternity clothing out there... great twin sets and workout wear... fun outfits for different occasions—work, play and formal... trendy maternity wear made for smaller women... extremely comfortable and flattering... pricey but she does have a fabulous line at Target that's reasonably priced... her clothes will make you feel sexy even when you really feel like you're busting-out-of-the-seams pregnant..."

Medela ★★★☆☆
(www.medela.com)
Parent Reviews: "...seamless bra with matching boxers and briefs.... super soft and comfortable... you can bet their bras are of as high quality as their breast pumps... comes in 3 colors in very simple styles..."

Meet Me in Miami ★★★★☆
Parent Reviews: "...flirty and sexy as their ads say—true enough, you will feel like a flirty and sexy pregnant woman... fun and fabulous clothes especially for going out and special occasions..."

Michael Stars Maternity ★★★★½
(www.michaelstars.com)
Parent Reviews: "...if you are fan of Michael Stars tshirts, you will love these maternity versions... great for everyday in and out of the house... incredibly durable—mine have lasted more than it's fair share of washings... shirts are pretty easy to find online..."

Mimi Maternity ★★★½☆
(www.mimimaternity.com)
Parent Reviews: "...I love Mimi maternity jeans—I wore them a lot in the beginning because they look good and were comfortable... reasonably priced for the working woman's wardrobe... draconian return policy... I still wear the underwear... adorable, hip, trendy clothes for working pregos..."

Motherhood Maternity ★★★★☆
(www.motherhood.com   800.466.6223)
Parent Reviews: "...the slightly 'lower-end' version of A Pea In The Pod... shop wisely and you'll find some great items... reasonable prices... plenty of fun, casual clothes to choose from... great bathing suit and underwear selection... cute things for under $20... dismal return policy..."

Naissance On Melrose
(www.naissanceonmelrose.com   800.505.0517)
Parent Reviews: "*...trendy styles that mesh with your pre-pregnancy style... great basics... great price, especially when on sale...very stylish... love the panels in their pants for different belly sizes... pretty intimates...clothes that I would wear if I weren't pregnant... great return policy even for online purchases... great that most things are available online so you don't have to go to LA to get these super cool clothes...*"

Nursing Wear
Expressiva (www.expressiva.com)
Parent Reviews: "*...bras, underwear and other clothing that were thoughtfully designed for nursing mothers... basic designs in mixed cotton and lycra are extremely comfortable and durable... you'll want to wear these every day... their dresses don't look like your typical nursing gowns...*"

Old Navy
(www.oldnavy.com   800.653.6289)
Parent Reviews: "*...super cheap and stylish... love the long length in pants... lots of variety... sexy halter dresses for the summer months... plenty of room to grow, unlike many brands that get too small in the final trimester... great for basics like t-shirts, yoga-style pants and bathing suits... the return policy is much better than any other maternity store I have shopped... clothes can look kinda worn after a few washings... for the price, who cares if they don't last more than one pregnancy?...*"

Olian Maternity
(olianmaternity.com)
Parent Reviews: "*...beautiful and elegant clothes you can't resist... original and unique designs a welcome relief to the basic stuff that's all over the place... some styles run small so if you have a local store carrying this brand, go in for a fitting... mostly sold in boutique maternity stores but also available online...*"

Velvet Maternity
Parent Reviews: "*...such comfortable 100% cotton tops that are great for everyday and mixing with everything... stock up on these as you can probably live in them until after your baby is born...*"

parenting books

★★★★★ "lila picks"

- ★ Baby Book, The (William & Martha Sears)
- ★ Expectant Father, The (Arming Brott)
- ★ New Basics, The (Michael Cohen, MD)

Attachment Parenting Book, The

(Sears, William & Martha www.sears.com)
Price .... $13.95; 224 p
ISBN 0316778095 (2001)

Parent Reviews: *"...they deal with all of those controversial attachment parenting issues in such a positive way... a very loving, nurturing and relaxed approach... they offer many ideas and approaches, and understand that some things will work and some will not... overly repetitive—they could have made the book half as long... an amazing guide to real, down-to-earth parenting..."*

Baby Book, The
★★★★★
(Sears, William & Martha Little, Brown & Company)
Price .... $21.95; 704 p   ISBN 0316778001 (2003)

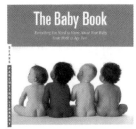

Parent Reviews: **"**...the Sears' are my gurus—they believe in co-sleeping, breastfeeding and an overall gentle and nurturing way of parenting... any time I have a question or problem, I either get out this book or go to the web site... thoroughly covers newborn to 2 years... an enormous book that could be made smaller, but it's incredibly valuable... if you want to sleep with your baby and aren't sure how to stand up to the people who think you're crazy, this book will give you lots of ammo... I buy this book for all my expectant friends... **"**

Breast Feeding Book, The
★★★★☆
(Sears, William & Martha www.sears.com)
Price .... $14.95; 272 p   ISBN 0316779245

Parent Reviews: **"**...an 'everything breastfeeding' guide from the gurus of attachment parenting... it helped reassure me that things were going fine with the way I was breastfeeding my first child—it took away the doubts I was having... if you don't practice attachment parenting and want to do extended nursing, then this book isn't for you... encouragement, how-tos for positioning, multiples, thorough home care instructions for mastitis and other breastfeeding maladies—even funny stories and anecdotes... **"**

Caring for Your Baby and Young Child: Birth to Age 5
★★★★☆
(Shelov, Steven et al Bantam)
Price .... $20; 784 p

ISBN 055338290X (2004)
Parent Reviews: **"**...an enormous amount of information... this is my 'know when to call the doctor' book... it covers all the basic medical questions as well as basic baby care... heavy and dense but extremely thorough... this book features no-nonsense descriptions of the common issues facing new parents... a must-have reference for all new parents... **"**

parenting books

www.lilaguide.com

Complete Book of Breastfeeding, The

(Eiger, Marvin et al Workman Publishing Company)
Price .... $10.95; 432 p
ISBN 0761109021 (1999)

Parent Reviews: **"**...it answered just about every question I ever had about breastfeeding... doesn't sugarcoat the truth but rather gives you the facts... informative with diagrams and good explanations... it offered not only the physiological information but covered the psychological aspects too... informative, but it lacks the scientific depth I was looking for... why so many pages?...**"**

Expectant Father, The

(Brott, Armin Abbeville Press, Inc.)
Price .... $11.95; 272 p
ISBN 0789205386 (2001)

Parent Reviews: **"**...a great month-by-month guide for first time dads... an excellent way to help him feel engaged in the process and knowledgeable about the changes that occur... it offers sound, down-to-earth advice to help guide him through mom's pregnancy and birth... very 'touchy-feely'... I love the fact that this is a book clearly designed to engage dads more in the early months—I know my husband often felt like a third wheel even though he really wanted to help...**"**

Ali's Notes: **"**...finally, a book for dads that's something other than the baby encyclopedias... good on the basics with an accessible voice... I'm amazed at the range of men that are fans of this book...**"**

Girlfriends' Guide to Pregnancy, The

(Iovine, Vicki Pocket Books)
Price .... $14; 288 p
ISBN 0671524313 (1995)

Parent Reviews: **"**...a fun, tell-it-like it is account of pregnancy... a gift that will make even the crankiest mom-to-be smile... well-written and comprehensive... Vicki is a godsend— she has a great, positive outlook and reminds you to keep a sense of humor... the 'go girlfriend!' voice got kind of annoying... it comes across as if she's telling you what to do, rather than setting out options... this definitely shouldn't be the only book you buy about pregnancy, but it's good to have for the entertainment value... hip, hilarious, trustworthy and comforting pregnancy advice...**"**

Ali's Notes: **"**...some expectant moms love this book— some don't at all... what this book does do better than others is get the main points about the stages of pregnancy across in a way that's *informative without trying to be encyclopedic... some of the humor can get annoying, but overall, it's a great place to start...* **"**

Girlfriends' Guide to Toddlers ★★★★½
(Iovine, Vicki Perigee)

Price .... $13.95; 271 p
ISBN 039952438X (1999)

Parent Reviews: **"***...this fun book offers strategies for dealing with toddlers... it made me laugh out loud several times... it makes you feel so much better, especially when you're struggling with toddler issues... the perfect blend of humor and advice... I've bought this as a gift for all my new parent friends... I didn't find this one as helpful as her guide to pregnancy... more entertaining than informative...* **"**

Ali's Notes: **"***...whether you liked the Girlfriends' Guide to Pregnancy or not, most who read it are fans of this toddler version... like the first book it's written with a balance of humor and advice... a good sanity check...* **"**

Happiest Baby on the Block ★★★★½
(Karp, Harvey www.thehappiestbaby.com)
Price .... $13.95; 288 p   ISBN 0553381466 (2003)

Parent Reviews: **"***...a must-read for parents of fussy babies... useful suggestions that lead to immediate results... it made perfect sense and helped me understand why the first three months are so different for babies... lots of easy to follow examples... it was a bit repetitive, but given that I wasn't able to remember anything during my first few months anyway, it was kind of a handy feature... a quick easy read with advice that really works... nothing too revolutionary—you can get the gist just by browsing through it at the book store...* **"**

Healthy Sleep Habits, Happy Child ★★★★½

(Weissbluth, Marc Ballantine Books)
Price .... $14.95; 528 p
ISBN 0449004023 (1999)

Parent Reviews: **"***...this very large book answers all of your sleep questions from newborn to adolescent... I read 3 books on sleep and this was by far the best... it was nice to have the author acknowledge the different types of baby personalities and encourage parents to treat their newborn like a person... didn't seem terribly practical for anyone not completely committed to the program... you'll need to take the whole thing with a grain of salt... it makes you feel like the*

parenting books

only option is to allow your child to cry, which I didn't like... extremely informative and logical, saved our life when we had a sleepless baby... "

New Basics, The ★★★★★
(Cohen, Michel MD HarperCollins)
Price .... $14.95; 368 p
ISBN 0060535482 (2004)

Parent Reviews: "...wonderful advice presented in an easily accessible manner... the alphabetical listing makes it easy to look up topics... the approach and advice takes a refreshing tone and perspective... I've been getting this book as a gift for all my 'first-time parent' friends... sensible advice delivered in a relaxed, yet reassuring manner... he covers it all—it truly is the A to Z guide of baby care... "

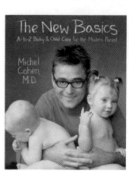

Ali's Notes: "...highly popular and, from my own experience, quite useful... he has an amazingly vocal following... one of the hottest 'parenting books' around... "

No-Cry Sleep Solution, The ★★★★☆
(Pantley, Elizabeth McGraw-Hill/Contemporary Books)
Price .... $14.95; 208 p
ISBN 0071381392 (2002)

Parent Reviews: "...an alternative to letting your baby cry it out... a wonderfully systematic approach to teaching your baby to sleep without letting him or her cry through it... basically the attachment parenting approach, but with concrete advice on how to get sleep right now... the book gives you ideas on designing your own sleep program, which is great if you are a planner and can think, but if you are exhausted and brain-dead you might find it daunting that there is no plan to follow... their technique just plain doesn't work for some babies—I was frustrated to no end... "

Nursing Mother's Companion, The (5th Ed) ★★★★½
(Huggins, Kathleen et al National Book Network)
Price .... $14.95; 336 p
ISBN 155832304X (2005)

Parent Reviews: "...my daughter is 11 months old and I still have this book on my night table... it answers all questions without being preachy... the author accounts for the fact that every woman is different and is very nonjudgmental... I find it lacks information about resources to go to if you have problems... this book is of limited value if you are having nursing problems and really need advice and direction... terrific information on how to breastfeed and pump,

with specific tips for each age group... well laid-out and gives lots of useful advice on things you might not think of... **"**

Pregnancy Journal, The

(Harris, Christine Chronicle Books)
Price .... $19.95; 205 p
ISBN 0811846970 (2005)

Parent Reviews: **"***...this was such an awesome journal to have during my pregnancy... each day I had something to read about the baby, myself and changes taking place... it gives you a countdown to the delivery date... filled with facts, fun questions, history and places to fill out information and journal thoughts and feelings... spiral bound with high quality paper... doctors generally use a 40 week calendar and this book doesn't—it gets a little confusing...* **"**

Sign With Your Baby

(Garcia, Joseph)
Price .... $14.95; 112 p   ISBN 0966836774 (2002)

Parent Reviews: **"***...a great guide to help teach your baby how to sign... both of my kids were early talkers and I attribute that to using his sign language technique... keep in mind that this is not true to American Sign Language, but it seems to work nonetheless... not only practical, but fun to use...* **"**

Ali's Notes: **"***...a favorite technique for minimizing the terrible twos, baby sign is gaining great momentum... this book provides a readable tool for developing a skill that's worst outcome is a fun activity...* **"**

Super Baby Food

(Yaron, Ruth www.superbabyfood.com   866.222.9266)

Price .... $19.95; 608 p
ISBN 0965260313 (1998)

Parent Reviews: **"***...a great guide to healthy food options for your baby... it explains allergens and all kinds of other things that were real eye-openers to me... it appears well-researched and provides good practical advice... a gold mine of nutritional info... a nice reference with lots of helpful recipes... some of the info was overwhelming and a bit difficult to digest— no pun intended... the food contamination part was a little over-the-top paranoid for me... good info for making your own baby food and which foods to choose for your baby...* **"**

Touchpoints: Guide to the First Six Years of Life

★★★★☆

(Brazelton, T Berry)
Price $34.95
ISBN 0738207934 (2002)

Parent Reviews: **"**...this book helped us understand the physical and emotional stages of our son and learn to grow with him... although the tone may not appeal to all readers it is a good resource... a great resource that gives you more than mere milestones... written with love, this book helps you to understand things like toddler tantrums, eating habits and more... the author ties a lot of ideas and topics together—many important lessons/ideas for parents... **"**

What To Expect The First Year (2nd Ed)

★★★★☆

(Eisenberg, Arlene et al Workman Publishing Company 800.722.7202)
Price .... $15.95; 806 p
ISBN 0761129588 (2003)

Parent Reviews: **"**...a must have—I referred to this book countless times during my son's first year... I didn't like the pregnancy version of this book, but loved this one... great first aid section... it prepares you without scaring you if your child is not hitting milestones... usable suggestions for introducing solids, tackling bedtime and weaning... not crazy about the question and answer format... written for people who have never been around babies... kind of repetitive... the same topics could have been covered in about half the number of pages... easy to follow index... **"**

What To Expect When You're Expecting (3rd Ed)

★★★★★

(Eisenberg, Arlene et al Workman Publishing Company 800.722.7202)
Price .... $13.95; 624 p
ISBN 0761125493 (2002)

Parent Reviews: **"**...easy-to-read format—month-to-month events during pregnancy... includes a handy, complete list of development milestones... this book left no stone unturned... calmed my nerves and explained the kinds of things I wanted to ask my doctor but felt kind of silly about... almost too much info... referred to this book time and time again during my pregnancy—it was my bible... **"**

Womanly Art of Breastfeeding (7th Ed), The

★★★★☆

(Gotsch, Gwen et al Plume)
Price .... $17; 480 p
ISBN 0452285801 (2004)

Parent Reviews: "*...a must-have for nursing moms—really, it's all in here... easy to follow layout... it answers all nursing questions and then some... especially good for first-timers... they have been around forever helping mothers to successfully breastfeed... you might find their approach a bit preachy... it seems to be written primarily for stay-at-home moms... overkill, if you ask me—they could have distilled this information into a much smaller book... easy to refer to and read small chunks at a time...*"

Your Pregnancy Week by Week (5th Ed)

★★★★½

(Curtis, Glade et al DaCapo Press)
Price .... $15.95; 428 p
ISBN 1555613462 (2004)

Parent Reviews: "*...this nicely designed book provides a weekly synopsis of what is going on with the baby and the expectant mom... so fun to read about the baby week by week... very well laid out... the end chapters were a little skimpy... they don't just tell it like it is, rather they tiptoe around some of the touchier issues... practical, sane advice that didn't cause me to panic—very helpful for first-time moms...*"

parenting books

highchairs

What kind of chair you'll want depends on your lifestyle, the age of your baby and how much space you have to store the chair. Here are several things you'll want to consider:

Size: If your space is limited and your preference is to have your baby at the table with you as soon as they're in a chair, you probably don't want the traditional American highchair. A better fit might be a European-style highchair, built more like a booster chair with an infant seat.

Multi-Stage: If you think you'll want a traditional highchair with a tray, consider a multi-stage chair that can take you from highchair to booster to toddler seat. Then you don't have to buy a separate accessory or chair for each stage.

Washability: Highchairs see a lot of spills and messes, so you'll want to make sure yours is easy to wash. Be sure it's easy to disassemble when it's time to clean and that the cushions stand up well to washing. This may sound obvious, but chairs can vary a lot in how easy they are to keep clean.

Adjustability: If you're looking for a one-size-fits-all solution that will last as long as possible, get a chair that's easy to adjust. Look for chair size adjustment, height adjustment and harness adjustment, and make sure the adjustments are easy enough that you'll actually want to make them.

Collapsibility: Seriously consider how much space you have to allocate to your highchair. If you'll need to put it away when it's not being used, make sure it collapses and releases easily.

Wheels: Wheels make highchairs easier to roll out of the way, and they will also give you more flexibility to adjust to your growing baby's eating habits, times and styles.

Reclining: If your baby is sitting up on his or her own, don't worry about getting a seat that reclines, as you've missed most of the value of that feature.

Portability: The best bet for the frequent traveler or the parent with two homes is a reliable, everyday solution at the location where you and your baby will be most often, and a sturdy, collapsible clip-on that's easy to take on the road.

by Ali Wing at egiggle.com

standard highchairs

"lila picks"

- ★ KinderZeat (Stokke)
- ★ Prima Pappa Rocker (Peg Perego)
- ★ Svan Chair (Svan of Sweden)

Dondolino

Peg Perego (www.pegperego.com 800.671.1701)
Price .... $200-$230
Features ......folds; 7 height pos

Parent Reviews: *"...stylish and robust... it rolls, rocks, and reclines... dishwasher-safe trays and nice plush washable seat covers... it converts into a rocking chair which means that after feeding my baby can take a nap in the same seat... 7 height positions and the seat reclines to 4 different positions... it's like a highchair and rocker in one..."*

Easy Chair

Graco (www.gracobaby.com 800.345.4109)
Price ....$30-$40
Features .... no fold

Parent Reviews: *"...a very basic highchair for a great price... it reclines slightly for bottle feeding... the vinyl pad comes right out and can be washed in the sink... the T-bar works great so I rarely have to use the harness... no wheels makes it a bit of a pain to move around, but it was so cheap I can't really complain... it still looks good after two kids... tray is really easy to put on and take off... not too big and bulky... the straps can be difficult to adjust, but we never use them anyway..."*

www.lilaguide.com

Envision

Evenflo (www.evenflo.com 800.233.5921)

Price .... $40-$50
Features .... folds; 7 height pos

Parent Reviews: *"...basic highchair with most of the features you might need... it folds really flat and even fits into the trunk of my car... plenty of height adjustments make it suitable to use for a while... three recline positions for bottle feeding or activities... the double tray doesn't stay together and I always end up having to clean two trays which kind of defeats the purpose... overall pretty durable and good value for the price..."*

Harmony

★★★½☆

Graco (www.gracobaby.com 800.345.4109)

Price .... $120-$150
Features .... folds; 6 height pos

Parent Reviews: *"...curved legs let you bring the chair closer to the table than some other models... seat reclines to 4 positions... toy bar comes with several critters that entertain while I'm getting food ready... wheels are convenient... folds and stands by itself... removable tray that's dishwasher safe..."*

Healthy Care Deluxe High Chair

★★★★½

Fisher-Price (www.fisherprice.com 800.747.8697)

Price .... $85-$90
Features .... folds; 7 height pos

Parent Reviews: *"...I love the 3 dishwasher-safe trays—one for each meal... 7 height settings—I haven't needed them yet, but it's nice to know they are there for the future... locking wheels... the seat reclines quite a bit which allows my baby to bottle feed himself... the one-hand release sometimes requires two hands... the assembly process was a bit of a drag... they also make a Link-a-doos version so you can attach the Fisher-Price Link-a-doos toys... the pad is machine-washable... excellent value for the money..."*

Healthy Care Highchair

★★★★︎

Fisher-Price (www.fisherprice.com   800.747.8697)
Price .... $20-$25
Features .... 2 height pos

Parent Reviews: *"...a great little seat at a great price... the feeding tray comes off and fits into the dishwasher... it adjusts to 3 different heights and we can pretty much take it anywhere... it reclines and has a nice molded plastic seat... the snap-on lid works pretty well although it invariably comes off by the time we've unpacked it from the car..."*

IKEA Highchair

★★★★︎

IKEA (www.ikea.com)
Price $20
Features .... no fold

Parent Reviews: *"...so cheap and so easy to clean... lightweight and simple... at only $20 you can get several—for grandparents' and friends' houses... all plastic so you can literally hose it down... you get what you pay for—no adjustments possible... no wheels or recline... not the prettiest piece of furniture— it's more functional-looking..."*

Ali's Notes: *"...classic IKEA—functional and inexpensive... talk about minimalist... you get virtually none of the features most other highchairs have (reclining seat, height adjustment, etc) but then again you're paying only a fraction of the price... perfect as a second seat at grandma's house..."*

(value)

KinderZeat

★★★★★

Stokke (www.stokkeusa.com   877.978.6553)
Price .... $175-$200   Features ....no fold

Parent Reviews: *"...not cheap, but very cool and versatile... it's made out of wood and looks so much nicer than those plastic seats... solid construction and made out of beautiful wood... many height adjustment options... not really useful for kids that can't sit up and balance completely on their own... since it works for kids of varying heights, you can use it for a while..."*

Ali's Notes: *"...the best of the European approach to highchairs... a chair that works as a highchair (no tray), but is loved by most as a stylish and contemporary toddler chair... so many fun colors and such great styling that this chair is sold at modern art museums as well as standard baby stores... adjustable seat and foot rest allows your child to sit comfortably at any height without having to dangle his or her feet... oh yeah, it costs almost $200..."*

(multi-use, style)

Mamma Double Tray ★★★★½
Chicco (www.chiccousa.com 732.805.9200)

Price .... $110-$120
Features .... folds; 6 height pos

Parent Reviews: "...it folds very nicely and stands on its own... we used the adjustable heights and reclining seat even when we weren't feeding the baby—it's a nice place to play... the cover doesn't feel like plastic and it's super easy to clean... the plastic leg divider attached to the tray makes it awkward to clean... 6 chair heights and the seat even reclines... the double tray makes the transition from feeding to eating quick and easy..."

Peas & Carrots Highchair ★★★★☆
Zooper (www.zooperstrollers.com 503.248.9469)
Price .... $130-$150
Features ...... folds; 4 height pos

Parent Reviews: "...neat, modern-looking colors... adjustable heights... seat leans back for bottle feeding... the snack tray is dishwasher-safe... wheels for easy moving around... folds and stands on its own... looks almost like a car seat turned highchair... nice storage compartment under the seat..."

Ali's Notes: "...it has many of the bells and whistles that the Peg Perego chairs offer for a lot less money... Zooper is a safe value pick for the parent who wants a solid highchair without paying a ton of money..."

Polly Highchair ★★★★☆

Chicco (www.chiccousa.com 732.805.9200)
Price .... $100-$110
Features .... folds; 6 height pos

Parent Reviews: "...it folds very nicely and stands on its own... the seat cushion is so easy to clean—it's vinyl and I just wipe all the dirt off... you can take the tray off which is nice so we can slide the chair to a table... it reclines for that post-meal nap... 7 height positions..."

Prima Pappa Rocker

Peg Perego (www.pegperego.com 800.671.1701)
Price..........................$160-$190
Features..........folds; 7 height pos

Parent Reviews: **"**...*functional and nice to look at... I can't imagine getting through mealtime without it... it has several heights and a 4-position reclining seat... double tray feature has removable and machine-washable inserts... the tray is easy to remove with one hand... food does get stuck in the cracks of the upholstered seat... a monthly hose-down does the trick to clean it right up... nice large tray... wheels make it easy to move from the dining room to the kitchen... it folds flat for storage...* **"**

Ali's Notes: **"**...*if you want all the bells and whistles, then this is the highchair for you... the ultimate in toddler luxury... it reclines, it rocks, it cleans easily and best of all, it folds very well... we call it the 'Cadillac' of highchairs...* **"**

Simplicity

Evenflo (www.evenflo.com 800.233.5921)
Price ....$70-$80
Features ......folds; 8 height pos

Parent Reviews: **"**...*we love the different heights and reclining positions... the removable tray is dishwasher safe... great price considering all the features... it doesn't fold up too well, but for the low price it seems like a pretty minor thing... good mobility—wheels work pretty well except on carpeting... nice plush seat cushion...* **"**

SmartSteps Discovery Highchair

Evenflo (www.evenflo.com 800.233.5921)
Price ....$100-$110
Features ......folds; 8 height pos

Parent Reviews: **"**...*at first I thought the 'game tray' was an unnecessary gimmick, but my boy loves it... sometimes he just sits in the chair to play before or after meals... 8 height settings for the seat... it reclines a lot so I don't need to move my baby if she falls asleep after eating... easy to clean...* **"**

highchairs: standard

www.lilaguide.com

Svan Chair

★★★★★

Svan of Sweden (www.scandinavianchild.com   866.782.6222)
Price .... $200-$220

Parent Reviews: **"**...a piece of art—stylish, small and practical for the long run... it converts from a highchair to a simple chair that can be used by anyone... beautiful wood... pricey, but truly exceptional quality... detachable tray is not dishwasher-safe... **"**

Ali's Notes: **"**...the Svan begins as a high chair, becomes a booster chair, evolves to a toddler seat and eventually converts to a child's desk chair—the ultimate in multi-stage... this chair takes the best of the plastic American-style highchair (with every bell and whistle) and combines it with the minimalist (typically wooden) European style without a tray or booster.... if you don't fall in love with it the first time you see it, you will once you start using it... **"**

Trend High Chair

★★★★☆

Baby Trend (www.babytrend.com   800.328.7363)

Price............................ $85-$90
Features..........folds; 6 height pos

Parent Reviews: **"**...all the features you'll need... several recline options make it easy to feed a baby or use the chair as an activity chair... the height adjustment feature is really handy not just as your baby grows, but also for little guests... never thought I would need wheels but I'm surprised at how much we end up pushing it from the kitchen to the dining room and back... the cover is machine-washable... **"**

hook-ons

★★★★★ "lila picks"

- ★ Caddy Table Seat (Chicco)
- ★ Hook On High Chair (Me Too!)

Caddy Table Seat ★★★★★

Chicco (www.chiccousa.com 732.805.9200)
Price ....$35-$40
Features .... 3 pt harness

Parent Reviews: *"...we don't have room for a stand-alone highchair and find this one great... well-made and good-looking... seems to fit securely on to pretty much any table surface in our house... a handy pocket on the back to stow bibs, toys and more... easy to assemble and dissemble... I don't like having to take the arms off every time I put it in the bag... rubberized pads prevent the table from getting scratched... it's plush, easy to use and folds flat for travel..."*

Easy Diner ★★★★☆

Regalo (www.regalo-baby.com)
Price $20

Parent Reviews: *"...it attaches very easily and quickly to table tops—we take ours everywhere so we always know our son can eat at the same level with us... rubber prevents scratches to the table's surface... strong metal frame..."*

highchairs: hook-ons

Fast Table Chair

★★★★☆

Inglesina (www.inglesina.us 877.486.5112)
Price ....$55-$65
Features .... folds

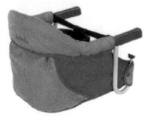

Parent Reviews: **"**...secures firmly to most table tops... pretty easy to put on and take off most tables at restaurants... the main problem is that you can only hand wash it...**"**

Hook On High Chair

★★★★★

Me Too!
Price ....$40-$50   Features..................................folds

Parent Reviews: **"**...very sturdy—it clips onto almost all types of tables... not just a chair for feeding—we use it as our son's coloring chair... folds flat and is convenient to take with you... lightweight and very portable... comfortable and safe—it really locks on tight... I like having our daughter sitting in her own highchair in restaurants instead of the grimy ones they usually provide... it was the best gift we received and we plan to always give this to friends having babies...**"**

Ali's Notes: **"**...stylish, simple and secure... so collapsible (with no folding parts) that it fits in suitcases and bags... unlike a lot of similar 'hook-on' solutions, it won't hurt your (or your relative's!) nice dining room table... some parents like this solution so much that they skip a high chair altogether and make it their everyday solution... fun colors...**"**

Travel Lite Table Chair

★★★★☆

Graco (www.gracobaby.com 800.345.4109)
Price ....$30-$35   Features................... removable tray

Parent Reviews: **"**...sturdy and locks on to most table tops we've come across... easy to fold and take with you... small enough so we take it to restaurants and grandparents' house... can be used with or without the tray... vinyl padding is easy to clean... 3 point harness keeps my son from falling through the bottom... stiff, bare-bones design is less ideal for the 'early eater' who need a little more support...**"**

booster seats

"lila picks"

- ★ 4-Stage Feeding Seat (The First Years)
- ★ Baby Sitter (Bumbo)
- ★ Cooshie Booster Seat (Baby Smart)

4-Stage Feeding Seat

The First Years (www.thefirstyears.com 800.317.3194)
Price .... $30-$35   Features .... 3 pt harness

Parent Reviews: *"...we take it everywhere—restaurants, grandma's house, even the movie theater... I like the reclining feature—I could give my baby a bottle in this seat but still use it as a real booster when she got older... easy cleaning—I just throw the tray and seat in the dishwasher... you can adjust the height so it fits any table... fits securely to pretty much any chair... it works best for infants and smaller kids..."*

Ali's Notes: *"...why get a standard highchair when you can get this cool booster with a tray?.. although it's a lot to haul around as a booster seat, customers who swear by boosters (many of whom skip the highchair purchase altogether) love its bells-and-whistles approach... ideal for the young/early eaters (not toddlers)..."*

multi-use

All-in-One Reclining Booster Seat

Safety 1st (www.safety1st.com   800.544.1108)
Price .... $25-$35
Features .... 3 pt harness

Parent Reviews: "*...sturdy, spacious but also pretty big... it comes with a cushion and a nice high seat back... the seat reclines to six different positions... three height adjustments... comes with a 3 point harness but also has a T-bar so my son can't fall through the bottom... you don't need the feeding tray—your child can safely eat with you on the table... tray is dishwasher-safe...*"

Ali's Notes: "*...similar in style to the 4-Stage Feeding Seat (by The First Years)... ideal for parents who prefer the simplicity of a booster to the bigger and bulkier standard highchair...*"

Baby Sitter ★★★★★

Bumbo (www.bumbobabyseat.com)
Price $40

Parent Reviews: "*...so simple and practical... we have several of them because you can use them at the dinner table or even on the floor for playing... made of soft, rubbery material that doesn't scratch tables and chairs... lots of colors to choose from... we even use it in the bathtub which makes washing much easier...*"

Ali's Notes: "*...innovative and clever... very durable and sturdy... talk about multi-use—parents tell us they use it for almost everything around the house that requires sitting up... not the best for travel...*"

Cooshie Booster Seat ★★★★★

Baby Smart
Price .... $25-$30

Parent Reviews: "*...a foam version of those boosters you typically get at restaurants... I like it because it's easy to move around and can be stowed away when not being used... it doesn't scratch wooden chairs and doesn't have to be strapped down to keep it from slipping... basically a glorified piece of foam padding...*"

Ali's Notes: "*...simple, functional and inexpensive... a true booster seat (not for use instead of a highchair)... works with any chair and won't scratch surfaces (a big complaint with the hard plastic boosters)...*"

Grow With Me Portable Booster Seat

★★★★☆

Safety 1st (www.safety1st.com 800.544.1108)
Price ....$20-$25
Features .... 3 pt harness

Parent Reviews: "...good replacement for a highchair once your child is stable in a chair... great value—significantly cheaper than a stand-alone highchair... cleans easily... folds easy for storage or travel... we keep one in the trunk of our car for when we go out to restaurants... doesn't recline... attaches to any chair in seconds... "

Hisita Booster Chair

★★★☆☆

Hisita (www.hisita.com 866.879.1395)
Price ....$45-$55

Parent Reviews: "...not really a booster seat, but a very cool platform onto which you can place most chairs... it raises the chair up so your baby can sit at the table... no safety harnesses or reclining options... at least our dining room looks somewhat normal and doesn't have a big, ugly, plastic baby chair in it—we just use our existing chairs... "

On-The-Go Booster Seat

★★★★☆

The First Years (www.thefirstyears.com 800.317.3194)
Price ....$18-$22
Features .... 3 pt harness

Parent Reviews: "...perfect for when you're on the road or going to visit friends who don't have kids... amazing how quickly it inflates on its own... a small, compact alternative to the other hard, plastic travel chairs... good for occasional travel but not as your daily booster... it's actually hard to get all the air out of it... not the most sturdy, but easy to take with you... weighs less than 2 pounds... packs flat and has its own zipper case... "

On-the-Go Fold-Up Booster

★★★★☆

Safety 1st (www.safety1st.com 800.544.1108)
Price ....$20-$25
Features .... 3 pt harness

Parent Reviews: "...made out of hard, durable plastic... my daughter used this until she was 3 years old... easy to clean... folds up into a compact little package for storage or travel... 2 height settings... removable tray so you can move the chair right up to the table... 3 point harness... it attaches to the chair via straps that recoil into the seat base when they're not being used—it makes storage a little neater... the slip-resistant pads on the legs prevent scratches on our wooden chairs... "

highchairs: booster seats

Safety Seat

★★★½☆

Baby Bjorn (www.babybjorn.com 800.593.5522)

Price $30

Parent Reviews: **"**...about as simple as it gets... easy to use and very easy to clean... it's a big piece of plastic that you can put on most chairs so your baby gets a bit of a lift... if your child is not old enough to climb in and out of it, make sure to buy it with the safety bar... **"**

Swing Tray Portable Booster ★★★★☆

The First Years (www.thefirstyears.com 800.317.3194)

Price .... $18-$25   Features .... 3 pt harness

Parent Reviews: **"**...the swing-away tray makes it so much easier for me to get my boy in and out of the chair—he even manages to get in the seat on his own now... 3 height adjustments lets you use it with most tables... the whole thing comes apart and is easily stored when we're not using it... the tray is helpful when you're not feeding at a table... it secures firmly to any chair with several straps... I love that the tray swings out and I don't have to find a place to put it while getting my baby out... **"**

monitors

Short of standing in your baby's nursery all day long, nothing will bring you more peace of mind during naptime than a good baby monitor. There are a lot of different features that will help you rest assured your baby's sleeping peacefully, so know which ones are important to you before you start shopping.

Two-way Talk: This feature makes your monitor work like a walkie-talkie, allowing you to soothe your crying baby as you make your way to the nursery.

Video Monitors: If you really want to keep an eye on your baby, a video monitor can help you see what they're up to while you're out of the room.

Movement Monitors: Some parents invest in movement monitors, but few report back that they find them useful.

Sound Quality: The most common criticism we hear about baby monitors is that they can be difficult to hear or that they pick up neighboring sounds. Your best bet is a monitor made by an established electronics company that's entered the baby market, rather than a baby company that's entered the electronics market.

Compatibility: If you have more than one type of monitor, make sure the brands and models are compatible and don't interfere with each other's signal.

Bonus Features: Last but not least, other great features to look for are rechargeable base units and sound level lights on the parent unit that visually indicate the volume of your baby's voice, even if you are not within earshot.

by Ali Wing at egiggle.com

monitors

★★★★★
"lila picks"

- ★ Angelcare Movement Sensor (Unisar)
- ★ Baby's Quiet Sounds Video Monitor (Summer Infant)
- ★ MobiCam Baby Monitor (Mobi Technologies)
- ★ UltraClear (Graco)

2.4 GHz Ultra-Range Monitor ★★★★½
The First Years (www.thefirstyears.com 800.225.0382)
Price ....$60-$70   Features 2 ch; bat/AC; 1 rec; 2.4 GHz

Parent Reviews: **"**...a monitor system with a really long range... it comes with rechargeable batteries but also works with AC adapters... the receiver has a belt clip... sound lights let me see when my baby's crying... one of the few 2.4 GHz monitors out there...**"**

49 MHz Two Receiver Monitor ★★★★☆
The First Years (www.thefirstyears.com   800.225.0382)
Price ....$30-$45
Features ......2 ch; 2 rec; 49 MHz

Parent Reviews: **"**...the 2 receivers are really convenient in our 3-level house... the parent unit can be used plugged in or with batteries, so you can clip it to your belt if you are moving around... good range—I can go out to my separate garage and still get sound...**"**

participate in our survey at

900 MHz BabyCall Monitor ★★★★☆
Sony (www.sony.com)
Price .... $40-$50
Features 27 ch; 1 rec; 900 MHz

Parent Reviews: "...great Sony quality and great value for the money... the sound is very clear... no problems with static or reception... easy to clip on to your belt if you need to move about the house... the receiver battery is rechargeable or the unit can be plugged in... it also has a light to let you know when it's out of range..."

900 MHz Long Range ★★★★½
Fisher-Price (www.fisherprice.com   800.747.8697)
Price .... $30-$35
Features . 2 ch; 1 rec; 900 MHz

Parent Reviews: "...great distance—I can visit with my neighbor outside while my baby sleeps... I love that the lights tell you if your baby is crying in case you don't hear him... the vibrating option is cool if there's a lot of noise and you can't hear the monitor that clearly... we've used it for two kids and it's still going strong..."

Angelcare Movement Sensor with Sound Monitor ★★★★★
Unisar (www.bebesounds.com   800.430.0222)
Price .... $75-$100   Features .... 2 ch; bat/AC; 2 rec

Parent Reviews: "...this monitor senses the slightest movement—including breathing... if no motion is detected for 20 seconds the alarm sounds... first-rate sound quality... no static or interference... my baby is a tummy sleeper and this lets me feel safe letting her sleep on her belly... you can buy the option that comes with 2 receivers or just 1..."

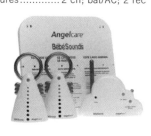

Ali's Notes: "...keep in mind that the movement sensor only works if you set up the crib monitor for movement... the first on the market to offer this potentially SIDS-preventive (Sudden Infant Death Syndrome) feature... the biggest drawback is that many parents we talk to never feel like they've set it up correctly (or are constantly questioning whether or not they did it properly)..."

Baby's Quiet Sounds Video Monitor

★★★★★

Summer Infant (www.summerinfant.com 800.268.6237)
Price ....$85-$100
Features 2 ch; bat/AC; 1 rec; 900 MHz

Parent Reviews: **"**...superior quality—the TV image is clear, even in a dark room... the sound is excellent and I love being able to both see and hear my baby... when our monitor had problems they sent us a new one right away... the power light on the camera is too bright—it lights up a whole room and sometimes disturbs my baby's sleep... we've been totally satisfied with this product from day one...**"**

Ali's Notes: **"**...the parents' popular choice for a video monitor... I'm a fan of their line because Summer Infant has a long history of developing a multitude of electronics products... a brand that deserves its good reputation for developing and supporting quality nursery electronics...**"**

Family Listen N Talk

★★★☆☆

Graco (www.gracobaby.com 800.345.4109)
Price ....$60-$70   Features .... 2 ch; 2 rec; 900 MHz

Parent Reviews: **"**...even though it was a bit pricey, we've been happy with the performance in our 2-story home... we can keep tabs not only on our baby, but can monitor and talk to our toddler via the intercom feature... we have to make sure the walkie-talkies are not too close to each other or anything electrical— or the interference is overwhelming... the receivers work with either batteries or power cord...**"**

In Sight

★★★★☆

Safety 1st (www.safety1st.com 800.544.1108)
Price ....$115-$130
Features .3 ch; 1 rec; 900 MHz

Parent Reviews: **"**...I love being able to watch and listen to my little one sleep or play... it takes the guessing out of whether they are okay or not... I like being able to peek in on them without waking them up... the black and white screen produces a decent picture... ideal for a nervous parent like myself—I can both listen and watch...**"**

Ali's Notes: **"**...if you can't stand just being able to hear your tot breathing and feel the need to be able to see him too, then this little high-tech gadget is for you... the biggest downside with video monitors is that you now also have picture quality to worry about in addition to that occasional annoying static...**"**

participate in our survey at

MobiCam Baby Monitor ★★★★★

Mobi Technologies (www.getmobi.com 310.551.1120)
Price .... $175-$200

Parent Reviews: "...the best monitor out there... rather expensive compared to a $20 Graco unit... manufactured by an electronics company that also makes all kinds of neat, high-end electronics... you can feel the quality difference just by picking the units up... very clear picture, sound and it's quite sturdy (ours has been dropped a bunch of times)... it works great in complete darkness..."

Ali's Notes: "...if you can't stand just being able to hear your tot breathing and feel the need to be able to see him too, then this little high-tech gadget is for you... winner of The Wall Street Journal's 2005 monitors review... best-of-class for video monitoring... keeps growing with baby as a nannycam, playroom monitor, etc...."

multi-use

On-the-Go Monitor ★★★★★

Safety 1st (www.safety1st.com 800.544.1108)
Price $20
Features .... 2 ch;1 rec; 49 MHz

Parent Reviews: "...great for taking with you on a trip... the base and receiver can be clipped together instead of having to pack 2 separate pieces... it works either on battery or AC... sound lights let you 'see' noise instead of having to hear it... the cord is stored in the base unit..."

Ali's Notes: "...hats off to Safety 1st for innovating a smart, simple monitor particularly suited to travel..."

value

Safe Glow 2 Receiver Monitor ★★★★☆

Safety 1st (www.safety1st.com 800.544.1108)
Price .... $25-$30
Features 2 ch; bat/AC; 2 rec; 49 MHz

Parent Reviews: "...it's like a soft light built into a monitor... just touch the light and it turns on and off... it comes with 2 receivers... sound lights let me know if my baby is crying even when I can't hear the monitor that well... it works on batteries or AC..."

www.lilaguide.com

Sound Sleep

★★★★☆

Graco (www.gracobaby.com 800.345.4109)
Price ....$25-$30   Features.........................2 ch; 2 rec

Parent Reviews: "...having 2 receivers is a great feature—you avoid having to move it around all the time... pretty basic monitor... worked fine in our house as well as when we took it on the road... way too much static—it was incredibly frustrating... sound lights let you see if baby is making noise in addition to hearing it... all units work on both batteries as well as AC adapter..."

Sounds 'N Lights

★★★★☆

Fisher-Price (www.fisherprice.com 800.747.8697)

Price ....$20-$30
Features ......2 ch; 1 rec; 49 MHz

Parent Reviews: "...I love the light sensors—even when I'm in a noisy room, the lights let me know if my baby is asleep or awake... you can get it with 2 receivers or just 1... works with battery or wall socket... after numerous drops and 2 kids, it still works great... cheap, but does the trick..."

Sweet Dreams Monitor

★★★☆☆

Fisher-Price (www.fisherprice.com 800.747.8697)
Price ....$35-$40
Features ... 2 ch; 1 rec; 49 MHz

Parent Reviews: "...being able to activate the music and light show without being in the room is really cool... I love being able to talk to my baby—or husband—with the two-way communication feature... the reception is good... it has a light show, lullabies and nature sounds in addition to being a monitor... we had trouble initially with static however we were able to resolve this after a while..."

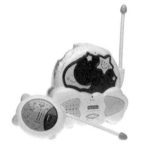

Ali's Notes: "...with music, lights and monitoring, this monitor is as much an activity toy as a sleep aid..."

multi-use

participate in our survey at

UltraClear

Graco (www.gracobaby.com 800.345.4109)
Price ....$45-$55   Features.........................2 ch; 2 rec

Parent Reviews: *"...good sound quality—I can hear my baby babbling and snoring... good for apartments and small homes—does not pick up other signals... get the ultra model with 2 receivers—you won't have to move it around as much... reception was okay... didn't work in our house—we were getting all kinds of noises and sounds... "*

Ali's Notes: *"...2 units are definitely better than 1... parents rave as much as they rant about how much or little static these receivers pick up (I guess it just depends on where you live)... fair price given the standard 2 receiver package... "*

nursery & furniture

When it comes to your baby's nursery, there are a few key things to consider beyond the color scheme or wallpaper design - you've also got furniture to pick! Spending a little more up front can be well worth it if you get something that will last your child for years. Look for multi-stage furniture (such as cribs that convert into toddler beds or day beds) to really get the most for your money.

Drop-rail cribs vs. fixed-side cribs: What's the difference? Drop-rail cribs have a side that moves up and down for easier access, while fixed-side cribs tend to have a lower overall height and sturdier construction. Drop-rail cribs can make it easier to lay a sleeping baby down (or, for the petite folks, make it even possible). But again, fixed-side cribs are sturdier and longer lasting, generally speaking. Safety heights and regulations are standard for both and are achieved by multi-level mattress settings.

Multi-Stage Cribs: Some innovative crib systems actually allow you to buy a kit to convert your crib into both a bassinet and a toddler bed - meaning you can cover all your baby's sleeping stages until childhood with one purchase.

Bassinets: Bassinets are a popular method of creating a smaller sleeping area in the parents' room when they want the baby nearby, but not necessarily in the same bed. As another alternative, look for co-sleepers and snuggle-nests - both convenient and space-saving.

by Ali Wing at egiggle.com

bedding

★★★★★ "lila picks"

- ★ Amy Coe
- ★ Dwell Baby
- ★ Pottery Barn Kids
- ★ Wendy Bellissimo

Amy Coe ★★★★★
(www.amycoe.com 415.252.1300)

Parent Reviews: "*...the quality is lovely and the patterns are beautiful... tres chic... my daughter's crib set still looked great after 2 years... worth it if you have the extra cash... high-end quality and wonderful soft, light cotton... $345 for a dust ruffle and bumper set—you've got to be kidding... they also make lower-end versions that are sold at non-boutique stores like Target... absolutely gorgeous items that will make your nursery look spectacular...*"

Ali's Notes: "*...known for her commitment to quality construction and very comprehensive collection, Amy Coe has been doing baby bedding for more than 10 years... Amy's particularly strong East Coast following led her to be selected as Target's featured baby bedding designer... true to her Connecticut home-base, Amy Coe's traditional, vintage cottage-style bedding is a best-of-category...*"

BabyGap ★★★★½☆
(www.gap.com)

Parent Reviews: "*...bright, colorful and just fabulous... the quality is just like everything else Gap sells—good quality for a reasonable price... the selection isn't huge, but what they have is darling... hard to find so you might have to buy online...*"

Ali's Notes: "*...this isn't Gap's first time around at baby bedding... just out in Summer 2005 and only available in a few stores nationwide, we'll have to wait and see if the second time's the charm...*"

Blue Moon Baby
(www.bluemoonbaby.com   626.455.0014)
Parent Reviews: **"**...20 different patterns to choose from... the only bedding with chenille fabric... you can choose soft or bright color patterns... a vintage feel... the fabric is so soft... found only in specialty stores... they really pay attention to quality... highly decorative... very expensive... customer service will help you coordinate fabrics to complete your nursery...**"**

Brandee Danielle
(www.brandeedanielle.com   800.720.5656)
Parent Reviews: **"**...so cute and so many designs to choose from... classy, clean designs... ours lasted through 2 active boys... they produce very good quality and don't skimp on their fabrics... bumpers are wonderfully soft and padded... so far so good—our set has withstood several washings and still feels great... too much money for baby bedding—you can find comparable brands for less money... their designs are a little too 'froufy' for my taste...**"**

Carter's ★★★★☆
(www.carters.com   888.782.9548)
Parent Reviews: **"**...Carter's has been around for so many years, I know I can trust their products... durable, still soft after repeated washings... cute styles, all the basics... I can stock up on essentials because the prices are so reasonable... they change their styles every year, so it is hard to find pieces once they are discontinued... affordable, high-quality bedding... a name you can trust...**"**

Celebrations
(www.baby-celebrations.com   310.532.2499)
Parent Reviews: **"**...over 25 styles and 100 fabrics to choose from... I love that each style is carried through for many seasons—I can transition my baby's bedding to toddler bedding without having to start all over... created by a mom and daughter who know what babies need... great customer service... I can coordinate my whole nursery with ease...**"**

CoCaLo
(www.cocalo.com   714.434.7200)
Parent Reviews: **"**...great selection of bedding for boys... bright, colorful designs... great combination of fabrics... clever designs... simple, chic and elegant... really interesting details... excellent customer service... high-quality products, made well, built to last... created by a designer with an eye for detail and interesting patterns...**"**
Ali's Notes: **"**...includes brand labels found in the market known as Baby Martex, Oshkosh and Kimberley Grant... one of the few bedding manufacturers making crib sets for the new Stokke Sleepi System (round vs. traditional crib)...**"**

Cotton Tale
(www.cottontaledesigns.com   714.435.9558)
Parent Reviews: **"**...cute and practical linens for a wonderful, adult look... the bumper has fabric attached to the bottom so there aren't any gaps and the material has held up beautifully over time... very practical, yet high-end looking...**"**

Dwell Baby ★★★★★
(www.dwellshop.com)
Parent Reviews: **"**...gorgeous designs and materials—I love my daughter's nursery... not cheap, but the quality is fantastic... Egyptian cotton sets that are reversible... more patterns and colors than you can imagine...**"**

Ali's Notes: **"**...out of nowhere just a few years ago, Dwell Baby Bedding took the market by storm and became one of the most popular collections today... known for being sophisticated but still sweet, Dwell Baby Bedding uses simple geometric patterns and shapes and rich colors with a contemporary twist... Dwell Bedding is a best-of-category for modern contemporary style and a lila pick for sophistication and high quality...**"**

Lambs & Ivy ★★★★☆
(www.lambsivy.com   800.345.2627)
Parent Reviews: **"**...everything for a gorgeous looking nursery—sheets, bumpers, blankets, etc... bright colors that are stimulating and create a wonderful ambiance... prices are reasonable and all the pieces have held up well over the 2 years we used them...**"**

Land of Nod ★★★★½
(www.landofnod.com   800.933.9904)
Parent Reviews: **"**...whimsical designs you can't find anywhere else... super-soft, good quality fabric... unusual prints... cute, tasteful designs that aren't over-the-top... great cotton pieces... they don't seem to develop new product lines very often—their catalog showcases the same things time after time... I wish there were a few more solid color simple things... beautiful stuff—creative and colorful... excellent customer service...**"**

Ali's Notes: **"**...now a joint-venture with Crate and Barrel, let's hope Land of Nod can keep its individual, whimsical style... smart styles with fun themes, the Land of Nod bedding wins another style pick for their chic sets...**"**

Lands' End ★★★★½
(www.landsend.com   800.963.4816)
Parent Reviews: **"**...the best quality for the price... the only problem is not being able to see and feel their products before you order online, but everything I've ordered I've liked... they use great fabrics that are almost as soft as my baby's bottom... the jersey crib sheets are great, elastic gathering goes completely around the sheet for a snug fit and added safety... great quality and easy online ordering...**"**

Ali's Notes: **"**...Lands' End's baby bedding separates match their famously simple and conservative style... despite a rather limited selection to date, their collection leverages their company's roots in textiles to earn a value pick for well-priced, nicely made baby bedding basics...**"**

Nava's Designs ★★★☆☆
(www.navasdesigns.com   818.988.9050)
Parent Reviews: **"**...gorgeous and luxurious handmade items... I actually wouldn't mind having her stuff on my bed let alone my baby's... I love how she uses silks and other fancier material in many of her designs... nice accessories... extremely expensive, but if you are looking for something really special, then look no further...

this bedding costs more than my king size bedding when you add all of the accessories... "

NoJo
(www.nojo.com 800.854.8760)
Parent Reviews: "*...detailed, unique designs... very high-end and expensive... the matching accessories helped me create a beautiful nursery... sophisticated bedding with a high price tag... superb quality... the soft fabrics are great for my baby... high fashion for the baby who has everything...* "

Nurseryworks
(n/a 888.508.9540)
Parent Reviews: "*...truly different from the other bedding manufacturers out there... you'll pay a price for having a cool looking nursery... not frilly and virtually no pink or blue... refreshingly modern...* "
Ali's Notes: "*...a relatively new entrant into the contemporary baby bedding arena... if design is your thing, then be sure to check out this on-the-rise new competitor to collections like Dwell Baby and LuLu... contemporary and chic...* "

Pine Creek
(www.pinecreekbedding.com 503.266.6275)
Parent Reviews: "*...soft, comfortable and attractive bedding... you can't purchase through the website, only at individual retailers... so many patterns and fabrics to choose from... the website will only deal with retailers, not with customers...* "

Pottery Barn Kids ★★★★★
(www.potterybarn.com 800.993.4923)
Parent Reviews: "*...they have the greatest designers and everything is mix and match... they turn over their patterns frequently so you don't end up with the same bedding as you neighbor... you can return anything with a receipt up to a year after purchase... holds up well in the wash—colors haven't faded in 2 years... I found amazing deals at their outlets... some of the accessories are overpriced—you have to wait for your favorite item to go on sale before you'll find it to be a great buy...* "
Ali's Notes: "*...Pottery Barn Kids Bedding earns both a value and overall lila pick this year for their high quality mix-and-match sheet basics in a range of fun colors for as little as $17 each...* "

Rachel Ashwell
(www.shabbychic.com)
Parent Reviews: "*...shabby chic for your baby... cozy, relaxed styles... I love the reversible receiving blankets... the T-shirt sheets are the softest sheets on the market... impeccable designs... I would never spend this much money on sheets... a wide variety of fabrics and patterns to choose from... elegant, stylish bedding... I like the warm, open feel to the designs...* "

Silk Baby Throw
Kumi KooKoon (www.kumikookoon.com)
Parent Reviews: "*...made of the finest silk... luxurious bedding... there is no higher quality on the market... this bedding is so comfortable—it wraps my baby up in softness and luxury... the beautiful pastel colors are muted and elegant... for the baby that has everything... as much as $240 for a fitted sheet...* "

Ali's Notes: **"**...Kumi's 100% hypoallergenic silk baby throws have a growing following in the super-luxury baby market... **"**

Sumersault ★★★★☆
(www.sumersault.com   800.232.3006)

Parent Reviews: **"**...nice selection of patterns—festive and fun, not run-of-the-mill... very good quality... fits snugly on mattress... colors don't fade when washed... one of the nicest selections for boys I've ever found... sheets are soft and sturdy... a little pricey, but I though it was worth it because our nursery looked so bright and cheery... colors haven't faded even after numerous washings... **"**

Wendy Bellissimo ★★★★★
(www.wendybellissimo.com   818.348.3682)

Parent Reviews: **"**...handmade, custom designs... she uses the most luxurious fabrics and the nursery looks absolutely stunning... really thick bumpers and wonderfully soft cotton... convenient bumper covers unzip for easy washing... love how simple and elegant the designs are... exquisite fabrics... high-end for sure, both in quality and price... a crazy amount of money for sheets—your baby doesn't even know the difference... so beautiful, classy and tasteful... **"**

Ali's Notes: **"**...Wendy Bellissimo is the name for flowery, romantic luxury for the baby nursery... traditionalists and grandparents delight in her style, making Wendy Bellissimo's traditional baby bedding (particularly her great whites) both a best-of-category for their romantic style and an overall lila pick for her best-of-class textiles... **"**

standard cribs

★★★★★
"lila picks"

- ★ Bellini
- ★ IKEA
- ★ Pali
- ★ Stokke

Baby's Dream ★★★★☆
(www.babysdream.com 800.835.2742)
Parent Reviews: **"**...they manufacture beautiful, classic-looking pieces that also are very functional... solid, wonderfully finished wood—no veneer... the crib becomes a toddler bed, then a full-size bed... higher sides keep my budding acrobat inside his crib... easy to coordinate with other items to create a beautiful nursery... wonderful workmanship but you pay for it—their cribs certainly aren't cheap... in order to convert my crib to a toddler bed we had to buy an additional conversion kit... yes, the conversion kit cost more money, but it's still less than buying a whole new bed... my crib's railing and headboard aren't a standard size so some of our crib accessories won't fit properly... prices can be a little high, but the quality is well worth it... **"**
Ali's Notes: **"**...they produce great mid-priced cribs and other nursery furniture... parents seem highly satisfied that they've found a good balance between style and budget... available in many local baby retailers... **"**

Bellini ★★★★★
(www.bellini.com 914.472.7336)
Price .... $475-$550   Features .... convertible
Parent Reviews: **"**...lovely designs made of solid wood... nice clean lines... the crib will easily last through several children without showing signs of wear... timeless designs—easy to add matching accessories years later... functional with four mattress settings, wheels and drawers... eventually can be converted into a smart looking toddler bed... tons of store locations nationwide so

you can actually go, look and touch the model before you buy... finishing colors include white, coffee, antique white, natural, bleach and mahogany... service at the stores ranges from great to nonexistent... all of their cribs are manufactured in Italy which may explain the high price tag... **"**

Ali's Notes: **"**...so you want some of that Italian style in your nursery?.. Bellini has plenty for you to choose from, but it does come at a price ($500 plus)... their popularity soared when Miranda of 'Sex In The City' outfitted her nursery with one of their cribs... well-made and lots of styles to choose from... **"**

Bonavita/Babi Italia ★★★★☆
(www.bonavita-cribs.com 866.266.2848)
Parent Reviews: **"**...classic Italian styles that are beautiful and expensive... it seems like they have a million different styles and models to choose from so you're bound to find something that works in your nursery... lots of 3-in-1 models and most have wheels and drawers... they also make models that convert all the way to a full-size bed... we found ours on sale and absolutely love it... the drawer underneath is handy and opens and shuts quietly... high quality wood... exactly what we were looking for—solid wood construction including the right finish... all the features you might want—knee push railing, wheels and comes in many colors... easy assembly... if Bonavita is what you're looking for, then be prepared to spend some serious cash... **"**

Ali's Notes: **"**...lots of cribs and furniture in every imaginable style and color... Babi Italia is sold through bigger chain stores while Bonavita is offered at specialty retailers... decent quality and lots of options both in terms of price ($300 and up) and style... **"**

Child Craft/Legacy ★★★★☆
(www.childcraftind.com 800.725.8625)
Parent Reviews: **"**...not as expensive or fancy as some of the ridiculously-priced imports but the quality is great... they make everything from cribs to dressers and beds—all of it looks nice... my son is now a toddler and we have converted his crib into a bed which doubles as a daybed—a great investment... basic, no muss, no fuss crib... easy access to child via dropdown side rail... nice color selections... the under-the-crib drawer is perfect for linens and clothes and slides in and out quietly... well-manufactured, nicely designed—they also offer many more color choices than some of the other brands out there... **"**

Ali's Notes: **"**...drawers, wheels, adjustable mattress heights, convertible beds, and every imaginable color... plenty to choose from at this low to mid-priced manufacturer... made in the USA... **"**

Delta ★★½☆☆
(www.deltaenterprise.com 800.377 3777)
Parent Reviews: **"**...family-owned and based in NY, these guys make some nice looking nursery furniture... cribs, dressers, tables and chairs... their cribs range from high-end to very basic and not that good-looking... mine is currently going through baby number three and it still looks like new... I love their 3-in-1 crib—it transforms into a toddler and full-size bed... made of really solid wood that can withstand the beating my son gives it... easy to put together... the mattress height can be adjusted to 5 positions... they have a couple of nice models that are worth checking out since you can probably save some money here compared to other brands... **"**

Ali's Notes: *"...you can get one of their cribs for $100 at one of the big chains (Target, etc.)... just remember that you get what you pay for..."*

ducduc
(www.ducducnyc.com   212.226.1868)
Ali's Notes: *"...a new entrant on the market, aiming to provide 'best-of' contemporary nursery furnishings... all American-made... prices are not for the faint of heart... stay tuned for reviews next year..."*

Forever Mine
(www.forevermine.com   800.356.2742)
Parent Reviews: *"...the best buy out there—stylish, good-looking cribs for $200-$250... the trick is ordering through their web site and getting product shipped straight from their warehouse... we gambled and bought our crib based on the price and the pictures we saw on their web site— we couldn't be happier... they also make changing tables, dressers and other nursery furniture... delivery time can be up to 2 months so plan accordingly—we were without a crib for 2 weeks because we didn't anticipate the long wait... all the features you might want in a crib at rock bottom prices (and delivered straight to your door!)..."*

IKEA
(www.ikea.com)
Parent Reviews: *"...IKEA is simply amazing—the quality is great and you can't beat the price... they all have strange Swedish names... a good-looking crib for less than $100— sure, it doesn't have all the fancy contraptions that other manufacturers try to sell you, but it works just fine... the sides don't go down so you have to keep reaching over... looks expensive, but it's cheaper than anything out there... sturdy and really easy to put together... ours converts into a toddler bed... smaller than other cribs which makes it easy to get the baby in and out... watch out because the shipping can cost as much as the crib—still you end up saving lots of money... it took my husband a couple of hours to piece it together so make sure you have a mechanically-minded person to help out... their products are well-designed, inexpensive and just make sense..."*
Ali's Notes: *"...get out your thinking cap and screwdriver... this is a great low-cost crib and furniture supplier... designs are clean and functionality is generally simpler (no drop sides, varying mattress heights, etc.) but the price is right if you're okay with (a lot of!) do-it-yourself assembly..."*

Little Miss Liberty Round Crib Company
(www.crib.com   310.281.5400)
Parent Reviews: *"...we really wanted a round crib, but when we found out how much they charge for it we changed our minds!... $600+ for a crib—are they kidding?.. made out of a special plastic that looks modern but not cold... I love the canopy that you can hang toys or decorations on... easy to access baby from all sides... a round crib is great in a smaller room and we move ours around all the time... fun shape that is a little out of the ordinary... expensive and kind of gimmicky—we got ours as a gift and I would frankly never spend that much for a crib... now you need round sheets... you seem to be pay a lot extra for something that isn't really that much better than an ordinary wooden crib..."*

Million Dollar Baby/DaVinci
(www.milliondollarbaby.com 323.728.9988)

Parent Reviews: *"...they make just about everything—cribs, dressers, cradles, beds, etc... prices are reasonable but vary quite a bit... they carry several 3-in-1 models that allow you to convert the crib to a day bed and then finally to a full bed—it's an economical way to stretch your dollars... nice, classic styling... the side railing lowers easily and quietly... prices are very reasonable given the quality... plenty of colors to choose from which makes it easy to find something that will fit into your nursery... the conversion kit is not included with your initial purchase so if you're planning on converting make sure you factor that into the price... it took us a while to assemble— the instructions could have been better... good value for the money..."*

Morigeau-Lépine
(www.morigeau.com)

Parent Reviews: *"...original designs from a great Canadian company... they make everything from cribs to dressers to beds and shelving units... if you have the money you can fill your whole nursery or tot's room with their gorgeously designed furniture... they make the kind of furniture that will still look good for years to come... good color choices and the craftsmanship is outstanding... made of beech or maple which are nice strong woods... stands up to an active toddler... love the look and they have many different styles to choose from—several different 'collections' ranging from old-fashioned to more modern looking... matching furniture looks great in adult rooms too..."*

Natart
(www.natartfurniture.com 819.364.3189)

Parent Reviews: *"...expensive but beautiful nursery and bedroom sets by a Canadian company... definitely high-end both in terms of price and quality—my friend spent over $600 for a crib!.. hard to find since not that many stores seem to carry them... solid hardwood construction with all the bells and whistles you would expect for the money..."*

NettoCollection ★★★★☆
(www.nettocollection.com 212.343.1545)

Parent Reviews: *"...I like that their cribs have some style—not your typical 'baby' look... ultra-modern and also ultra-expensive... you don't have to give up style just because you have a baby—these guys understand that... clean lines... it doesn't look like a crib—it's more like a cool, modern-looking piece in my daughter's room... well-made furniture..."*

Ali's Notes: *"...sophisticated, modern and streamlined... the NettoCollection has been the leader in the 'modern' baby furniture market... fixed side rails, 3-position adjustable mattress support and a pull-out blanket shelf for easy-access storage... beautifully manufactured for 'best-of' quality... the biggest downside is price..."*

Oeuf
(www.oeufnyc.com 718.965.1216)

Parent Reviews: *"...their cribs are simple and straightforward—no gimmicks... expensive, but so versatile—it converts into a toddler bed and even comes with a changing station that attaches to the frame... well-made and designed..."*

Ali's Notes: *"...minimalist... it easily converts into a junior bed, making it a great transitional piece that will take your child from infant to toddler... a nice, clean, modern look in contrast to some of the more traditional models out there... fixed sides keep it sturdy and stable, but a lower overall height makes it a lot easier to reach your baby and change the sheets... pricey, but super nice..."*

OFFI & Co ★★★★½
(www.offi.com 800.958.6334)

Parent Reviews: *"...not only good-looking, but super functional... so well-made and sturdy... 3 mattress heights and a huge drawer on wheels underneath... I like that I can combine practicality with a sense of design in my baby's nursery..."*

Ali's Notes: *"...a top choice for a great value, low investment modern crib (under $600)... solid pine and fiberboard... convenient drop side and a trundle-style drawer underneath that's deep enough to accommodate extra bedding, clothing and even toys... as your child gets older, simply remove the drop side and use it as a toddler daybed..."*

Pali ★★★★★
(www.paliitaly.com 877.725.4772)

Parent Reviews: *"...very pretty, high quality furniture for my baby's nursery... beautifully made with many styles to choose from... color choices include natural, white, cherry, cognac—all of which are beautiful... many functional models that convert from cribs to daybeds to full-size beds... our crib is a hand-me-down from 3 other boys and it still looks and works great... the rails and headboard have rounded edges so if my son falls and bumps his head he's okay... truly a one-hand drop side... the extra drawers are spacious and slide easily... assembly instructions are convoluted, but once you get it set up it works great... definitely not the cheapest crib out there... I sometimes wake my son when I pop the side up..."*

Ali's Notes: *"...mid-priced and extremely popular Italian crib and furniture maker... they carry pretty much any type of crib you could ask for—traditional to modern... the biggest gripe is that their assembly instructions are convoluted and just plain terrible..."*

Ragazzi ★★★★½
(www.ragazzi.com)

Parent Reviews: *"...everything from cribs to children's furniture... their warranty for cribs covers 15 years or 3 kids... I like that I can coordinate my entire nursery with their furniture sets... the furniture is beautiful, and will grow with my child... the crib has the quietest dropdown of any cribs I've seen... drawers have nice sliding features... love the non-toxic lacquer finish... well built, holds up to our son's constant kicking and shaking... wonderful quality but prices are sky high... crazy expensive... top-of-the-line good looking stuff that costs a lot but also lasts forever—we handed down our changing table and crib to friends and they are as thrilled with it as were we..."*

Ali's Notes: *"...higher-end with prices ranging in the $650+ range... good features and plenty of styles to choose from... generally good customer service... made in Canada..."*

Sorelle ★★★½☆
(www.sorellefurniture.com 201.461.9444)

Parent Reviews: "*...nice European design at a fair price... they offer almost 30 different models but they are based on the same basic design... they have basic and simple designs as well as fancier ones with lots of decoration on them... love the under-crib drawer—great for diapers, pacifiers or blankets... easy to raise and lower the sides... both the drawer and drop bar operate quietly... ours converts into a day bed... simple design that will work well pretty much anywhere... the drawer is kind of small—seems like other models have more space... wheels are cheap and scratched our hardwood floor... several color choices—all look great...*"

Ali's Notes: "*...low to mid-priced cribs... manufactured in Canada and South America and sold in big box chain stores like Babies R Us and Baby Depot (under different names)...*"

Stokke ★★★★★
(www.stokkeusa.com 877.978.6553)

Parent Reviews: "*...we love our Sleepi—it started as a bassinet and is now being used as our crib... 4 mattress heights... down the road we can convert it to a toddler bed and then ultimately into 2 chairs... yes it costs a bundle, but it's the best money we ever spent... it looks cool and works very well...*"

Ali's Notes: "*...every parent we know that has bought one is totally happy... very versatile... and talk about multi use— the complete Stokke Sleepi System morphs from a bassinet to a crib to a toddler bed to a junior bed and then into two kids' room chairs!.. the biggest downside is having to go with their specific bedding—then again, if you've already decided to buy this neat crib, then go all out and get the extras too...*"

Storkcraft Baby ★★★☆☆
(www.storkcraft.com 604.275.4242)

Parent Reviews: "*...more reasonably priced and simply designed than many of the other high-end manufacturers... many different styles to choose from and most convert to day beds... they sell them at discount outlets like Wal-Mart, Sears, Toys R Us and JCPenney... cheap in price, so-so in construction... we spent several hundred dollars less on our crib than many of our friends and quite frankly are just as happy...*"

Ali's Notes: "*...very low-priced ($100 and up)... available at most chain stores like Babies R Us... a good option if you're looking to save money or simply need another 'occasional-use' crib at the grandparents' house...*"

portable cribs

"lila picks"

★ Pack N Play (Graco)

BabyGo Portable Playard

★★★★☆

Evenflo (www.evenflo.com 800.233.5921)
Price .... $50-$80

Parent Reviews: **"**...it's very portable and the price is right... it comes with a bassinet and a couple of side pockets... 2 wheels on the rear make moving it around easy—it also collapses quickly, but you don't want to have to do that if you're just moving it from one room to the next... I like the music option—it's very soothing... the bassinet and changing area are both great, though my baby tends to sag when in the bassinet... **"**

P140 LP Aluminum Play Yard

★★★★☆

Compass (www.compassbaby.com 888.899.2229)
Price .... $90-$110
Features .... 32" x 40"

Parent Reviews: **"**...larger than the other manufacturers which is good and bad—good because baby has more room, bad because I can't get it out of the room without breaking it down... comes with a changing pad and mesh storage basket... very well-made—it's sturdy and feels like it will hold up for a long time... carry bag included... **"**

www.lilaguide.com

Pack N Play ★★★★★

Graco (www.gracobaby.com 800.345.4109)
Price .... $80-$100

Parent Reviews: *"...so convenient for when we go to Nana's house—we don't have to lay my baby on the couch anymore... a trusted classic—it seems like all of my friends have this one... it comes with wheels on the back two legs... quick to set up and relatively easy to transport—it comes with its own travel bag... mesh on all sides so my baby can look out and not feel like she's all cooped up... I can put my son in the Pack N Play and let him play in a safe place while I'm taking care of things around the house—by the time I'm done, he's usually fast asleep... I'm now using my same Pack N Play with my fourth child..."*

Ali's Notes: 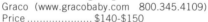 *"...Graco owns the market for portable cribs... a lot of manufacturers have tried to emulate the Pack N Play without much success (in fact many parents refer to their portable crib as their 'Pack N Play')... factoring in functionality and price the choice is pretty clear—Graco is the way to go..."*

Pack N Play Sport ★★★★½

Graco (www.gracobaby.com 800.345.4109)
Price .... $140-$150

Parent Reviews: *"...huge, but light as a feather... we use it as a play yard and even take it to the beach... the floor is not as well padded as the regular Pack N Play... the sides are pretty high and I had trouble putting my sleeping baby into it without waking him up... it's great for when you're up and about with baby—it provides a safe place to play as well as for mom to change diapers and make sure he/she isn't getting into any trouble... I like the mesh sides and the large sun canopy..."*

Travel Solutions Playard ★★★★☆

Combi (www.combi-intl.com 800.992.6624)
Price .... $140-$160

Parent Reviews: *"...a great solution if you have to travel with your little one... it works for several ages—the bassinet attaches to the inside, and when you don't need it you just take it out... it also has a diaper changing mat so you don't have to put your baby on the floor... wheels on the back two legs make moving it around pretty easy... the whole package weighs about 45 lbs so it's a chunk to be carrying around, but it will make your travels so much easier..."*

Travelin' Tot 4-in-1 Activity Gym

★★★★★

Kolcraft (www.kolcraft.com 800.453.7673)
Price .... $80-$100

Parent Reviews: *"...it does everything—I use it as a crib at night in our room, as a playpen, and as well a safe waiting area while I'm getting ready in the morning... all the bells and whistles you'll need—changing pad, music, vibrations and activity bar with toys on it... wheels make it easy to maneuver about... it comes with a convenient travel bag that has a shoulder strap for carrying..."*

cribs: portable

nursing & bottle feeding

One question all new moms must ask is whether or not to breastfeed. There are advocates for each side, but it really just comes down to personal preference, biological limitations and whether your schedule actually allows it. Even if you choose breastfeeding, you're going to need bottles for storing breast milk or the occasional bottle of formula when you're away. You'll also want to look into ways to pump and store your milk for times when you're not around. Whichever your choice, here are some things you'll want to consider:

Bottle Systems: Don't rush out and buy an expensive, automated pump until you're sure you need it. Until you know how successful you're going to be at breastfeeding, you might want to consider renting one instead. You might love it and want your own, decide a hand pump would be sufficient, or realize you don't need one at all. You will have to buy a kit with the personal accessories you'll need for pumping, but if you decide to buy the machine, the kit is usually deducted from the overall purchase. If you don't want the machine, you just saved yourself a couple hundred dollars!

Simplicity: Breastfeeding moms will want a storage system for saving up breast milk in the freezer. One great option is a breast milk ice cube tray that works like a regular ice cube tray with a lid. Another option is disposable bottle inserts that work with the breast pump. Simply pump, seal and freeze, then serve the milk straight from the bag. This is a great option for moms who don't want to waste a drop!

Renting: Many bottle makers offer grow-with-you systems so you don't have to buy a whole new set-up every few months. Not only are these systems great for the environment and your wallet, they also help ensure you can stick with whatever method you and your baby like (such as nipple style).

Storage: If your breast pump or bottle system feels like it's too much work, try another! There are a lot of different brands out there that offer great, no-fuss products. Besides, you've got other more important things to deal with.

by Ali Wing at egiggle.com

bottles & accessories

"lila picks"

- ★ Breastbottle Nurser (Adiri)
- ★ Natural Feeding Bottle (Avent)
- ★ Wide Neck Bottle (Dr Brown's)

Angled Tri-Flow Bottle System ★★★★☆
Munchkin (www.munchkininc.com 800.344.2229)
Price ....$4-$5
Features ..... 4 or 8 oz; reusable

Parent Reviews: *"...I love the angled bottle—it makes it much easier to feed and there is less air for baby to swallow... the only nipple my baby would take... they seem softer than most breast-shaped nipples... the angled bottle allows my son to hold it on his own... be careful though... sometimes the nipples can leak when on their side..."*

Breastbottle Nurser ★★★★★
Adiri (www.adiri.com 888.768.4459)
Price ....$10-$20

Parent Reviews: *"...it really does feel like a breast... so innovative... I absolutely love this bottle—it doesn't leak and my baby took to it immediately... a little more expensive than other bottles, but they've done such a good job designing it that I think it's well worth it..."*

Ali's Notes: *"...Adiri definitely gets points for innovation on this one... parents that use them swear by them... they are a fair bit more expensive than regular bottles, but think of it as the price of creativity..."*

Comfi Nursers

★★★☆☆

Evenflo (www.evenflo.com   800.233.5921)
Price .... $8-$10 (3 pack)
Features ..... 6 or 9 oz; reusable

Parent Reviews: **"** ...these are good if your baby has a small mouth... my daughter hates bottles, but she likes these... they don't have huge nipples... the nipples didn't work well for my baby—it kept caving in when she was trying to suck... **"**

Disposable Nurser

★★★★½

Avent (www.aventbaby.com   800.542.8368)

Price .... $5-$12
Features ...... 4 & 8 oz; disposable

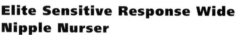

Parent Reviews: **"** ...easy to use and easy to transport... we just put dry formula into the bags and then add water when we need to feed... great for traveling when you don't want to lug around a bunch of bottles... the only time it leaked on us was when I screwed the top on too tightly... very easy to clean, since you're basically swapping out the bags on the inside... **"**

Elite Sensitive Response Wide Nipple Nurser

★★★★½

Evenflo (www.evenflo.com   800.233.5921)
Price .... $6-$8 (2 pack)
Features ..... 5 or 9 oz; reusable

Parent Reviews: **"** ...it has a great wide mouth and is easy to clean... the angle seems to really helps cut down on air intake... staged nipples means you don't have to keep changing bottles as the baby grows... they come in multi-packs of different pastel-colored bottles which is great if you want to color-code for multiple kids... wish the nipples were a little longer, my daughter had trouble

latching on to them...hard to reach the bottom of the taller bottles for cleaning...difficult to find the Stage 3 wide mouth nipples in stores, I had to go the their website... **"**

Ali's Notes: **"** ...Evenflo is known as one of the baby bottle market leaders... basic system purchase upgrades as baby grows for multi-use savings... **"**

Express Bottle & Babyfood Warmer

★★★★☆

Avent (www.aventbaby.com 800.542.8368)
Price .... $46-$70
Features ....

Parent Reviews: "...I love this thing because it heats just about anything for my baby— from frozen breast milk to baby food in jars... I can even use my Avent bottle liners... heats evenly and works reliably... another great product from Avent..."

Express Electric Steam Sterilizer

★★★½☆

Avent (www.aventbaby.com 800.542.8368)
Price............................ $75-$85

Parent Reviews: "...it sterilizes a bunch of stuff at the same time—bottles, breast pump parts, nipples etc... works quickly and effectively... large in size, so can take up a bit of space..."

Express Microwave Steam Sterilizer

★★★★½

Avent (www.aventbaby.com 800.542.8368)
Price .... $30-$35

Parent Reviews: "...easy to use, fits into a standard microwave and takes up very little space in your kitchen... big enough for 4 to 5 bottles and cups... your bottles and nipples are sanitized within minutes... fabulously easy to use for everything from teething toys to the kitchen sponge... it even keeps parts sterilized for a few hours if you leave the lid on..."

Ali's Notes: "...designed for your bottles, but so easy and good this will be a keeper in your kitchen... a true multi-use product that is worth the extra money..."

MultiFlow Bottle

★★★★½

Tigex (www.tigexusa.com 866.698.4439)
Price................................ $5-$7
Features................ 5oz/8oz/11oz

Parent Reviews: "...we got a starter kit that contained a few of everything (different sized bottles, nipples, etc.)... handles available... the best part of this system is the different nipples that accommodate various flow rates and formula thicknesses... easy to clean... a simple design that really works... no valves and easy to drink from... love the cover to keep the nipple clean..."

Natural Feeding Bottle ★★★★★
Avent (www.aventbaby.com 800.542.8368)
Price ....$12-$15 (3 pack)   Features.............4/9/11 oz; reusable

Parent Reviews: "...mine have lasted through three babies... the various nipple flows are great for babies as they transition from breastfeeding... easy for baby to hold and easy for mom and dad to clean... I like that the entire beverage line has interchangeable parts... dishwasher and microwave safe... sometimes my two-year old son pushes the nipple through the bottle and spills milk everywhere... more expensive than other brands but they are the best I've tried... "

Ali's Notes: "...Avent is a popular favorite for the American new-parent market... my vote, and the vote of many... you really can't go wrong with this choice... "

multi-use value

Night & Day Bottle Warmer ★★★⯨☆
The First Years (www.thefirstyears.com)
Price ....$35-$45

Parent Reviews: "...a very convenient way to warm the baby's bottle and also jars of baby food... it has a simple design so it doesn't look bad sitting on the counter... great to prepare bottles and warm up for middle of the night feedings... heats up quickly... easy to use once you figure out the timing for your size bottle... it didn't seem to warm the bottle evenly... you have to be careful how much water to add because it heats the bottle very quickly and can overheat easily... "

Premium Eazy Feed Nurser ★★★★⯨
Playtex (www.playtexbaby.com 800.222.0453)
Price .... $14-$16 (starter set)   Features.............. 4 or 8 oz; reusable

Parent Reviews: "...the unique liner system makes for easy cleaning... the liners can be used to freeze breast milk... many different sizes and shapes of nipples available for the finicky bottle drinker... the air release system is neat since it lets you get rid of extra air that has built up while filling... disposable liners make sterilization unnecessary... you have to keep buying liners which at $7 per hundred starts adding up... you can't use a bottle warmer with the bottles that use disposable liners ... "

participate in our survey at

Standard Neck Bottle

Dr Brown's
Price .... $12-$18 (3 pack)
Features ..... 4 or 8 oz; reusable

★★★★½

Parent Reviews: "...a must-have for babies that get gassy easily... they are miracle workers and I wouldn't use anything else... a lot of pieces to clean, but it's definitely worth it—these bottles work... unique 'reflux-free' design... all the parts are dishwasher safe..."

VentAire Bubble Free Bottle

★★★★☆

Playtex (www.playtexbaby.com 800.222.0453)
Price .... $11-$15 (2 pack)   Features .... 6 or 9 oz; reusable

Parent Reviews: "...venting the air out while my baby drinks makes for less air that he gets in his tummy... my son had bad reflux, but the VentAire bottles really helped... the bottom vent helped my infant when she was having problems with spitting up—this is the only bottle that seemed to work for her... the tilted design makes feeding baby easier when he is in a sitting position... the discs can be tricky to clean..."

VIA Nurser

★★★☆☆

Avent (www.aventbaby.com 800.542.8368)
Price $8
Features .. 4 or 8 oz; disposable

Parent Reviews: "...disposable bottles that really can be used several times over... the system works well—all the parts fit together tightly so there's no leaking... 2 sizes, great for storage in fridge or freezer... they attach directly to pump, use same attachments as regular Avent bottles... they stack inside each other so they take up less room in your cupboard..."

Wide Neck Bottle

★★★★★

Dr Brown's
Price .... $15-$20 (3 pack)
Features ..... 4 or 8 oz; reusable

Parent Reviews: "...the vent inside the bottle helps cut down on the air bubbles for baby... helped stop gas and spit-up in its tracks... this bottle made meal times more enjoyable for us... my baby loves the wide-mouth bottles... a little harder to clean since it has the vent and other little pieces... extra-tall bottles don't fit into the standard diaper bag bottle compartment..."

breast pumps

★★★★★
"lila picks"

★ Isis Breast Pump (Avent)
★ Pump In Style Advanced (Medela)

Easy Comfort Double Electric/Battery Breast Pump ★★★★☆
The First Years (www.thefirstyears.com)
Price .... $150-$160   Features......... electric; single/double

Parent Reviews: "...a good double pump that costs a fair bit less than Medela and Ameda pumps... I love the battery powered option since I can't always get to a power outlet when I need to pump... the bottles can have a nipple attached directly on to them for feeding right away... I only wish there was more control over the suction speed and strength... also available in a single pump... fits wide neck bottles..."

Easy Comfort Manual Breast Pump ★★☆☆☆
The First Years (www.thefirstyears.com)

Price .... $20-$22
Features .... manual; single

Parent Reviews: "...a manual pump that comes at a good price but frankly isn't worth it... very time-consuming and uncomfortable... you get what you pay for and I spent a lot of time getting frustrated... easy to use, clean and assemble..."

participate in our survey at

Hands-Free Breast Pump ★★★½☆

Whisper Wear (www.whisperwear.com)
Price .... $200-$220   Features......... electric; single/double

Parent Reviews: "...yes, it really is a handsfree pump—you wear the cups under your clothing and you can pump while reading, working at your computer and even driving... the pump is well-made, easy to use and clean... so much quieter than other pumps on the market and easier to transport... compared to other pumps this system makes it so much easier to incorporate breastfeeding into your daily life..."

Ali's Notes: "...can a breast pump really be a 'style pick'?.. the Whisper Wear can because it helps the nursing mom not look like she is overtly nursing... Whisper Wear's hands-free pump gets marks for hiding in mom's clothes and being as low-impact as the not-always-glamorous act of pumping can be..."

Harmony Breast Pump ★★★★☆

Medela (www.medela.com 800.435.8316)
Price .... $35-$45   Features .... manual; single

Parent Reviews: "...easy manual pumping and small enough to take with you wherever you go... it provides surprisingly good suction... easier on your hands than some of the other manual pumps... the biggest problem with this manual pump is that it takes a while to get the job done... it works in two settings—one for expression and one for letdown... very convenient for travel since it fits into a quart sized bag..."

Ali's Notes: "...the perfect travel solution... too slow and cumbersome to serve as your only pump, but great when 'on the road'..."

Isis Breast Pump ★★★★★

Avent (www.aventbaby.com 800.542.8368)
Price .... $40-$60   Features .... manual; single

Parent Reviews: "...a very efficient hand pump... small, light and easy to carry... no noise and best of all no electricity needed... the storage bottles that come with the kit are great and stay closed without leaking... nice carrying case... easy to carry along to work or even road trips... it takes a while to get the hang of manual pumping... all parts can be cleaned in the dishwasher... I love that even though it's a manual pump, I can still pump one-handed..."

Ali's Notes: "...smart, portable and easy to use... once you've got the hang of it, the Isis offers the most productive handheld approach..."

www.lilaguide.com

Pump In Style Advanced Breastpump ★★★★★

Medela (www.medela.com 800.435.8316)
Price .... $200-$280   Features .... electric; double

Parent Reviews: "...I can't imagine having any other breast pump—hospital-grade quality that never failed... it lasted through two kids and has been passed on... it comes in a briefcase-like bag that can go in the office without comment... the pump bag contains everything you need, right down to a mini-cooler... it works well with Medela bras so you can pump and check email at the same time... wonderful for work since it cuts down the time needed for pumping..."

Ali's Notes: "...the mac-daddy of breast pumps made for hospital-grade pumping in your living room... looks like a briefcase or backpack, and only the wiser know what's really in the bag... a one-time 'parenting investment', since it's useful life is for as many kids as you have!.. Medela really sets the market standard for quality in nursing... with such market dominance, Medela offers the most complete line of accessories and alternatives for varying lactation needs, challenges and stages..."

multi-use

Purely Yours Dual Electric Breast Pump ★★★★½

Ameda (www.ameda.com 877.992.6332)
Price .... $165-$185   Features .... electric; double

Parent Reviews: "...good suction and great control over the speed and level of suction... once I got into the groove, I could empty both breasts in 10 minutes, yielding up to 14 ounces... sealed system so only collection system and bottles need regular washing... it comes with cool-packs and insulated tote... much less expensive than other hospital-grade pumps and it works just as well..."

Single & Double Deluxe Breastpumps ★★★★☆

Medela (www.medela.com 800.435.8316)
Price .... $100-$160

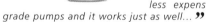

Features ....electric; single/double

Parent Reviews: "...very portable and easy to use... it comes in a single or double pump option... you can set the suction speed to a couple of different settings... it doesn't work with batteries, but I use it as a second pump at work so I don't have to lug one around all the time... it comes with a smart-looking black case..."

Ali's Notes: *"...Medela's solution for the 'occasional use' mom... works with an adapter or battery so super easy to travel with... a nice low-cost solution that is perfect for enabling those first year date nights!..."*

Symphony

Medela (www.medela.com)
Price ....$1,250   Features..........electric; single/double

Parent Reviews: *"...the 2 phase system is pretty slick and I do think it works better than ordinary pumps... it first works in 'stimulation' mode and then switches to 'expression' mode after 2 minutes... expensive, but it's by far the best pump out there... it's nice and quiet so I don't mind pumping at work... the digital display is nice... it feels like they have taken pumping to a whole new level... too expensive to buy, but definitely the model to rent..."*

sippy cups

★★★★★
"lila picks"

★ Fun Grips Soft Starter Spill-Proof Cup (Gerber)

★ Take & Toss (The First Years)

Big Sipster Spill-Proof Cup ★★★★½
Playtex (www.playtexbaby.com 800.222.0453)
Price .... $7-$8 (2 pack)   Features................................10.5oz

Parent Reviews: "*...a big cup for big kids... machine washable, withstands being dropped and still doesn't leak... my daughter was weaned off her bottle after using these cups for about two weeks... the colors and designs are great, makes the cups easy to spot... I love the easy-to-clean valves... my son would throw his around and nothing ever seeped out of the valve... valves have a tendency to get lost...*"

Clean & Simple Spill-Proof Sports Bottle ★★★★☆
The First Years (www.thefirstyears.com 800.317.3194)
Price ....$4-$6   Features................................. 12oz

Parent Reviews: "*...a simple design that really works... no valves and easy to drink from... love the cover to keep the spout clean... I just pop off the lid and use these as cups for older kids too... they are incredibly durable, they have been bounced out of a mini van, chewed on by a teething toddler, rolled around by curious cats and stepped on by distracted parents... the spout is easy for curious tots to take off...*"

First Sipster Spill-Proof Cup

★★★★☆

Playtex (www.playtexbaby.com 800.222.0453)
Price .... $7-$8 (2 pack)
Features 7oz

Parent Reviews: "*...I love the fact that they have handles but still fit into the car seat cup holder... the design is fun, but more importantly they don't leak... durable and dishwasher-safe... great value for the money—we've never had problems with them...*"

Fun Grips Soft Starter Spill-Proof Cup

★★★★★

Gerber (www.gerber.com 800.443.7237)
Price ....$4-$8   Features .... 7 or 10oz

Parent Reviews: "*...much easier for young infants to grasp than any other cup I tried... very durable—ours have been dropped and chewed on and still don't leak... perfect for learning to use a big kid cup... replacement parts are pretty easy to come by... won't fit in many drink holders because of the wide base...*"

Ali's Notes: "*...anything but multi-stage, these cups are perfectly named 'starters'—for that stage, they're great... as soon as your child gets into regular use (in cars, on the go, etc.) you'll want to graduate to a new style...*"

Insulator Spill-Proof Cup

★★★★½

Playtex (www.playtexbaby.com 800.222.0453)
Price .... $6-$7 (2 pack)
Features 6oz

Parent Reviews: "*...the double-walled insulation feature does help keep things cool or hot—I thought it was a bunch of marketing hype at first... easy to hold and they come in all kinds of character themes... they don't leak and seem easy to drink from... a great cup to graduate to since you can also use it without the lid... ours were dropped a couple of times and then basically stopped working—somehow the seal was damaged and they were basically useless after that...*"

www.lilaguide.com

Insulator Sport Straw Cup

Playtex (www.playtexbaby.com 800.222.0453)
Price ....$5-$6   Features 9oz

Parent Reviews: **"**...my son loves the graphics and the fun of drinking through a straw... it keeps drinks very cold and the sliding top that 'closes' the straw is a lifesaver... my son couldn't figure out a sippy cup, but did great with this straw cup starting at six months... doesn't leak... takes a beating, but withstands all abuse... kind of hard to get the straw and lid clean... the "no-spill" straw isn't exactly no-spill, although if you close the straw with the sliding lid, it doesn't leak... **"**

Magic Cup

Avent (www.aventbaby.com 800.542.8368)
Price .... $5   Features .... 7, 9 or 12oz

Parent Reviews: **"**...I love the soft tip... easy for my son to transition between the bottle and the cup especially while teething... nice looking and long-lasting... easy for little hands to hold... interchangeable with all Avent bottles and nipples... could never get it to not leak... too expensive for a sippy cup that my kids lose all the time... the handle hooks are nice to attach to your pants or belt should you want to leave the diaper bag at home... **"**

Ali's Notes: **"**...lots of mixed reviews about whether or not they leak—some parents love them, others seem to hate them... they aren't that expensive so if you're up to it, give them a try and decide for yourself... **"**

My First Cup

Munchkin (www.munchkininc.com 800.344.2229)
Price .... $5-$6 (2 pack)   Features 6oz

Parent Reviews: **"**...it evolves into a regular cup... the soft, rubbery band around the outside makes it easy for little hands to hold onto... valve stays in place... reasonable price for good quality... these cups have helped my son transition into 'big boy' cups... you can buy extra valves quite easily... not totally leak-proof over time—mine have started to leave dribbles in the diaper bag... **"**

Take & Toss

The First Years (www.thefirstyears.com 800.317.3194)
Price ....$2-$3   Features..........................4.5 or 7oz

Parent Reviews: **"**...*very handy to take on the road... lightweight and cheaper than anything else out there... originally designed to be thrown away, but we just keep using ours over and over... they come in tons of different colors which makes it easy to color code when other kids are around... they aren't designed to last for a long time and will leak after extensive use... a little hard to get open... I noticed the little ridge around spout can trap a lot of gunk...* **"**

Ali's Notes: **"**...*the truth is very few parents end up just tossing these cups after a single use, so they end up sticking around for a while... the nice thing is that once they start leaking (from being thrown around), you really can toss them... the best overall value for your everyday toddler use...* **"**

sippy cups

potty training

Your product needs for potty training are simple: start with a sturdy potty seat that's independent from the toilet (ones that attach to the toilet are often too advanced for beginners). Then, as your little one starts wanting to sit on the toilet like mom and dad, pick a simple, secure toilet seat trainer. Grab your copy of *Everybody Poops* and you're all set!

Simplicity: Avoid seats that are overly complicated, awkward to use or that kids might have difficulty getting on and off of. The simpler the better. Remember, if they look difficult to use, they probably are.

Sturdiness: Whatever you get, make sure it's sturdy and stable. Nothing will hamper toilet training like a seat your child is afraid they're going to fall off of!

Travel: Another benefit of the toilet seat trainer is that they're great for travel, making a sanitary seat for a little one who doesn't get the idea of a public restroom.

by Ali Wing at egiggle.com

potty seats

★★★★★

"lila picks"

★ Potty Chair (Baby Bjorn)
★ Toilet Trainer (Baby Bjorn)

3-In-1 Potty 'N Step Stool   ★★★★½

Safety 1st (www.safety1st.com   800.544.1108)
Price $10

Parent Reviews: *"...I like it because it's simple and straightforward... versatile and convenient for small bathrooms... it can be used as a training toilet—low to the ground... removable plastic bowl for easy cleanup... a big-potty converter seat that goes right on a standard toilet... the step stool's good for teeth-brushing and hand-washing... priced right..."*

Ali's Notes: *"...a potty chair turned potty trainer with the bonus of being able to use it as a stool... a good, economical, all-in-one purchase that you'll be able to use for potty training, as well as after your toddler is 'trained'..."*

Folding Potty Seat   ★★★★☆

Primo (www.primobaby.com 973.926.5900)
Price .... $9-$12

Parent Reviews: *"...it folds and fits into most bags... pretty sturdy as long as your tot isn't too big and heavy... perfect for use in dirty public restrooms... more trouble than it was worth... you are still going to want to wash it after using it in a public bathroom... we have one in the car for when my boy needs to go to a public restroom..."*

participate in our survey at

Ali's Notes: *" ...using the restroom when you're away from home can be a scary experience—even more so for tots who are just learning to use the potty... this handy folding potty seat acts as a bathroom barrier, keeping germs at bay and adding extra stability for your child... it folds compactly and will easily fit in most diaper bags... a nice solution for taking your training tot to that 'not-so-clean' restroom at the park... "*

Little Potty ★★★★½
Baby Bjorn (www.babybjorn.com   800.593 5522)
Price $10

Parent Reviews: *"...easy to clean, single piece construction... built-in spray guard... small enough to take with you on road trips... a great space saver in our little bathroom... comfortable and ergonomic... very durable and easy to use... an overpriced piece of plastic... it's a pain to clean—it doesn't come apart and it's too big to fit in the sink... "*

One Step Trainer Seat ★★★☆☆
Safety 1st (www.safety1st.com   800.544.1108)
Price......................................$6

Parent Reviews: *"...it fits right on to your regular toilet but is designed for small bottoms... it frequently doesn't stay in the up position and pokes me in the back while I'm sitting on the toilet... nothing fancy, but it works well for our family... my daughter likes it because she can use the same toilet we use—it makes her feel like a 'big girl'... "*

Potty Chair ★★★★★
Baby Bjorn (www.babybjorn.com   800.593 5522)
Price $23

Parent Reviews: *"...the Little Potty's big brother... a very simple design that is easy to clean—just dump and rinse the little inner potty... my daughter loves being able to pour the contents into the toilet herself... high splash guard for boys... reasonable price for a basic, but practical potty... just a plain potty—no silly music or lights... "*

Ali's Notes: *"...a special design that allows your child to sit comfortably for as long as necessary... durable, PVC-free and recyclable plastic, with an inner potty that is easily removed for emptying and cleaning... most importantly, it won't slip and create any unnecessary setbacks in your tot's toilet training... "*

Potty N Step Stool

★★★★⯪

Safety 1st (www.safety1st.com 800.544.1108)
Price .... $12-$18

Parent Reviews: **"**...it works as a step stool, potty and also fits onto your regular toilet... easy to clean... our boy likes it enough to sit on it just to 'play' potty... the fact that the seat comes off and fits onto an adult-sized toilet seat makes the transition to the big toilet much easier... the only downside is that it slides on our tiled floor a little too easily...**"**

Soft Trainer Seat

★★★★⯪

The First Years (www.thefirstyears.com)
Price .... $9-$12

Parent Reviews: **"**...my daughter's seat looks more comfortable than our regular toilet seat—I wish they made one of these for adults... I like the handles and soft seat... my little boy puts the seat on the toilet, does his business and then puts the seat away all by himself...**"**

Toilet Trainer

★★★★★

Baby Bjorn (www.babybjorn.com 800.593 5522)
Price .... $25-$30

Parent Reviews: **"**...we skipped the little potty seats and went straight to this fabulous toilet trainer... kids sit on the big toilet just like mommy and daddy... adjustable to most toilet seats... good looking design and well made... I never know where to put it when my daughter isn't using it...**"**

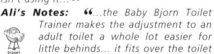

Ali's Notes: **"**...the Baby Bjorn Toilet Trainer makes the adjustment to an adult toilet a whole lot easier for little behinds... it fits over the toilet seat so that the child can sit securely and comfortably... most importantly, children can put it on and take it off all by themselves, making potty training and early potty usage a lot less intimidating... a nice 'stage 2' follow-up to the Baby Bjorn Potty Chair...**"**

strollers & joggers

Strollers are one of your bigger-ticket items, so you'll want to make sure you pick the right one. Luckily, you can narrow your choices quite a bit just by considering how you're going to be using it. For example, are you a city dweller who has to navigate curbs, rough surfaces and public transportation? Are you a suburban mom who drives most places and only uses the stroller on smooth, paved surfaces? Keep the following things in mind when choosing a stroller and your choice will be more obvious.

Size and Weight vs. Durability: For the most part, you'll find there's a trade-off between a stroller's size and weight and its durability. If you live in the city and want something that's easy to get around with, you may want a stroller that's smaller, leaner and easier to handle. However, if you don't have to navigate stairs and storage isn't an issue, you might want a bigger, sturdier stroller that can take a lot more abuse and will last through more than one child.

Car Seat Compatibility: If you're going to spend a lot on a standard stroller, look for one that's compatible with your car seat, especially if you're going to be in and out of your car a lot. This is particularly important early on when you don't want to wake your baby and they're too young to hop in and out on their own.

Joggers vs. All-Terrain Strollers: Serious runners will probably want a jogger in addition to their stroller, and should consider collapsibility, overall weight, size and style of the wheels, and the availability of replacement parts and service. However, if you're a speed walker or casual jogger, you don't really need a separate jogger. There are a lot of great all-terrain strollers now that will easily take you from street to trail, and they're great for anyone who's extra-active.

Durability: The more you spend, the more you're going to want a stroller that lasts, and with any luck, you might be able to use your stroller for more than one child. Be sure to consider wheel construction, as plastic wheels can get sticky and difficult to maneuver over time.

Washability: Another factor for long-term use is the washability of the stroller. Make sure you consider the stickiness factor and get one that is easy to clean.

by Ali Wing at egiggle.com

umbrella strollers

"lila picks"

- ★ Techno XT (Maclaren)
- ★ Triumph (Maclaren)

Caddy Umbrella

★★★★☆

Chicco (www.chiccousa.com 732.805.9200)

Price .... $40-$50 Seat .... 2 pos recline; 5-pt harness
Weight .... 11 lbs Wheels .... 8x6"; plastic

Parent Reviews: "...the most affordable umbrella stroller out there... sturdy yet lightweight... so light and small I can take it anywhere... able to handle the worst city sidewalks, but not ideal for long strolls... flimsy sun canopy that really isn't very effective... I wish it would recline more—my baby is always slumped over when he falls asleep... the storage basket that goes underneath the seat is an extra item... my feet often hit the wheels while walking... better wheels than most comparably priced umbrella strollers... you can't beat the price, but you can beat the quality and features..."

Ali's Notes: "...like most 'mini' version umbrella strollers, this one is better for quick trips than heavy use... very compact fold... not great for tall parents... sun canopy doesn't provide much coverage... partial recline only so check against your planned usage before purchasing..."

City Savvy ★★★⯪☆

Combi (www.combi-intl.com 800.992.6624)
Price .... $100-$120   Seat .... full recline; 5-pt harness
Weight.......................... 11 lbs   Wheels .... 8x6"; plastic

Parent Reviews: "...solid and easy to wheel around... I love that the seat reclines all the way—you wouldn't believe how much easier my baby fall asleep... the wheels are a little small, but as long as I'm not 'off-roading' they roll fine... easy to fold and really compact—if fits behind our front door... I wish the canopy were a little bigger, but overall it works fine... great deal—you get most of what you need without having to take out a second mortgage... the seat covers comes off and are machine washable... works with the Combi Infant seat... "

Ali's Notes: "...sturdy everyday stroller in a lightweight package... easy to carry with strap so nice for the busy, urban family who's also navigating subways, airports and/or buses... the basket doesn't hold everything, but holds enough... very compact... with their car seat it's designed as a total travel solution... "

Deluxe Comfort Ride Umbrella ★★☆☆☆

Cosco (www.coscojuvenile.com 800.544.1108)
Price .... $18-$20   Seat .... 2 pos recline; 3-pt harness
Weight............................ 7 lbs   Wheels .... 6x4"; plastic

Parent Reviews: "...it hardly gets cheaper than this... not the world's best-designed umbrella stroller, but who cares—it only cost me $20... folds pretty easily... good-sized storage bin... flimsy wheels that rattle unless you're on smooth ground... works great for quick stop-and-go errands... very cheap and you get what you pay for... "

Ali's Notes: "...super-lightweight... cute, but not made to last... minimal cushioning... very small... poor steering... "

Global Buggy ★★★⯪☆

Maclaren (www.maclarenbaby.com 877.442.4622)
Price .... $275-$299   Seat .... full recline; 5-pt harness
Weight.......................... 20 lbs   Wheels .... 8x6"; plastic

Parent Reviews: "...I love that this stroller can hold a car seat (none of the other Maclaren strollers do)... the seat goes all the way flat and is nice and plush for the baby... it holds up great and isn't too heavy... no cup holder for mom, and no activity bar for baby... too bad the handles don't adjust like the Techno XT because then this stroller would have it all... not cheap, but all of Maclaren's stuff is high quality... "

Ali's Notes: "...known principally for their easy-to-collapse, lightweight umbrella strollers, this is one of Maclarens full-service strollers... it fits most car seats... plastic wheels limit ease of wheeling... small storage basket... "

Micro Stroller

★★★★½

Silver Cross (www.silvercrossbaby.com)
Price .... $110-$130   Seat .... no recline; 5-pt harness
Weight .... 9 lbs   Wheels .... 8x6"; rubber

Parent Reviews: "...the seat doesn't recline at all, which is a big bummer... the folding mechanism is cool and it goes almost completely flat... once folded you can use the carrying strap to throw it over your shoulder—that's key for us subway riders... nice umbrella stroller with smooth rolling rubber wheels... good-sized mesh basket and well-positioned handles... the sun shade really doesn't do much and the rain cover is extra... padded seat, while most other umbrella strollers just have a basic mesh seat..."

Ali's Notes: "...a long-time high-end pram manufacturer, Silver Cross does a high quality chassis with rubber tires for improved durability and maneuverability, and has taken that know-how into the everyday stroller market... while all reports to date on their quality are good, the recent closure of their US distributor makes it a little difficult to predict where this company is going with their new breed of strollers..."

Mini Stroller

Silver Cross (www.silvercrossbaby.com)
Price .... $110-$130   Seat .... recline; 5-pt harness
Weight .... 9 lbs   Wheels .... 8x6"; rubber

Parent Reviews: "...same as the Micro except that the seat does recline a little..."

Quest

★★★★½

Maclaren (www.maclarenbaby.com   877.442.4622)
Price .... $175-$200   Seat .... 4 pos recline; 5-pt harness
Weight .... 14 lbs   Wheels .... 8x5"; plastic

Parent Reviews: "...this is our mall/car/errand/travel stroller—it works for everything but jogging... super lightweight... great for both short and especially tall people—you're not constantly kicking the wheels when pushing... the basket is tiny and hard to reach especially when the seat is back... does not stand on its own when folded... if you are looking for an umbrella stroller, but also want a smooth ride, storage for your stuff and durability, then this is the stroller for you... best everyday mall crawler and errand stroller... not cheap, but typically Maclaren—first rate!..."

Ali's Notes: "...a couple steps up from Maclaren's Volo stroller in terms of plushness... easy one-handed folding (what Maclaren is known for)... great for urban areas or parents-on-the-go for whom an umbrella stroller is a must, but frequent use requires more comfort than a made-for-travel-only umbrella can offer... known for their great colors and fabrics, the Quest is even available in a 'Mod' version for the contemporary chic mom..."

Savvy EX

Combi (www.combi-intl.com 800.992.6624)
Price .... $200-$220 Seat .... full recline; 5-pt harness
Weight .... 18 lbs Wheels .... 8x6"; plastic

Parent Reviews: "...works well with Combi infant car seats—it locks securely into the frame... nice big canopy provides lots of coverage... I love their folding mechanism—just push the button on the handle and voila!... the wheels aren't the greatest and the slightest bit of dirt or gravel throws them off... big storage basket... great everyday-use stroller with all the gizmos like cup holder and big sun canopy... it works great for us..."

Ali's Notes: "...a stroller that's still fairly lightweight but more plush than travel-friendly umbrellas... easy fold and carry... great sun shade, cup holders and pockets for things like keys and wallet... nice big storage basket... the biggest complaint is that the wheels get sticky and squeaky after heavy usage (no different than most plastic-wheeled umbrella strollers)..."

Soho DX

Combi (www.combi-intl.com 800.992.6624)
Price .... $80-$100 Seat ...... partial recline; 5-pt harness
Weight .... 12 lbs Wheels .... 8x6"; plastic

Parent Reviews: "...a great choice for city dwellers... light, but still quite sturdy... the front bar unsnaps so you can swing it forward and junior can jump right in... folds up small enough to fit on the floor behind the back seat of our car... the seat has only a partial recline... it's so small that I was afraid it would be snug and tight, but my son seems comfortable... the handles are a bit low and cannot be adjusted... don't plan on doing all your shopping on foot—the storage basket is quite small... it works with the Combi Connection Infant seat (you need to buy the connection kit separately)..."

Ali's Notes: "...very lightweight, but still sturdy and compact... biggest downside is the partial recline—decide that's what you want before buying, to avoid frustration... plastic wheels mean two-handed steering..."

Soho Sport

★★★★☆

Combi (www.combi-intl.com 800.992.6624)

Price ....$80-$95   Seat ....recline; 5-pt harness
Weight......................... 12 lbs   Wheels .... 8x6"; plastic

Parent Reviews: "...super lightweight and nice compact fold... small canopy, basket and wheels—but I guess that's the trade-off for the mobility... the ideal 'public transportation' stroller—it folds easily into a compact package... our main stroller for air travel... good price point... "

Ali's Notes: "...like Combi's Soho DX, the Sport is very lightweight, sturdy and compact, but with the same downsides... the 'Sport' version adds a little cushion and style that makes it a little better for longer outings (and from the vantage point of your baby's comfort, probably worth the incremental additional weight during transport)... "

Techno Classic

★★★★☆

Maclaren (www.maclarenbaby.com 877.442.4622)

Price ....$290   Seat ....4 pos recline; 5-pt harness
Weight......................... 17 lbs   Wheels .... 8x6.5"; plastic

Parent Reviews: "...a true one-hand fold that's convenient for travel on public transportation... a little heavier than other umbrella strollers, but also a fair bit sturdier... a small, robust little stroller that you can steer with one hand... the handles can be easily adjusted to 3 different height settings... seat reclines all the way... adjustable harness height has given our stroller a longer life... shopping basket is small and will hold just the basics... compact yet sleek looking... easy to carry with the shoulder strap... "

Ali's Notes: "...easy one-handed folding (what Maclaren is known for)... great compartments... compact and easy to carry over the shoulder... comfortable full recline seat... plastic wheels affect maneuverability over time... "

Techno XT

★★★★★

Maclaren (www.maclarenbaby.com 877.442.4622)

Price ....$299   Seat ....4 pos recline; 5-pt harness
Weight......................... 17 lbs   Wheels .... 8x6.5"; plastic

Parent Reviews: "...for newborns on up, this is an awesome stroller... sun shade and rain cover that actually work... my husband is a good 8 inches taller than I am and so we both appreciate the extendable handles (41-44 inches)... lightweight and easy to fold for trips down subway stairs or up into the bus... small enough to fit in the trunk of a taxi... folds like an umbrella stroller... so light that it tips backwards if you have too much stuff hanging from the handles... 4 position recline on seat... the canopy only provides limited protection...

amazing that the wheels survived our short hikes on unpaved roads... "

Ali's Notes: "...easy one-handed folding (what Maclaren is known for)... one of the sturdiest, lightest and most attractive umbrella strollers on the market... extendable handles for taller parents are a particularly rare option on umbrella-style strollers!... this model does the best job of balancing lightweight/travel-friendly with everyday functionality and durability for the value... "

Triumph ★★★★★

Maclaren (www.maclarenbaby.com 877.442.4622)
Price .... $150   Seat.. multi pos recline; 5-pt harness
Weight......................... 12 lbs   Wheels .... 8x4.5"; plastic

Parent Reviews: "...tiny and light as a feather... perfect for when you're on the move... so simple to fold... wheels swivel or lock, but either way they are too small for anything rough... locks itself when folded and carries well with the strap provided... no cup holders... available in lots of cool colors... excellent quality for a reasonable price... steers well with one hand... the seat reclines just enough for a nap... the sunshade doesn't provide a ton of coverage so be prepared to use lots of sunscreen... padded handles are angled and comfortable to push... a super umbrella stroller... "

Ali's Notes: "...a little bigger than the Volo stroller (Maclaren) and with a partially reclining seat... easy one-handed folding (what Maclaren is known for)... good basket access... only a partial recline... super lightweight travel solution (especially for toddlers)... no cup holders... fun colors to choose from... "

Umbrella Stroller ★★★⯪☆

Cosco (www.coscojuvenile.com 800.544.1108)
Price .... $10-$12   Seat .... no recline; 3-pt harness
Weight............................ 9 lbs   Wheels .... 8x4"; plastic

Parent Reviews: "...the smallest, lightest umbrella stroller around... truly tiny... I wasn't thrilled—too hard to push to be of real use... good idea to build such a tiny stroller, but in reality it doesn't hold up the way you want it to... it's so cheap, why wouldn't you get one—even if you only use it a couple of times... compact fold... "

Ali's Notes: "...tiny, tiny, tiny—strollers don't get any lighter... good for older kids... a good option if you need a quick, cheap stroller solution for when your stroller is lost by the airline... for very limited use... "

Volo ★★★★☆

Maclaren (www.maclarenbaby.com 877.442.4622)
Price ....$100   Seat .... no recline; 5-pt harness
Weight........................... 9 lbs   Wheels..................... 8x4.5"; plastic

Parent Reviews: "...a small, robust little stroller that you can steer with one hand... perfect for city cruising—subways, buses, zoo trips and traveling on an airplane... compact and great looking... the smallest stroller Maclaren makes... easy to steer, fold and carry with the built-in carry strap... comfy mesh seat... I can never keep the canopy down when it's windy... too bad the seat doesn't recline... rain gear is extra... handles don't height adjust, but they are tall enough that my husband doesn't keep kicking the wheels with his feet... front wheels lock for cruising or can swivel for easy maneuverability... the best umbrella stroller around... "

Ali's Notes: "...super lightweight—perfect for city, subway, busses, and trips to the zoo... gets pricey (for a lightweight umbrella) when you add up all accessories... surprisingly easy to push for plastic wheels... does not include sun shade or any recline positions (so think toddler use only)... nice shoulder strap for carrying... "

standard strollers

★★★★★
"lila picks"

- ★ Metrolite LE (Graco)
- ★ Pliko P3 (Peg Perego)
- ★ Queen B (BumbleRide)
- ★ Snap N Go (Baby Trend)
- ★ Swing (Zooper)

A3
★★★★☆

Peg Perego (www.pegperego.com 800.671.1701)
Price .... $320-$350   Seat .... full recline; 5-pt harness
Weight......................... 23 lbs   Wheels .... plastic

Parent Reviews: *"...we love how easy it is to use this stroller... the folding mechanism is simple and it even stands on its own when in the folded position... I'm glad I spent the money on this great stroller... big storage bin and very comfy seats... I basically bought it for the reversible handle feature—when my baby was smaller I liked being able to see him..."*

Ali's Notes: *"...think Pliko

stroller (also Peg Perego) but with a nifty reversible handle... sure, you pay a little more, but parents love the functionality... smooth glide and amazingly plush... easy to have baby face either way (a big bonus!)... huge basket for easy storage and shopping... works with Peg Perego car seats... standard plastic wheel issues over time..."*

Acella Alumilite

★★★★★

Safety 1st (www.safety1st.com 800.544.1108)
Price ....$55-$60 Seat ....recline; 5-pt harness
Weight..........................16 lbs Wheels .... 6x8"; plastic

Parent Reviews: "...lightweight and works great for both my kids—I can snap my infant car seat in or leave it as is for my toddler... the head rest is a nice feature for newborns and the child cup holder actually works and holds the cups tightly... the visor is large and really keeps sun and rain off your little ones... one-hand fold works great..."

Ali's Notes: "...nice storage basket... great child tray... fabric stains easily... plastic wheels affect manueverability over time..."

Aria

★★★½☆

Peg Perego (www.pegperego.com 800.671.1701)
Price ....$200-$220 Seat ....3 pos recline; 5-pt harness
Weight..........................13 lbs Wheels ....8X5.5"; plastic

Parent Reviews: "...compatible with the Primo Viaggio infant car seat, but not other brands... a nice-looking, lightweight everyday use stroller... tot tray with cup holder... smallish sunshade—my boy is always squinting... fabrics are wonderful and hold up well to the abuse my kids dish out... folds pretty easily and stands on its own when folded... collapses small and relatively smoothly... partial recline and big basket are amazing given how lightweight this stroller is..."

Ali's Notes: "...the Pliko stroller's (Peg Perego) little brother... a lightweight stroller that can still accommodate an infant seat (Peg Perego only)... smallish sunshade... small plastic wheels means maneuverability will deteriorate over time... very lightweight for such a complete system... good collapsibility..."

Bidwell 905

★★★★½

Bertini (www.bertinistrollers.com 800.746.6463)
Price ....$380-$450 Seat ....recline; 5-pt harness
Weight..........................38 lbs Wheels ...... 4x10" or 12"; air or solid

Parent Reviews: "...a gorgeous pram that converts into a stroller... works like a pram—comfy for baby, but heavy and harder to handle for mom and dad... loaded with cool features... height adjustable handles makes this work for both me and my husband... fully reclining seat for naps... cool turning system that lets both wheels turn at the same time— no more need to tip your pram on the back wheels... bassinet option for babies— but the bassinet and toddler conversion kits are costly and extra... heavy and not ideal for lugging up and down stairs... suspension and soft tires make for a sleep-inducing stroll..."

strollers: standard

Ali's Notes: *"...for the traditional pram lover—the romantic... nice big tires and shocks for even the roughest terrain... extremely sturdy (in part because it's so heavy)... built to last... a traditional-style classic with a very innovative steering mechanism..."*

Camden   ★★★½☆

Silver Cross (www.silvercrossbaby.com)
Price .... $200-$230   Seat .... full recline; 5-pt harness
Weight......................... 16 lbs   Wheels .... 6x6"; rubber

Parent Reviews: *"...nice, classic look and well-designed... I like the way it folds—easy and compact... storage basket is roomy and accessible from all sides... the canopy rolls forward and provides lots of protection and the seat reclines flat... good features but pretty pricey for what you get..."*

Ali's Notes: *"...a long-time high-end pram manufacturer, Silver Cross does a high quality chassis with rubber tires for improved durability and maneuverability and has taken that know-how into the everyday stroller market... while all reports to date on their quality are good, the recent closure of their US distributor makes it a little difficult to predict where this company is going with their new breed of strollers..."*

Comfort Dimensions   ★★★★☆

Evenflo (www.evenflo.com   800.233.5921)
Price .... $55-$80   Seat .... recline; 3-pt harness
Weight.......................... 22 lbs   Wheels .... 4x8" & 2x9"; plastic

Parent Reviews: *"...travel system compatible with the PortAbout and Discovery infant carriers... easy fold... fits well into the trunk of my car with room to spare... lots of storage space... cup holders for me and my baby... plastic wheels roll smoothly on flat surfaces... doesn't handle that well on gravel or dirt paths... I wish more of the padding was removable for laundering... front wheels swivel and all wheels have suspension... I didn't realize how bulky this was until I pushed someone else's lighter stroller..."*

Culla   ★★★★☆

Peg Perego (www.pegperego.com   800.671.1701)
Price .... $670-$690   Seat .... recline; 5-pt harness
Weight.......................... 14 lbs   Wheels .... 4x10"; air

Parent Reviews: *"...a versatile, lightweight pram that converts into a stroller... adjustable handlebar is great... includes a removable bassinet so I don't have to wake my baby when taking him out... baby can face front or back... smooth ride on nice big wheels, but they don't swivel so you constantly have to lift the front wheels in tight spaces... beautiful. Italian fabrics... comes with a mesh anti-bug netting...*

height adjustable handles are nice... truly beautifully crafted... "
Ali's Notes: "...the ultimate in comfort and function... converts from traditional pram to toddler seat... pram doubles as a nice bassinet that can be used apart from stroller... too large for convenient travel... nice Italian finishing... baby faces either way (a big bonus!)...a romantic approach... "

Flyer ★★★★☆

BumbleRide (www.bumbleride.com 800.530.3930)
Price .... $270-$275   Seat .... 4 pos recline; 5-pt harness
Weight .... 22 lbs   Wheels .... 8x8"; plastic

Parent Reviews: "...looks cool, and works really well too... I love the reversible seat so I can see my baby while pushing—it's almost like a pram that way... at first I thought the height adjustable handles were a gimmick, but now I'm amazed at how often we're changing the height... finally, a stroller that doesn't just come in navy blue or some funny checkered pattern... the seat reclines fully, creating a comfy bed... sun canopy provides ample shade... "

Ali's Notes: "...BumbleRide is a relatively new player in the stroller scene and has injected a little more color and style into the category... highly convenient key pocket... adjustable handlebar is great for taller people... no cup holder... heavier weight makes it tougher to travel with but sturdier for everyday usage... baby faces in or out—a must-have feature... "

Glider ★★★★½

Graco (www.gracobaby.com 800.345.4109)
Price .... $70-$100   Seat .... 4 pos recline; 5-pt harness
Weight .... 17 lbs   Wheels .... 6x6"; rubber

Parent Reviews: "...travel system with matching SnugRide infant carrier... 3 cup holders—2 for me and 1 for my baby... lots of undercarriage storage room... easy to use—steer, fold, snap car seat in and out... flat seat recline for nice long naps... foot rest does not height adjust... folds easily, but not as compactly as I'd like... "

Ali's Notes: "...light, but not too compact... works with popular SnugRide car seat for easy travel... solid construction... rubber wheels for better durability... "

strollers: standard

LiteRider ★★★★☆

Graco (www.gracobaby.com 800.345.4109)
Price ....$60-$90   Seat ..... 2 pos recline; 3/5-pt harness
Weight......................... 207 lbs   Wheels ....6x6"; rubber

Parent Reviews: "...you can buy just the stroller, but the real deal is when you buy the full travel system, with infant car seat and base unit for the car... nice rubberized wheels roll much more smoothly than the plastic ones on other strollers... parent and tot trays with cup holders... clock and storage on handle... seat does not recline flat... the height adjustable handle bar is a huge plus... big mesh basket... lots of different colors and patterns to choose from... sturdy, good general use stroller..."

Ali's Notes: "...car seat, carrier and stroller all-in-one... limited recline... nice large basket... rubber wheels for better durability..."

Metrolite LE ★★★★★

Graco (www.gracobaby.com 800.345.4109)
Price .... $160-$200   Seat .... full recline; 3/5-pt harness
Weight.......................... 18 lbs   Wheels ....6x6"; rubber

Parent Reviews: "...for use with the Graco SnugRide infant car seat or as a standalone stroller... great for quick trips or a walk around the neighborhood—the rubber wheels roll smoothly on most surfaces... front wheels swivel for easy maneuvering... high-end European look... love the adjustable handlebar... comes with all the features you might need—bottle holder, basket, roomy hood to keep the sun out of baby's eyes and even a lidded compartment for my keys and wallet... even the most upright position on the adjustable back is still pretty reclined and my daughter couldn't sit up straight, she had to hold onto the snack tray to pull herself up... I'd buy it again any day..."

Ali's Notes: "...generally sold as a travel system along with Graco's ever-popular SnugRide infant car seat... super popular because you get a lot of stroller/travel system for the money... lightweight but very sturdy... great maneuverability thanks to rubber wheels (instead of the usual plastic)... easy one-handed close..."

Pliko P3 MT ★★★★★

Peg Perego (www.pegperego.com 800.671.1701)
Price .... $270-$290   Seat .... full recline; 5-pt harness
Weight.......................... 15 lbs   Wheels ....8x6"; plastic

Parent Reviews: "...a full-size stroller with all the benefits of an umbrella stroller... 4 position seat recline that goes down all the way... 2 separate height adjustable handles... love how easily it folds... all the wheels have independent suspension which makes for a very smooth ride... works as a travel system with the Peg Perego infant car seat... bummer that you can't use other car seats without buying the extra converter bar... lightweight and sturdy... ours lasted through 3 kids... I like *all the rain gear that comes with it... excellent value—I would definitely buy it again...* **"**

Ali's Notes: **"***...the good old Pliko that has become a Peg Perego classic... it's a parent favorite for a reason—slick Italian styling with a plush seat cover (removable and machine-washable)... they are known for their high-quality, complete-system strollers... it works with Peg Perego car seats but you need to invest in an adapter if you want to use something else... if you've heard complaints about the folding mechanism you can relax—the new version has a much-improved folding mechanism...* **"**

Quattro Tour ★★★½☆

Graco (www.gracobaby.com   800.345.4109)
Price .... $100-$140   Seat .... full recline; 3/5-pt harness
Weight.......................... 28 lbs   Wheels .... 6x6"; rubber

Parent Reviews: **"***...the travel system comes with the awesome SnugRide infant car seat... seat reclines flat for comfy nap time... easy to open and close with one hand... roomy basket lets me take all the stuff we need to the park... fairly easy to handle and maneuver... big when folded which makes it hard to fit in the trunk of my small sedan... the fabric is machine washable but annoying to get off... cup holders for both parent and baby... big rubberized wheels can be locked or swivel... smooth ride on most city surfaces... awesome value for the price...* **"**

Ali's Notes: **"***...comfortable for baby and mom, but heavy... best for the suburban family that can stroll straight from home... don't even think about it if you're using public transportation...* **"**

Queen B ★★★★★

BumbleRide (www.bumbleride.com   800.530.3930)
Price .... $315-$340   Seat ....4 pos recline; 5-pt harness
Weight................................ 31   Wheels .... 4x12"; air

Parent Reviews: **"***...if a pram-style stroller is what you're looking for, then look no further... this is the modern version of the Mary Poppins pram but not nearly as expensive as other brands out there... you can use it as a pram or as a stroller... handle height can be adjusted and it's super-easy to push... it folds simply by collapsing in on itself (wheels have quick release)... lots of padding for infants and toddlers... a smooth, but pricey ride...* **"**

Ali's Notes: **"***...a cute old-fashioned-like pram that is reasonably priced (compared to other pram options like Silver Cross)... the best part is that you can reverse the seat to convert it from a pram into a stroller... it also has a nifty additional seat that can be attached just above the regular seat (limited use and for small tots only)... if your heart is set on a pram style stroller then, given these great features, this is the one to get...* **"**

Rhumba

★★★★½

Zooper (www.zooperstrollers.com 503.248.9469)
Price .... $125-$140   Seat ....recline; 5-pt harness
Weight......................... 17 lbs   Wheels .... 8x6"; plastic

Parent Reviews: "...a great versatile stroller... light enough for trips to the mall yet sturdy enough for lots of outdoor walks in the neighborhood... adjustable handle height is such a plus... the seat does not recline all the way... easy to fold one-handed and light enough to be lifted into the car while balancing my baby on my hip... I can easily loop a shopping bag or diaper backpack over the handles without tipping the stroller... comes with a nice big sun, bug and rain shield... all the wheels have separate suspension..."

Ali's Notes: "...Zooper continues to deliver on their growing reputation for quality at a midpoint price... this is Zooper's lightweight travel model..."

S300 Formula Wheel Deluxe Stroller

★★★★½

Compass (www.compassbaby.com 888.899.2229)
Price .... $120-$140   Seat ....3 pos recline; 5 pt harness
Weight......................... 27 lbs   Wheels ....6x8"

Parent Reviews: "...compatible with most major-brand infant car seats... fully reclining seat... super-sturdy aluminum frame with smooth-rolling wheels... sturdy child drink tray and soft, 'fanny pack-like' bag on the handle for parent... cool reversible handle so you can quickly and easily switch from toddler mode to having your babe face you... large storage compartment under the seat... sun shade provides ample coverage... a very innovative and well-made stroller..."

Ali's Notes: "...a solid and very durable stroller for the money... known for their clever designs, Compass delivers great quality for the price... it works well from infant to toddler (compatible with most major brand infant car seats)... nice reversible handle to face baby (front wheels don't swivel in carriage position so it can be difficult to maneuver when in this position)... plastic wheels translate to two-handed stroller maneuvering, particularly over time and with usage..."

Snap N Go

★★★★★

Baby Trend (www.babytrend.com 800.328.7363)
Price .... $30-$60   Seat .... n/a
Weight ....   Wheels .... 6x7"; plastic

Parent Reviews: "...a pretty basic design that works so well for infant car seats... all the features you'll need in an umbrella stroller... quite sturdy for its size... you can't beat the price... the 4-way fold is very compact but it took me a few tries to figure it out... little wheels don't provide the smoothest ride over longer distances... huge amount of storage space for such a little thing... for the price you can't go wrong with this one... "

Ali's Notes: 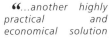 "...another highly practical and economical solution by Baby Trend... light and easy to use... enormous basket for holding a diaper bag and other gear... a universal system that works with almost every car seat... the perfect, occasional-use car seat companion... "

Swift

★★★☆☆

Inglesina (www.inglesina.us 877.486.5112)
Price .... $100-$110   Seat .... 3 pos recline; 5-pt harness
Weight .... 11 lbs   Wheels .... 8x6"; plastic

Parent Reviews: "...not quite a full-size stroller, but sturdier than an umbrella stroller... good for traveling... folds down quickly which is a plus when boarding a bus or plane... I love that it has a big basket, how far the seat reclines back and how easy it is to handle and steer... it's a pain getting at the basket when the seat is reclined... the one-hand fold isn't as easy as they make it sound... no cup holders for parents... too flimsy for long- distance strolling, but perfect for everyday outings... "

Swing

★★★★★

Zooper (www.zooperstrollers.com 503.248.9469)
Price .... $200-$210   Seat .... full recline; 5-pt harness
Weight .... 19 lbs   Wheels . 4x6" front; 4x7" rear; plastic

Parent Reviews: "...this stroller takes a beating and just keeps on going...smooth and comfy ride... comes with all the bells and whistles, like rain cover and extra sunshade... seat has full recline... height adjustable handles... infant carrier compatible, but can be used for infants even without the carrier, as it comes with an infant head support... pretty limited storage space and no place for a cup holder... reasonably light, folds easily and is very cool-looking... "

Ali's Notes: "...known for its swivel front wheel and suspension seat built for baby's comfort, the Zooper is all about easy maneuverability... all the bells and whistles... the basket could be bigger... "

Towne

Silver Cross (www.silvercrossbaby.com)
Price .... $300-$320   Seat .... full recline; 5-pt harness
Weight.......................... 21 lbs
Wheels 2x10" back/2x6" front; rubber

Parent Reviews: *"...one of the neatest-looking strollers I've seen—it's sleek and looks kind of like a space ship... long and sleek with lots of extras (for an extra price) like the foot muff... front wheels swivel or can be locked which makes it pretty versatile in terms of maneuverability... there's barely any storage though... although it has shock absorbers, it's not ideal for hiking... first class fabrics..."*

Ali's Notes: *"...a long-time high-end pram manufacturer, Silver Cross does a high quality chassis with rubber tires for improved durability and maneuverability and has taken that know-how into the everyday stroller market... while all reports on their quality to date are good, the recent closure of their US distributor makes it a little difficult to predict where this company is going with their new breed of strollers..."*

Universal Car Seat Carrier

Kolcraft (www.kolcraft.com 800.453.7673)
Price ....$50-$60   Seat .... separate infant car seats
Weight.......................... 13 lbs   Wheels .... 6x7"; plastic

Parent Reviews: *"...truly the best thing ever for hauling a little one around with you... compatible with pretty much every brand of infant car seat... easy to fold... easily accessible basket is generously sized for all of my stuff... I lamented when my son grew out of this product—it was his bed, rocker, car seat—all in one... I've even wheeled it around the house from room to room—it's so maneuverable... connecting the car seat to the stroller is a snap... dual front wheels that swivel and roll over pretty much anything you'll encounter in the city..."*

Ali's Notes: *"...the 'other Snap N Go'... small, lightweight, easy to use with almost any infant car seat... generous basket... good value for first stage stroller..."*

participate in our survey at

Venezia

★★★☆☆

Peg Perego (www.pegperego.com 800.671.1701)
Price .... $350-$380   Seat .... full recline; 5-pt harness
Weight.......................... 21 lbs   Wheels .... 8x6.5"; plastic

Parent Reviews: *"...easy to push infants in carriage mode and then switch to stroller for larger kids—simply change the position of the handle... handle height can also be adjusted... can be used with Peg Perego's Primo Viaggio car seat, but not other brands... canopy folds down completely over baby providing protection against sun and rain... the foot rest folds up for small babies to rest their feet... the storage basket is large, but can be hard to get to... front wheels lock or swivel... plastic wheels provide an average ride on anything less than smooth sidewalk... love the classic look and fabric..."*

Waltz

★★★★☆

Zooper (www.zooperstrollers.com 503.248.9469)
Price .... $150-$175   Seat .... full recline; 5-pt harness
Weight.......................... 16 lbs   Wheels .... 6x6"; plastic

Parent Reviews: *"...great Zooper quality and design... fully reclining seat with ample padding... works with infant carriers from several different manufacturers... small wheels aren't ideal for anything but really smooth surfaces... really big storage basket with room for everything you might need... front wheels swivel or lock with a snap... handles cannot height adjust which drives my husband crazy... a great product that I'd definitely recommend to other parents..."*

Ali's Notes: *"...great value for the money... compared to other strollers in the 'light' stroller category, this one gives you a lot for the money... all about easy maneuverability... it works well with infant car seats... full reclining seat is a big draw... ample padding... like other strollers with little wheels it's not great on uneven surfaces..."*

strollers: standard

Xplory

Stokke (www.stokkeusa.com   877.978.6553)
Price .... $750-$775   Seat ....3 pos recline; 5-pt harness
Weight.......................... 23 lbs   Wheels................................ rubber

Parent Reviews: *"...I love the unique design—it looks like the 'un-stroller'... quite functional and very easy to maneuver... quite expensive, but I guess if you want style you have to be willing to pay for it... nice rubber wheels and very lightweight..."*

Ali's Notes: *"...the Xplory is all about city dwelling with your baby—making it easier to go up and down stairs (with one hand), and bringing your baby to eye level (rather than street level)... plan extra time into your journey to take into account all of the people that are going to stop you to ask you about it... the biggest drawback is that it doesn't work with infant car seats... cool, contemporary design with easy handling... adjustable handles are great for tall parents..."*

participate in our survey at

all terrain strollers

★★★★★ "lila picks"

- ★ Boogie (Zooper)
- ★ Cameleon (Bugaboo)
- ★ e3 Explorer (Phil & Ted's)
- ★ Urban Single (Mountain Buggy)

Boogie ★★★★★

Zooper (www.zooperstrollers.com 503.248.9469)
Price .... $250-$290   Seat .... full recline; 5-pt harness
Weight .... 31 lbs   Wheels .... 3x12"; air

Parent Reviews: "...a slick, all-around stroller that will roll over anything, anywhere... it's true, the pivoting front wheel literally lets it turn on a dime... works great both as a city stroller and a jogger... compatible with most major-brand infant carriers... front wheel locks or swivels with the flick of a switch on the handle... handle can be adjusted to different heights... great pouch holds extra blankets, toys and mommy's drink... decadent—but it was by far the coolest gift we received... I worry about leaving it unattended because it looks like a stroller that's worth a lot of money... a bit heavy for actually jogging with, but works well for hiking... "

Ali's Notes: "...talk about features—it comes fully loaded with a fully reclining, reversible seat, smooth-riding wheels (the front wheel locks or swivels) and an enormous storage bin... Zooper deserves their great reputation for quality at a reasonable price and this is the stroller that proves it... "

www.lilaguide.com

Breeze ★★★½☆

Mountain Buggy (www.mountainbuggyusa.com 866.524.8805)
Price .... $280-$310   Seat .... full recline; 5-pt harness
Weight.......................... 14 lbs   Wheels .... 3x10"; air

Parent Reviews: "...the Terrain's little brother—same great design and features but lighter and smaller... definitely not for running, but great if you have to roll over some rough patches with your baby... the handle can be adjusted to different heights... aluminum frame is sturdy and doesn't rust... the sun shade is pretty skimpy so bring some sunscreen in that big mesh basket..."

Cameleon ★★★★★

Bugaboo (www.bugaboo.com 800.460.2922)
Price .... $879   Seat .... 3 pos recline; 5-pt harness
Weight.......................... 20 lbs   Wheels .... 2x6" front/12" back; air

Parent Reviews: "...the 'souped-up' version of the original Frog... very expensive, but it has so many features other strollers don't have... well-made... height adjustable handle (up to 44.5 inches!)... large seat and sun canopy... you can pick a base color for the stroller and then pick different colors and fabrics for the seat inlay, apron and sun canopy... all the bells and whistles you may (or may not) want... it rolls so smoothly and the handlebar is reversible so you can have the big wheels in front or in the back... suspension on the little wheels... a very well-designed piece of equipment... do try it out before you buy, as it's quite an investment..."

Ali's Notes: "...nice improvements upon the original Frog (the stroller responsible for strollers being a big celebrity me-too press topic in recent years!) in 3 important ways—you can lock out suspension during pram stage (better for baby); it offers height adjustable steering for different-sized parents, and it makes the 'lifetime' promise more palatable by allowing you to change/update colors (hence the 'chameleon-inspired' name)... finishing touches are upgraded (fabrics, bassinet, cushioning by Aerosleep, etc.)... so far reviews are mixed about the new fleece fabric, and at almost $900 (almost $200 more than the original Frog) it's inarguably expensive... if you're a designer-inspired shopper, keep your eye out for their 'designer feature' model appearing next year..."

e3 Explorer

★★★★★

Phil & Ted's (www.philandteds.com)
Price .... $375-$395   Seat .... 3 pos recline; 5 pt harness
Weight .... 21 lbs   Wheels .... 3x12"; air

Parent Reviews: "...very cool-looking and very useful... spend the extra dollars to get the extra, low riding seat... at first I thought my kids wouldn't like riding in the back, but now my kids actually squabble over who gets to sit in the 'cool' seat... the best alternative to those enormous double strollers... air filled tires and a swivel wheel in the front make it easy to use both on rough surfaces and at the mall... sun canopy doesn't provide very much sun coverage... we get stopped all the time by other parents asking us about our stroller... worth every penny... the most versatile single/double stroller out there... the only design flaw is that I kick the bottom seat when it's attached..."

Ali's Notes: "...the latest edition from this innovative New Zealand gear manufacturer... kids seem to love being in the low-rider back seat... narrow and nimble (particularly for navigating urban streets with 2!)...rugged enough for trails... my favorite mid-priced stroller with a real 2-kid solution..."

Gecko

★★★★⯨

Bugaboo (www.bugaboo.com 800.460.2922)
Price .... $679   Seat .... 3 pos recline; 5-pt harness
Weight .... 18 lbs   Wheels .... 2x6" front/12" back; air

Parent Reviews: "...the trimmed down and cheaper version of the Frog... it's like NASA engineered this thing... everything about it is well made... it reverses so you can push with small wheels in front for maneuverability, or with large wheels in front on rugged terrain... such a cool-looking stroller and so well-designed... if you can afford it, you'll definitely get your money's worth... the same basic functionality as the Frog, but with less padding and extras... before you buy, carefully compare with the Cameleon and other brands to make sure you get all the features you want..."

Ali's Notes: "...a 3-in-1 system that accommodates a bassinet, seat and car seat in one lightweight, easy-to-maneuver package... the tradeoffs for the reduced weight are a slightly less convenient seat-adjustment mechanism and a pram that doesn't work as a bassinet off the stroller quite as well as the original Frog afforded... all the styling of the original Frog with a little savings..."

Jazz

★★★★☆

Zooper (www.zooperstrollers.com 503.248.9469)
Price .... $250-$270   Seat .... recline; 5-pt harness
Weight .... 18 lbs   Wheels .... 3x10"; rubber

Parent Reviews: "...height adjustable handle and rolls so smoothly... so modern looking—I love the design... it comes with all the extras you might want—lockable front swivel wheel, full boot, big basket... you can lock the front wheel by clicking a button on the handle bar—no need to stop, crouch down and get your hands dirty... incredibly light and easy to push... huge shopping basket—I fit my whole backpack under there..."

Ali's Notes: "...great for joggers, good height adjustable handle... great design... terrific storage bin... nice accessory options... not good for newborns—too large for them... no reversible mode... good front wheel option, lock or swivel..."

Rocket Stroller

★★★★☆

BumbleRide (www.bumbleride.com 800.530.3930)
Price .... $285-$295   Seat .... 4 pos recline; 5-pt harness
Weight .... 25 lbs   Wheels .... 3x12"; air

Parent Reviews: "...almost like a jogger, but not quite... love the front swivel wheel—it definitely extends the stroller's usefulness in tight spaces like the mall... good shade, plush material and nice big air-filled tires—a cozy ride for my baby and easy pushing for me... I'm short and my husband is tall, so this was one of the only options as far as the height adjustable handle... nice color choices... the backrest can be put down all the way so you basically end up with a rolling bassinet..."

Ali's Notes:  "...a competitively priced all-terrain stroller that rolls smoothly and wears well... BumbleRide is known for manufacturing a robust stroller with more interesting colors than the standard navy blue... cute, but on the heavier side..."

Runabout

★★★★½

Valco Baby (www.valcobaby.com)
Price .... $340-$360   Seat .... full recline; 5-pt harness
Weight.......................... 25 lbs   Wheels .... 3x10"; air

Parent Reviews: "...solid and well-built... smooth steering beyond belief... nice double compact fold... swiveling front tire makes it a jogger when locked or a mall stroller when in swivel mode... the coolest thing is the add-on toddler seat that sits in front of the main seat... why buy a big double for kids of different ages?.. great quality, nice fabrics, and easy pop-off tires... the storage basket could be bigger, but it works well enough for basics like jackets and sunscreen... padded cushion fits into the seat to provide extra support for infants..."

Ali's Notes: "...fantastic steering, nice option for swivel or locked front wheel... accommodates toddler seat in front (but with no head support—so not for off-roading or a sleeping toddler... heavy..."

Shuttle

★★★★½

Bertini (www.bertinistrollers.com   800.746.6463)
Price .... $270-$330   Seat ....recline; 5-pt harness
Weight.......................... 30 lbs   Wheels .... 4x12"; air

Parent Reviews: "...the ultimate strolling machine... combines the best features of a pram with a jogging stroller... Bertini's steering system is very cool—both sets of wheels turn at the same time or can be locked... classy European design and so well made... it handles pretty much any terrain and is completely steerable... the handle moves up and down to accommodate my husband's height... it's huge even when folded... it's pretty heavy for a single stroller, but surprisingly steerable... unlike the other Bertini models, the seat in the Shuttle is only forward-facing..."

Terrain Single

★★★★☆

Mountain Buggy (www.mountainbuggyusa.com   866.524.8805)
Price .... $340-$360   Seat ....recline; 5-pt harness
Weight.......................... 21 lbs   Wheels .... 3x12"; air

Parent Reviews: "...simple, solid build that offers a high weight limit—up to 100 pounds... well-made... basic, lightweight but solid construction... nice big treaded tires... front wheel does not swivel which is good when you're on rough surfaces, but cumbersome at the mall... full recline on the seat is nice... additional accessories can turn this stroller into a pram with the optional carry cot or car seat adapter... I love the large storage baskets and extra pockets for blankets, IDs, etc... no height

adjustment on handlebar... probably not ideal for the serious runner... as bare-bones as it gets... "

Ali's Notes: "...known for its solid construction, this Mountain Buggy stroller is a big hit among parents who need to roll their tots over more than the smooth floor of the local mall... basic, no-frills construction... not the cheapest all-terrain stroller out there, but I rarely meet owners who aren't highly satisfied with their purchase... if only the US distributor would bring over the fun, bright fabrics available in Europe... "

TT Safari ★★★★½
InStep (www.instep.net)
Price .... $160-$175   Seat .... recline; 5-pt harness
Weight .... 21 lbs   Wheels .... 1x12" & 2x16"; air

Parent Reviews: "...so easy to push and turn that we use it as our 'regular' stroller... jogger type design with a nice front swivel wheel... lightweight... big pocket in back for parents to store supplies... my husband is 6'4" and even he can walk or jog with this stroller... smooth ride... the canopy doesn't block the sun well enough... good value as far as jogging strollers go... "

Urban Single ★★★★★
Mountain Buggy (www.mountainbuggyusa.com 866.524.8805)
Price .... $400-$410   Seat .... full recline; 5-pt harness
Weight .... 22 lbs   Wheels .... 3x12"; air

Parent Reviews: "...the front wheel swivels or can be locked depending on where you are... extra accessories can turn this stroller into a pram with the optional carry cot or car seat adapter... I love the large storage baskets and extra pockets for blankets, IDs and extras... full seat recline... no height adjustment on handlebar... the seat padding isn't the most plush... super-easy fold doesn't require having to take off the wheels... a considerable investment but you're going to love every minute using it... "

Ali's Notes: "...known for its solid construction, this Mountain Buggy stroller is a big hit among parents who need to roll their tots over more than the smooth floor of the local mall... the secret to the Urban Single's success is its basic, no-frills construction... not the cheapest all-terrain stroller out there, but I rarely meet owners who aren't highly satisfied with their purchase... "

Zydeco

★★★★½

Zooper (www.zooperstrollers.com 503.248.9469)
Price .... $350-$390   Seat ....recline; 5-pt harness
Weight.......................... 31 lbs   Wheels........................... 3x12"; air

Parent Reviews: "...all the fancy European brands rolled into one... infant carrier compatible... the swiveling front wheel makes it easy to steer in tight spaces (it locks by pushing a button on the handle bar)... the seat is reversible and reclines fully so you can use it when your tot is a baby as well as sitting upright... my husband loves being able to adjust the height of the handlebars... huge, spacious and easily accessible storage bin... easy to fold... people are always commenting on its sporty design... shock absorbers under the seat and big air-filled wheels make for a smooth, snooze-inducing ride... comes with all the bells and whistles, including rain and sun cover..."

Ali's Notes: "...known for its swivel front wheel and suspension seat built for baby's comfort, the Zooper is all about easy maneuverability... as plush as it is functional, this stroller provides lots of style and value... the fully-loaded Zydeco is not well-suited to travel given its weight... Zooper continues to deliver on their growing reputation for quality at a midpoint price..."

multi-use

joggers

"lila picks"

★ Ironman Sport Utility (BOB Strollers)
★ Speedster Deluxe (Kelty)

Deluxe Sport Utility Stroller ★★★★☆

BOB Strollers (www.bobstrollers.com 800.893 2447)
Price .... $349   Seat .... recline; 5-pt harness
Weight .... 21 lbs   Wheels .... 3x16"; air

Parent Reviews: *"...just like the original Sports Utility Stroller but a little lighter and with aluminum wheels... large, smooth-rolling wheels—it's a pleasure pushing it... the suspension offers a smooth ride on both trails and city streets... extra-wide seat is more comfortable for my boy... rounded canopy with variable positions to block the sun... easy to fold and unlike other models I've tried, it actually stays together... storage space behind and below the seat... a slick jogger that's worth every penny..."*

Ali's Notes: *"...smooth ride over bumpy terrain... great for off-road... has great wind/sun/insect shield attachment option... BOB joggers defined the stroller 'cross-trainer' market and continue to be the all-sport-utility of baby joggers..."*

Expedition LX

★★★★☆

Baby Trend (www.babytrend.com 800.328.7363)
Price ....$150   Seat ....recline; 5-pt harness
Weight.......................... 24 lbs   Wheels ....3x16"; air

Parent Reviews: **"**...a sturdy, steel frame jogger... the huge tires are great for bumpy dirt roads... the moveable sun visor is key... the mud guard helps keep everyone clean on those wet, muddy days... cup holders for everyone... I love the fact that the top has a window in it so I can see my daughter while I'm pushing her... bulky and difficult to put in my car... not ideal for use as your only stroller—too big for everyday/city use... **"**

multi-use

Ali's Notes: **"**...great, easy-to-use car seat adapter allows jogging with infant... easy folding system... great, easy safety elements, easy to use without restricting jogging... Baby Trend makes some of the most popular all-utility joggers on the market today... **"**

EZ Strider Single

InStep (www.instep.net)
Price ....$120-$125   Seat ....recline; 5-pt harness
Weight.......................... 26 lbs   Wheels ....3x16"; air

Ali's Notes: **"**...quite long in all positions... works in any environment... fantastic as jogging stroller... a bit light on padding for the seat... sufficient storage... great maneuverability... **"**

Ironman Sport Utility

★★★★★

BOB Strollers (www.bobstrollers.com 800.893 2447)
Price ....$349-$359   Seat ....recline; 5-pt harness
Weight.......................... 20 lbs   Wheels ....3x16"; air

Parent Reviews: **"**...for the serious runner... light weight with slick tires... made for cruising on all kinds of surfaces—my son loves it... suspension you can adjust as your baby gets heavier... huge aluminum wheels... the canopy provides a decent amount of protection even when it drizzles... not the easiest to steer when shopping... extra large basket is easily accessible even when the seat is reclined... quick-release wheels, but we virtually always leave them on when we fold it up... this stroller rocks... **"**

travel

Ali's Notes: **"**...the ultimate for road runners (though a bit big/heavy for long-distance runners)... very easy to fold up... great canopy... made for cruising on all kinds of surfaces... adjustable suspension as baby grows... BOB joggers defined the stroller 'cross-trainer' market and continue to be the all-sport-utility of baby joggers... **"**

Performance Series Single
Baby Jogger (www.babyjogger.com 800.241.1848)
Price .... $320-$340   Seat .... recline; 5-pt harness
Weight .... 22 lbs   Wheels .... 3x16"/20"; air

Q Single
Baby Jogger (www.babyjogger.com 800.241.1848)
Price .... $300-$350   Seat .... recline; 5-pt harness
Weight .... 18 lbs   Wheels .... 3x12"/16"; air

Reebok Velocity Extreme   ★★★★☆
Baby Trend (www.babytrend.com 800.328.7363)
Price .... $190-$200   Seat .... 2 pos recline; 5-pt harness
Weight .... 25 lbs   Wheels .... 3x16"; air

Parent Reviews: *"...a fast jogger for those of us who like to run versus jog... lightweight aluminum with huge wheels... canopy is slick and doesn't catch too much wind... made from good-looking, durable fabric that can take a beating... wheels come off easily which makes transportation much more feasible... bulky if you're in a mall, but perfect out on a dirt trail... adjustable rear suspension depending on where we go to explore... great value for the price..."*

Ali's Notes: *"...great shock absorption, not great sun cover... stroller pulls to the side (instructions tell you how to correct)... very comfortable... huge basket..."*

Revolution   ★★★★☆
BOB Strollers (www.bobstrollers.com 800.893 2447)
Price .... $330-$360   Seat .... part. recline; 5-pt harness
Weight .... 23 lbs   Wheels .... 3x16"/20"; air

Parent Reviews: *"...the front wheel locks or swivels... it's a great jogger that can also be used easily at the mall... like all BOB strollers this one is super-sturdy and well-made... good for running, strolling and even quick trips to the store... great sun/rain canopy..."*

Ali's Notes: *"...BOB joggers defined the stroller 'cross-trainer' market and continue to be the all-sport-utility of baby joggers... the Revolution improves the classic for running without compromising the all-utility extras that make BOB the overall 'active parent' favorite..."*

Speedster Deluxe

Kelty (www.kelty.com 866.349.7225)
Price .... $300-$325   Seat ....recline; 5-pt harness
Weight........................... 24 lbs   Wheels............................3x16"; air

Parent Reviews: " ...nice big wheels... a long frame—works for bigger kids too... height adjustable handle—that means both my husband and I can run with the same jogger... well-balanced which makes it easy to push when running... not great for everyday use—too big and difficult to maneuver... very easy to fold... sturdy and steady even when you're running fast... great sun and rain shade... the seat does not recline at all, but is naturally angled backwards... good-sized storage bin under the seat... feels like it could last through 10 kids... "

Ali's Notes: " ...fantastic runner's stroller...not great for crowded places due to maneuverability... nice adjustable handlebar... great storage... very easy to fold... built to last... Kelty makes true runner's joggers... "

Sport Utility Stroller

BOB Strollers (www.bobstrollers.com 800.893 2447)
Price .... $240-$299   Seat ....recline; 5-pt harness
Weight........................... 22 lbs   Wheels............................3x16"; air

Parent Reviews: " ...a slick jogger that's worth every penny... if you're serious about running with your baby, this is the one to get... the suspension offers a smooth ride on trails and city streets... shock absorbers are adjustable... canopy with variable positions to block the sun... good height for taller people—but okay for shorties too... easy to fold and unlike other models it stays together... available in green, blue and black... it requires a fair bit of strength to collapse... no full recline, but it seems comfortable enough for long naps... sturdy aluminum frame... top of the line... "

Ali's Notes: " ...BOB joggers defined the stroller 'cross-trainer' market and continue to be the all-sport-utility of baby jogger... great maneuverability... requires a lot of space... terrific suspension... good height for tall people... better for off-road runners than long-distance runners... "

doubles & triples

★★★★★ "lila picks"

- ★ Duette (Peg Perego)
- ★ DuoGlider (Graco)
- ★ e3 (Phil & Ted's)
- ★ Twin Traveller (Maclaren)
- ★ Urban Double (Mountain Buggy)

Aria Twin ★★★★☆

Peg Perego (www.pegperego.com 800.671.1701)
Price .... $330-$360   Seat..recline; side-by-side; 5-pt harn
Weight......................... 15 lbs   Wheels .... 8X5.5"; plastic

Parent Reviews: "...the best lightweight double stroller—light enough to take everywhere... well-made... the sunshades are kind of skimpy and we end up having to improvise shade... small wheels can make it hard to maneuver especially when fully loaded with both kids..."

Ali's Notes: "...known for its super-light weight—only 15 lbs!.. seats don't recline all the way which can make stroller naps a little more challenging... a good choice for urban parents who need to wheel 2 tots around... better on smooth surfaces... although lightweight, still good quality..."

Axiom Ditto

★★★☆☆

Dreamer Design (www.dreamerdesign.net 509.574.8085)
Price .... $650-$670   Seat .. recline; side-by-side; 5-pt harn
Weight......................... 29 lbs   Wheels............................3x16"; air

Parent Reviews: "...huge wheels make for a smooth ride... separate sun canopies... nonadjustable padded handle with wrist strap... if you think you're going to go running with 2 tots then this is your best bet... hard to turn when fully loaded—this has less to do with the stroller than it does with the fact that you're pushing close to 60 pounds... well-made with nice materials... "

Bidwell Twin

★★★★½

Bertini (www.bertinistrollers.com 203.348.7466)
Price .... $585-$620   Seat .... side-by-side; 5-pt harness
Weight......................... 43 lbs   Wheels............................4x12"; air

Parent Reviews: "...very fancy double pram with fabulous air-filled tires... built for Mary Poppins and those bumpy cobblestone roads... all 4 wheels turn, making it really easy to maneuver... the handlebar adjusts to various heights... the bassinet is removable so you use the stroller for bigger kids too... independently reclining backrests, but only one canopy... extra accessories will put an added dent in your wallet, but are well worth it if you can afford it... enormous and bulky, but so cool looking—expect a few stares from other parents... "

Domino Trio

★★★★☆

Inglesina (www.inglesina.us 877.486.5112)
Price .... $675-$800   Seat .... recline; 5-pt harness
Weight......................... 69 lbs   Wheels...................... 6x10"; rubber

Parent Reviews: "...an enormous contraption, but how else am I going to get around with 3 babies... you can fit an infant car seat on each of the three seats... the seats swivel, so babies can face each other, forward, or face mommy while you walk... incredibly sturdy... not easy to steer and maneuver given how big it is, but given your options, the Trio works pretty well... front wheels can be either swiveling fixed... seats have multiple recline positions... large metal storage basket... removable, washable upholstery... "

strollers: doubles & triples

Domino Twin ★★★½☆

Inglesina (www.inglesina.us 877.486.5112)
Price .... $500-$550   Seat ...... recline; in-line; 5-pt harness
Weight.......................... 57 lbs   Wheels .... 6x10"; rubber

Parent Reviews: "...as far as doubles go, this is by far the best stroller I have ever pushed... it is well-built, and thoroughly thought-out... very comfortable for both babies... beautiful, eye-catching design... the biggest downside is that it's still huge, even when folded—it barely fits in our minivan..."

Duallie Sport Utility ★★★★½

BOB Strollers (www.bobstrollers.com 800.893 2447)
Price ....$429   Seat .... recline; 5-pt harness
Weight.......................... 30 lbs   Wheels .... 3x16"; air

Parent Reviews: "...a versatile double jogger... adjustable springs depending on the load you're carrying... adjustable height on the handles—a feature that goes a long way given how often my husband and I switch using it... a little light on seat cushioning... only one canopy for both passengers which isn't always very practical... nice big wheels make this a feasible choice even for more serious runners... reasonably light for a double... folds well... the Deluxe model comes with aluminum wheels rather than the plastic ones..."

Ali's Notes: "...BOB joggers defined the stroller 'cross-trainer' market and continue to be the all-sport-utility of baby joggers... heavier than some more streamlined-runner solutions... the upside of the cross-trainer approach is their all-utility appeal for on and off-road flexibility..."

multi-use

Duette ★★★★★

Peg Perego (www.pegperego.com 800.671.1701)
Price .... $550-$580   Seat ...... recline; in-line; 5-pt harness
Weight.......................... 33 lbs   Wheels .... 8X7.5 inch; plastic

Parent Reviews: "...a pretty cool contraption indeed... both seats can face forward, backwards or each other... it's one of the few doubles that works with infant car seats (Peg Perego only) in both seats at the same time... I love how my girls can entertain one another by facing each other... the suspension is wonderful for those uneven sidewalks... I love the ample cargo basket—more than enough room for all our stuff and groceries too... large, heavy and expensive... the stroller base folds nicely, but then you have 2 separate seats you need to store..."

Ali's Notes: "...it's heavy and loaded to the gills with features you'll like for lugging 2 kids and all their gear... the storage basket is enormous... best of all, both seats are reversible and you can attach 2 infant seats at the same time (absolutely necessary for parents of twins)..."

multi-use

DuoGlider

★★★★★

Graco (www.gracobaby.com 800.345.4109)
Price .... $130-$180   Seat .... in-line; 3-pt harness
Weight......................... 33 lbs   Wheels .... 6x9"; plastic

Parent Reviews: "...it fits both my kids and lots of stuff underneath... car seats snap in and out without problems... too bad it only works with Graco infant car seats... big wheels make pushing easy and comfortable... it became quite hard to steer once my little ones got bigger... huge storage basket... snack trays and cup holders for both kids... sun canopies provide a good amount of shade—especially the rear one... although the covers are washable they are a pain to take off and put back on... quite big and bulky even when folded, but still beats lugging 2 separate strollers around... "

Ali's Notes: "...parents love the 'stadium seating' so the tot in the back still feels like he can be part of the action.. accommodates infant carriers in either or both seats (at the same time)... seat cushions are not the easiest to remove and clean... with a Graco car seat purchase, this is an overall good value option, especially for twins... "

multi-use

DuoRider

★★★★½

Graco (www.gracobaby.com 800.345.4109)
Price .... $100-$130   Seat .... side-by-side; 3-pt harness
Weight......................... 23 lbs   Wheels .... 6x9"; plastic

Parent Reviews: "...a very lightweight and roomy double stroller... this stroller was so easy for our twins... car seats snap in and out without problems... both seats recline for napping... storage space that's actually usable and easily reachable... it was great with our twin babies and continues to work wonderfully with our now twin toddlers... it became quite hard to steer once my little ones got bigger... wheels were squeaky from the get-go... kinda bulky to transport and takes up a lot of space in the trunk... the patterns are not the prettiest... infant car seats are separate... "

Ali's Notes: "...independently reclining seats are key... both seats will take a SnugRide infant car seat (it feels strange to push when you have just one infant seat installed without any counterweight in the other seat)... very lightweight and you can't beat the price... "

strollers: doubles & triples

e3 Explorer ★★★★★

Phil & Ted's (www.philandteds.com)
Price .... $375-$395
Weight.......................... 21 lbs
Seat .... 3 pos recline; 5 pt harness
Wheels .... 3x12"; air

Parent Reviews: "...very cool-looking and very useful... spend the extra dollars to get the extra, low riding seat... at first I thought my kids wouldn't like riding in the back, but now my kids actually squabble over who gets to sit in the 'cool' seat... the best alternative to those enormous double strollers... air filled tires and a swivel wheel in the front make it easy to use both on rough surfaces and at the mall... sun canopy doesn't provide very much sun coverage... we get stopped all the time by other parents asking us about our stroller... worth every penny... the most versatile single/double stroller out there... the only design flaw is that I kick the bottom seat when it's attached..."

Ali's Notes: "...the latest edition from this innovative New Zealand gear manufacturer... kids seem to love being in the low-rider back seat... narrow and nimble (particularly for navigating urban streets with 2!)...rugged enough for trails... my favorite mid-priced stroller with a real 2-kid solution..."

Rally Twin ★★★★☆

Maclaren (www.maclarenbaby.com 877.442.4622)
Price .... $250-$300
Weight.......................... 27 lbs
Seat .... side-by-side; 5-pt harness
Wheels .... 12x4.5"; plastic

Parent Reviews: "...smaller and lighter than the Twin Traveler... perfect for city cruising—subways, buses, zoo trips and traveling on an airplane... not the most durable over the long term if used as you only stroller... small wheels make steering tricky at times, but this stroller's size is a blessing when I'm on the move with my twins... hard to push on anything other than a completely smooth surface—especially with the extra weight of two kids... folds surprisingly compact and even has a carrying handle... seats recline (2 positions) separately and have separate sun shades... I wish the sunshades provided more coverage..."

Ali's Notes: "...Maclaren—despite their recent move to Chinese manufacturing—sets the standard for "best-of" umbrella strollers... a skinny version of their well-loved Twin Traveler, the very light, easy to use Rally Twin is better for travel than everyday use..."

Speedster Deuce

Kelty (www.kelty.com 866.349.7225)
Price .... $385-$400
Weight.......................... 29 lbs
Seat .. recline; side-by-side; 5-pt harn
Wheels .... 3x16"; air

Parent Reviews: "...a nice wide jogger for two... big wheels make running smooth, but turning a bit of a drag... comes with a lifetime warranty... a one-handed folding system which actually works... love the way it folds over on itself... comes with extras like water bottles and bottle holders... handle height can't be adjusted, but they are tilted so you can select your hand placement based on your height... seats don't recline... the canopy covers both kids, so although it provides decent coverage you can't adjust it individually... "

Ali's Notes: "...Kelty owns the best-of for streamlined joggers well-designed for long-distance running... long and lean, but double-wide isn't the recipe for easiest-to-use for anything but long-distance running...... "

Take Me Too!

Evenflo (www.evenflo.com 800.233.5921)
Price .... $100-$120
Weight.......................... 29 lbs
Seat ...... recline; in-line; 3-pt harness
Wheels .... 4x7 & 2x8" inch; plastic

Parent Reviews: "...it has a nice big basket and reclining seats... very versatile for two kids—I like the fact that you can use it for infants, infant seats and toddlers... both seats get a sun canopy and it has 'stadium' seating so even the back seat gets a view of the world... if you're using an infant seat in the back, the front seat can't really recline anymore... one of the least expensive double strollers I found... I wish it came with a cup holder for me—I definitely have to push it with two hands and don't know what to do with my drink... "

Tango

Zooper (www.zooperstrollers.com 503.248.9469)
Price .... $250-$290
Weight.......................... 30 lbs
Seat .. recline; side-by-side; 5-pt harn
Wheels .... 8x6"; plastic

Twin Savvy EX

★★★★☆

Combi (www.combi-intl.com 800.992.6624)
Price .... $280-$300   Seat .... side-by-side; 5-pt harness
Weight .... 21 lbs   Wheels .... 12x6"; plastic

Parent Reviews: **"**...*as close to a double umbrella stroller as you're going to get... fits through a standard doorway... easy mobility and turning radius... tiny wheels easily get caught on rocks or twigs... very light... a dream come true for people who are not built like Schwarzenegger... canopies retract independently... seats recline separately so my tots can take turns napping... the optional acoustic canopy is cool if your tot needs entertainment on the go... not enough cargo space for all our stuff... canopies don't rotate enough to block the sun at all angles... the lightest double out there...* **"**

Ali's Notes: **"***...Combi's umbrella strollers are light and portable...among the smallest footprint available for side-by-side options for multiples... economical, but not likely to withstand heavy daily use well...* **"**

Twin Swift

Inglesina (www.inglesina.us 877.486.5112)
Price .... $190-$200   Seat .... recline; side-by-side; 5-pt harness
Weight .... 28 lbs   Wheels .... 12x6"; plastic

Twin Traveller

★★★★★

Maclaren (www.maclarenbaby.com 877.442.4622)
Price .... $300-$350   Seat .... side-by-side; 5-pt harness
Weight .... 32 lbs   Wheels .... 12x6"; plastic

Parent Reviews: **"**...*very narrow for a double stroller—side by side seating, but still fits through most doorways... kind of like an umbrella stroller for two... surprisingly lightweight... I'm so impressed with how durable they make it... both seats have 5 independent recline positions... clever design that manages to be both big enough for my toddler and cozy enough for my infant... easy to steer as long as the road isn't too rough... no snack or toy bar... a life saver—I would never have gotten out of the house with my twins without this stroller...* **"**

Ali's Notes: **"***...Maclaren—even with their recent move to Chinese manufacturing—sets the standard for "best-of" umbrella strollers... the Twin Traveller's small wheels make for good maneuverability in tight spaces, but not for long distance pushing... the highlight of this stroller is that both seats have an independent, full recline with 5-settings... for a double-wide umbrella stroller it's quite maneuverable, comfortable and durable...* **"**

Urban Double

Mountain Buggy (www.mountainbuggyusa.com 866.524.8805)
Price .... $590-$635   Seat .... recline; side-by-side; 5-pt harness
Weight.......................... 35 lbs   Wheels............................ 4x12"; air

Parent Reviews: *"...a side-by-side all-terrain stroller with front wheels that can swivel or lock... a double stroller that's actually easy to turn... surprisingly versatile—just as good for beach walks as for shopping in the mall... solid and sturdy—built like a tank... seats recline independently, but only one canopy for both seats... a truly easy folding mechanism... it doesn't lock when folded, which makes it hard to carry... the wheels can get a bit squirrelly on trails with lots of rocks and roots... the canopy doesn't fold forward far enough to provide full-body sun protection..."*

Ali's Notes: *"...the popular choice winners—especially for the parent who wants an 'everything, multiple-kid solution'... roomy, easy to maneuver and durable... basic and rugged looking..."*

multi-use

indexes

by model/product

by manufacturer

by model/product

2 in 1 Hair and Body Wash 83
2-in-1 Smart Fold Swing 60
2.4 GHz Ultra-Range Monitor 182
3-In-1 Potty 'N Step Stool 222
4-Stage Feeding Seat 177
49 MHz Two Receiver Monitor...... 182
5-in-1 Adjustable Gym.................... 44
900 MHz BabyCall Monitor 183
900 MHz Long Range.................... 183
A Pea in the Pod........................... 154
A3 234
Acella Alumilite 235
Adjustable Back Latch-Loc Car
    Seat.. 101
Adjustable Fleece Pouch 120
Agabang... 67
All-in-One Reclining Booster Seat.. 178
Alpha Omega Elite 106
Ambassador Booster..................... 113
Amy Coe....................................... 190
Angelcare Movement Sensor with
    Sound Monitor....................... 183
Angled Tri-Flow Bottle System 207
Anita G 67
Aquarium Take-Along Swing 60
Aria235
Aria Twin 256
Avatar.. 107
Axiom Ditto 257
B500 Folding Booster Car Seat...... 113
Baby Bag...................................... 131
Baby Bag...................................... 132
Baby Barrier Cream 145
Baby Bee Buttermilk Lotion for
    Sensitive Skin 89
Baby Bee Diaper Ointment............ 146
Baby Bee Shampoo Bar.................. 84
Baby Carrier 121
Baby Carrier Active....................... 121
Baby Carrier Original 122
Baby Einstein................................. 54
Baby Gentle Foaming Hair & Body
    Wash 84
Baby Healing Ointment................. 146
Baby Lounger................................. 48
Baby Lulu 67
Baby Magic Calming Milk Bath 84
Baby Magic Gentle Hair & Body
    Wash 85
Baby Moose Foaming Wash........... 85
Baby Papasan Infant Seat............... 48
Baby Playzone Take-Along Hop
    'n Pop...................................... 55
Baby Shampoo............................... 85
Baby Shampoo & Body Wash.......... 86
Baby Sit & Step 2-in-1 Activity
    Center 55
Baby Sitter 178
Baby Sitter 1-2-3 49

Baby Sling 122
Baby Tooth And Gum Cleanser....... 95
Baby Vitamin Barrier Cream.......... 146
Baby Wash & Shampoo 86
Baby Wit 68
Baby's Dream............................... 195
Baby's Quiet Sounds Video Monitor184
BabyGap 68, 190
BabyGo Portable Playard 201
Babystyle 68, 154
Back Pack Diaper Bag 132
Bambino Diaper Bag..................... 132
Bebe Cold Cream 89
Bedtime Lotion............................... 90
Bellini... 195
Belly Basics.................................. 154
Bidwell 905.................................. 235
Bidwell Twin 257
Big Kid 114
Big Sipster Spill-Proof Cup 216
Blue Moon Baby........................... 191
Bobux.. 74
Bodyguard 114
Bon Bebe 68
Bonavita/Babi Italia 196
Boogie... 245
Boppy 5-in-1.................................. 45
Bouncin' Baby Play Place 55
Boxy Backpack 133
Brandee Danielle 191
Brazelton, T Berry......................... 164
Breastbottle Nurser 207
Breeze... 246
Brott, Armin................................. 160
Bum Bum Balm 147
Butt Paste 147
Caddy Table Seat 175
Caddy Umbrella 227
Cadeau Maternity 155
Calendula Baby Cream 147
Calming Shampoo & Bodywash...... 86
Camden....................................... 236
Cameleon 246
Camellia 133
CarGo.. 114
Carter's................................. 68, 191
Catimini... 68
Celebrations................................. 191
Child Craft/Legacy........................ 196
Children's Place, The 69
Children's Sun Screen..................... 93
Children's Tooth Gel 96
City Savvy 228
Classic Johnny Jump Up 58
Clean & Simple Spill-Proof Sports
    Bottle 216
CoCaLo 191
Cohen, Michel MD....................... 162
Colorado Tote.............................. 133

266   participate in our survey at

index: by model/product

Comfi Nursers	208
Comfort Care Gum & Toothbrush Set	96
Comfort Dimensions	236
Comfort First Tub	79
Comfort Sport	107
Companion Infant Seat	102
Connection Infant Seat	102
Cooshie Booster Seat	178
Cotton Sling	122
Cotton Tale	191
Cover N Play Bouncer	49
Cricket	115
Culla	236
Curtis, Glade et al	165
Daily Baby Lotion	90
Decathlon	107
Delta	196
Deluxe 4-in-1 Bath Station	79
Deluxe Activity Rocker	49
Deluxe Comfort Ride Umbrella	228
Deluxe Jumperoo	58
Deluxe Quick Response Swing with Remote Control	61
Deluxe Sport Utility Stroller	252
Designer 22 Infant Seat	103
Desitin Original	147
Devi Baby	69
Diaper Backpack	134
Diaper Bag	134, 134
Diaper Case Bag	135
Diaper Champ	150
Diaper Cream	148
Diaper Daypack	135
Diaper DayPouch	135
Diaper Dekor Plus Diaper Disposal System	151
Diaper Genie	151
Diaper Pail	151
Diaper Pail	152
Diaper Rash Cream	148
Diaper Rash Ointment	148
Diaper Rash Spray	148
Discover And Play Bouncer	50
Discover & Play Activity Gym	45
Discovery Infant Car Seat	103
Disposable Nurser	208
Do-It-All Diaper Bag	136
Domino Trio	257
Domino Twin	258
Dondolino	169
Doorway Jumpster	59
Double Layer Slings	123
Dove Soap	87
Drop & Pop Activity Gym	45
Duallie Sport Utility	258
ducduc	197
Duette	258
Duo Diaper Bag	136
DuoGlider	259
DuoRider	259
Dwell Baby	192
e3 Explorer	247, 260
Easy Chair	169
Easy Comfort Double Electric/Battery Breast Pump	212
Easy Comfort Manual Breast Pump	212
Easy Diner	175
Eczema Baby Cream	90
Eiger, Marvin et al	160
Eisenberg, Arlene et al	164, 164
Elefanten	74
Elite Sensitive Response Wide Nipple Nurser	208
Emi Carrier	123
Envision	170
ERGO Baby Carrier	123
Essentials Diaper Bag	136
Euro Bath Tub	80
EuroRider	124
ExerSaucer Delux	55
ExerSaucer Mega Active Learning Center	56
ExerSaucer SmartSteps	56
ExerSaucer SmartSteps Jump & Go	59
ExerSaucer Ultra Active Learning Center	56
ExerSaucer Walk Around	57
Expedition LX	253
Express Bottle & Babyfood Warmer	209
Express Electric Steam Sterilizer	209
Express Microwave Steam Sterilizer	209
EZ Strider Single	253
Facial Cleansing Cloths	90
Family Listen N Talk	184
Fast Table Chair	176
First Sipster Spill-Proof Cup	217
Flutterbye Dreams—Flutter & Chime Bouncer	50
Flutterbye Dreams Swing	61
Flyer	237
Foam Shampoo For Newborns	87
Fold-up Tub	80
Folding Potty Seat	222
Forever Mine	197
Fun Grips Soft Starter Spill-Proof Cup	217
GapMaternity	155
Garcia, Joseph	163
Gecko	247
Gentle Baby Lotion	91
Gerber	69
Glider	237
Global Buggy	228
Gotsch, Gwen et al	165
Grins & Giggles Baby Wash	87
Grow With Me Portable Booster Seat	179
Gymboree	69
Gymini 3-D Activity Gym	45
Gymni Super Deluxe Light And Music	46
H&M Mama	155
Hands-Free Breast Pump	213

www.lilaguide.com

Hanna Andersson	69
Harmony	170
Harmony Breast Pump	213
Harris, Christine	163
Hartstrings	70
Head-To-Toe	87
HealthTex	70
Healthy Care Deluxe High Chair	170
Healthy Care Highchair	171
HipHugger Baby Sling	124
Hisita Booster Chair	179
Hook On High Chair	176
Huggins, Kathleen et al	162
Husky	108
IKEA	197
IKEA Highchair	171
IMaternity	155
In Sight	184
Infant Bath Seat	80
Infant Carrier	124
Infant Rocker	50
Infant to Toddler Rocker	51
Infant to Toddler Tub	81
Insulator Spill-Proof Cup	217
Insulator Sport Straw Cup	218
Intera	108
Iovine, Vicki	160
Iovine, Vicki	161
Ironman Sport Utility	253
Isis Breast Pump	213
Jacadi	70
Janie And Jack	70
Japanese Weekend	155
Jasmine	137
Jazz248	
Juicy Couture	156
Kangaroo	125
Karp, Harvey	161
Keds	74
Kelly's Kids	70
Kick and Play Bouncer	51
KinderZeat	171
Komfort Kruiser	115
Lambs & Ivy	192
Land of Nod	192
Lands End	156, 192
Le Top	71
Learn & Groove Activity Station	57
Lena Diaper Bag	137
Link-a-doos Bouncer	51
Link-a-doos Magical Mobile Swing	61
Link-a-doos Musical Play Garden	46
Link-a-doos Open Top Take-Along Swing	61
LiteRider	238
Little Me	71
Little Miss Liberty Round Crib Company	197
Little Potty	223
Little Tripper Diaper Bag	137
Liz Lange	156

Magic Cup	218
Magic Moments Learning Seat	52
Mamma Double Tray	172
Marathon	109
Marsupial Diaper Bag	138
Medela	156
Messenger Bag	138
Messenger Diaper Bag	138
Messenger Diaper Bag	139
Metro Back Pack	139
Metrolite LE	238
Michael Stars Maternity	156
Micro Stroller	229
Million Dollar Baby/DaVinci	198
Mimi Maternity	156
Mini Messenger Bag	139
Mini Stroller	229
MobiCam Baby Monitor	185
Moby Wrap	125
Moisturizing Lotion	91
Morigeau-Lépine	198
Motherhood Maternity	156
Mothership	140
MultiFlow Bottle	209
My First Cup	218
Naissance On Melrose	157
Natart	198
Natural Anticavity Fluoride Toothpaste for Children	96
Natural Feeding Bottle	210
Nature's Touch Baby Papasan Cradle Swing	62
Naturino	74
Nava's Designs	192
Neat Diaper Disposal System	152
NettoCollection	198
Night & Day Bottle Warmer	210
NoJo	193
Nurseryworks	193
Nursing Wear	157
Nurturing Cream for Face and Body	91
Ocean Wonders Aquarium Bouncer	52
Ocean Wonders Aquarium Cradle Swing	62
Odorless Diaper Pail	152
Oeuf	198
OFFI & Co	199
Oilily	71
Old Navy	71, 157
Olian Maternity	157
On-The-Go Booster Seat	179
On-the-Go Fold-Up Booster Seat	179
On-the-Go Monitor	185
One Step Trainer Seat	223
Open Top Swing Deluxe	62
Original Babysling	125
OshKosh B'Gosh	71
P140 LP Aluminum Play Yard	201
Pack Baby Carrier	126
Pack N Play	202
Pack N Play Sport	202
Pali	199

index: by model/product

Pantley, Elizabeth	162
Parent Survival Pack	140
Payless Shoes	75
Peaceful Time Open Top Swing	63
Peanut Shell	126
Peas & Carrots Highchair	172
Pedipeds	75
Perfect Height Swing With Mini Maestro	63
Performance Series Single	254
Petit Bateau	72
Pine Creek	193
Platy Paws	75
Playnest & Activity Gym	46
Pliko P3 MT	238
Polly Highchair	172
Polo Ralph Lauren	72
PortAbout Infant Car Seat	103
Pottery Barn Kids	193
Potty Chair	223
Potty N Step Stool	224
Preemie-Yums	72
Premaxx New Edition Baby Sling	126
Premium Eazy Feed Nurser	210
Preschoolians	75
Prima Pappa Rocker	173
Primo Viaggio	104
Protek Belt Positioning Booster	115
Pump In Style Advanced Breastpump	214
Purely Yours Dual Electric Breast Pump	214
Q Single	254
Quattro Tour	239
Queen B	239
Quest	229
Rachel Ashwell	193
Ragazzi	199
Rally Twin	260
Reebok Velocity Extreme	254
Revolution	254
Rhumba	240
Roadster	116
Robeez	75
Rocker	52
Rocket Stroller	248
Roundabout	109
Runabout	249
S300 Formula Wheel Deluxe Stroller	240
Safe Glow 2 Receiver Monitor	185
Safety Duck Tub	81
Safety Seat	180
Savvy EX	230
Sears, William & Martha	158
Sears, William & Martha	159, 159
Shelov, Steven et al.	159
Shoo Shoos	75
Shoulder Bag	140
Shuttle	249
Silk Baby Throw	193
Simplicity	173
Single & Double Deluxe Breastpumps	214
Sit n Stroll 5-in-1 Travel System	110
Smart Stages 3-in-1 Rocker Swing	63
SmartSteps Discovery Highchair	173
Snap N Go	241
SnugRide	104
Soft Trainer Seat	224
SoftWash	88
Soho DX	230
Soho Sport	231
Soothing Massage Bouncer	53
Soothing Vapor Baby Bath	88
Sorelle	200
Sound Sleep	186
Sounds 'N Lights	186
Speedster Deluxe	255
Speedster Deuce	261
SPF 30 Sunscreen	94
Splash Barnacle Activity Playmat	47
Sport Utility Stroller	255
Standard Neck Bottle	211
Starriser Comfy	116
Stokke	200
Storkcraft Baby	200
Stride Rite Shoes	76
Sumersault	194
Summit High Back	116
Sun Busters All-In-One Swim Gear	94
Sunblock Lotion SPF50	94
Super Sensitive Shampoo & Bodywash	88
Sure Comfort Newborn-to-Toddler Tub	81
Svan Chair	174
Sweet Dreams Monitor	186
Sweet Potatoes	72
Swift	241
Swing	241
Swing Tray Portable Booster	180
Swyngomatic Infant Swing	63
Symphony	215
Take Me Too!	261
Take & Toss	219
Talbots	72
Tango	261
Teacollection	72
Techno Classic	231
Techno XT	231
Terrain Single	249
Titan	110
Toilet Trainer	224
Tooth and Gum Cleanser	97
Touriva	111
Towne	242
Travel Lite Bouncer	53
Travel Lite Swing	64
Travel Lite Table Chair	176
Travel Solutions Playard	202
Travelin' Tot 4-in-1 Activity Gym	203
Trend High Chair	174
Triple Compartment Diaper Pack	141

Triple Paste Medicated Ointment
   For Diaper Rash 149
Triumph 232
Triumph 5 111
TT Safari 250
Tub-to-Seat Bath Complete 81
Tubside Bath Seat 82
TurboBooster 117
Twin Savvy EX 262
Twin Swift 262
Twin Traveller 262
Twist 'n Shout Bumper Jumper 59
Tyro II Infant Car Seat 105
Ultimate Diaper Bag 141
Ultra EZ Baby Carrier 127
UltraClear 187
Umbrella Stroller 232
Un-Diaper Bag 141
Universal Car Seat Carrier 242
Unscented Moisture 92
Urban Double 263
Urban Single 250
Urban Sling 142
Vanguard 111
Vantage Point High Back Booster .. 117
Venezia 243
VentAire Bubble Free Bottle 211
Ventura High Back 117
VIA Nurser 211
Vision 118
Volo 233
Wallaby 127
Waltz 243
Weissbluth, Marc 161
Wendy Bellissimo 194
Wide Neck Bottle 211
Wizard 112
Wraparound Baby Carrier 127
Wry Baby 73
Xplory 244
Yaron, Ruth 163
Zutano 73
Zydeco 251

by manufacturer

A Pea in the Pod
A Pea in the Pod 154

Adiri
Breastbottle Nurser 207

Agabang
Agabang 67

Allo Baby
Infant Carrier 124

Ameda
Purely Yours Dual Electric Breast Pump 214

Amy Coe
Amy Coe 190

Amy Michelle
Camellia 133
Jasmine 137

Anita G
Anita G 67

Aquaphor
Baby Healing Ointment 146

Attachment Parenting Book, The
Sears, William & Martha 158

Aveeno
Baby Wash & Shampoo 86
Daily Baby Lotion 90
Diaper Rash Cream 148

Avent
Disposable Nurser 208
Express Bottle & Babyfood Warmer 209
Express Electric Steam Sterilizer ... 209
Express Microwave Steam Sterilizer 209
Isis Breast Pump 213
Magic Cup 218
Natural Feeding Bottle 210
VIA Nurser 211

Baby Bjorn
Baby Carrier Active 121
Baby Carrier Original 122
Baby Sitter 1-2-3 49
Diaper Backpack 134
Diaper Bag 134
Little Potty 223
Potty Chair 223
Toilet Trainer 224

Baby Book, The
Sears, William & Martha 159

Baby Einstein
Discover And Play Bouncer 50
Discover & Play Activity Gym 45

Baby Jogger
Performance Series Single 254
Q Single 254

Baby Lulu
Baby Lulu 67

Baby Smart
Cooshie Booster Seat 178

Baby Trend
Adjustable Back Latch-Loc Car Seat 101
Diaper Champ 150
Expedition LX 253
Reebok Velocity Extreme 254
Snap N Go 241
Trend High Chair 174

Baby Wit
Baby Wit 68

Baby's Dream
Baby's Dream 195

BabyGap
BabyGap 190, 68

Babystyle
Babystyle 154, 68
Un-Diaper Bag 141

Balmex
Diaper Rash Ointment 148

Bellini
Bellini 195

Belly Basics
Belly Basics 154

Bertini
Bidwell 905 235
Bidwell Twin 257
Shuttle 249

Blue Moon Baby
Blue Moon Baby 191

BOB Strollers
Deluxe Sport Utility Stroller 252
Duallie Sport Utility 258
Ironman Sport Utility 253
Revolution 254
Sport Utility Stroller 255

Bobux
Bobux... 74

Bon Bebe
Bon Bebe 68

Bonavita/Babi Italia
Bonavita/Babi Italia..................... 196

Boppy
Boppy 5-in-1 45

Boudreaux's
Butt Paste 147

Brandee Danielle
Brandee Danielle 191

Breast Feeding Book, The
Sears, William & Martha 159

Britax
Bodyguard 114
Companion Infant Seat 102
Decathlon 107
Husky 108
Marathon 109
Roadster 116
Roundabout 109
Starriser Comfy 116
Wizard 112

Bugaboo
Cameleon 246
Gecko 247

BumbleRide
Flyer 237
Queen B 239
Rocket Stroller 248

Bumbo
Baby Sitter 178

Burt's Bees
Baby Bee Buttermilk Lotion for Sensitive Skin 89
Baby Bee Diaper Ointment 146
Baby Bee Shampoo Bar 84

Cadeau Maternity
Cadeau Maternity 155

California Baby
Calming Shampoo & Bodywash.... 86
SPF 30 Sunscreen 94
Super Sensitive Shampoo & Bodywash 88

California Innovations
Mini Messenger Bag 139

Caring for Your Baby and Young Child: Birth to Age 5
Shelov, Steven et al 159

Carter's
Carter's 191, 68

Catimini
Catimini 68

Catini Bags
Colorado Tote 133

Celebrations
Celebrations 191

Cetaphil
Moisturizing Lotion 91

Chicco
Caddy Table Seat 175
Caddy Umbrella 227
Mamma Double Tray 172
Polly Highchair 172

Child Craft/Legacy
Child Craft/Legacy 196

Children's Place, The
Children's Place, The................... 69

CoCaLo
CoCaLo 191

Combi
Avatar 107
City Savvy 228
Connection Infant Seat 102
Deluxe Activity Rocker 49
Metro Back Pack 139
Savvy EX 230
Soho DX 230
Soho Sport 231
Travel Solutions Playard 202
Twin Savvy EX 262
Tyro II Infant Car Seat 105
Urban Sling 142

Compass
B500 Folding Booster Car Seat ... 113
P140 LP Aluminum Play Yard 201
S300 Formula Wheel Deluxe Stroller 240

Complete Book of Breastfeeding, The
Eiger, Marvin et al 160

Cosco
Alpha Omega Elite 106
Ambassador Booster 113
Deluxe Comfort Ride Umbrella ... 228
Protek Belt Positioning Booster ... 115
Summit High Back 116
Touriva 111
Umbrella Stroller 232
Ventura High Back 117

Cotton Tale
Cotton Tale 191

DaRiMi Kidz
Sun Busters All-In-One Swim Gear 94

Delta
Delta 196

Desitin
Desitin Original 147

Devi Baby
Devi Baby 69

Dobre Goods
Bambino Diaper Bag 132

Dove
Dove Soap 87

Dr Brown's
Standard Neck Bottle 211
Wide Neck Bottle 211

Dreamer Design
Axiom Ditto 257

ducduc
ducduc 197

Dwell Baby
Dwell Baby 192

Eagle Creek
Parent Survival Pack 140

Eddie Bauer
Diaper Case Bag 135
Diaper DayPouch 135

Elefanten
Elefanten 74

Ella Bags
Ultimate Diaper Bag 141

EllaRoo
Wraparound Baby Carrier 127

Erbaviva
Baby Shampoo 85
Children's Sun Screen 93
Diaper Cream 148

ERGO Baby Carrier
ERGO Baby Carrier 123

Evenflo
2-in-1 Smart Fold Swing 60
BabyGo Portable Playard 201
Big Kid 114
Classic Johnny Jump Up 58
Comfi Nursers 208
Comfort Dimensions 236
Comfort First Tub 79
Discovery Infant Car Seat 103
Elite Sensitive Response Wide Nipple Nurser 208
Envision 170
ExerSaucer Delux 55
ExerSaucer Mega Active Learning Center 56
ExerSaucer SmartSteps 56
ExerSaucer SmartSteps Jump & Go 59
ExerSaucer Ultra Active Learning Center 56
ExerSaucer Walk Around 57
Infant to Toddler Tub 81
PortAbout Infant Car Seat 103
Simplicity 173
SmartSteps Discovery Highchair .. 173
Take Me Too! 261
Titan 110
Triumph 5 111
Vanguard 111
Vision 118

Expectant Father, The
Brott, Armin 160

Expressiva
Nursing Wear 157

Fisher-Price
900 MHz Long Range 183
Aquarium Take-Along Swing 60
Baby Papasan Infant Seat 48
Baby Playzone Take-Along Hop 'n Pop 55
Cover N Play Bouncer 49
Deluxe Jumperoo 58
Deluxe Quick Response Swing with Remote Control 61
Flutterbye Dreams—Flutter & Chime Bouncer 50
Flutterbye Dreams Swing 61
Healthy Care Deluxe High Chair .. 170
Healthy Care Highchair 171
Infant to Toddler Rocker 51
Kick and Play Bouncer 51
Link-a-doos Bouncer 51
Link-a-doos Magical Mobile Swing 61
Link-a-doos Musical Play Garden .. 46
Link-a-doos Open Top Take-Along Swing 61
Nature's Touch Baby Papasan Cradle Swing 62
Ocean Wonders Aquarium Bouncer 52
Ocean Wonders Aquarium Cradle Swing 62
Peaceful Time Open Top Swing 63
Smart Stages 3-in-1 Rocker Swing 63
Soothing Massage Bouncer 53
Sounds 'N Lights 186
Sweet Dreams Monitor 186

Fleurville
Mothership 140

Forever Mine
Forever Mine 197

index: by manufacturer

www.lilaguide.com 273

Galt
Playnest & Activity Gym 46

GapMaternity
GapMaternity 155

Gentle Naturals
Eczema Baby Cream 90

Gerber
Baby Moose Foaming Wash 85
Fun Grips Soft Starter Spill-Proof
    Cup 217
Gerber 69
Grins & Giggles Baby Wash 87
Tooth and Gum Cleanser 97

Girlfriends' Guide to Pregnancy, The
Iovine, Vicki 160

Girlfriends' Guide to Toddlers, The
Iovine, Vicki 161

Goo-Ga
Peanut Shell 126

Graco
Baby Einstein 54
CarGo 114
Comfort Sport 107
Cricket 115
Doorway Jumpster 59
DuoGlider 259
DuoRider 259
Easy Chair 169
Family Listen N Talk 184
Glider 237
Harmony 170
LiteRider 238
Metrolite LE 238
Open Top Swing Deluxe 62
Pack N Play 202
Pack N Play Sport 202
Quattro Tour 239
SnugRide 104
Sound Sleep 186
Swyngomatic Infant Swing 63
Travel Lite Bouncer 53
Travel Lite Swing 64
Travel Lite Table Chair 176
TurboBooster 117
Twist 'n Shout Bumper Jumper 59
UltraClear 187

Gymboree
Gymboree 69

H&M Mama
H&M Mama 155

Haiku
Messenger Diaper Bag 138

Hanna Andersson
Hanna Andersson 69

Happiest Baby on the Block, The
Karp, Harvey 161

Hartstrings
Hartstrings 70

HealthTex
HealthTex 70

Healthy Sleep Habits, Happy Child
Weissbluth, Marc 161

HipHugger
HipHugger Baby Sling 124

Hisita
Hisita Booster Chair 179

Hoohobbers
Infant Rocker 50

IKEA
IKEA 197
IKEA Highchair 171

IMaternity
IMaternity 155

Infantino
EuroRider 124

Inglesina
Domino Trio 257
Domino Twin 258
Fast Table Chair 176
Swift 241
Twin Swift 262

InStep
EZ Strider Single 253
TT Safari 250

Jacadi
Jacadi 70

Janie And Jack
Janie And Jack 70

Japanese Weekend
Japanese Weekend 155

JJ Cole
Essentials Diaper Bag 136
Premaxx New Edition Baby Sling . 126

Johnson's
Bedtime Lotion 90
Head-To-Toe 87
SoftWash 88
Soothing Vapor Baby Bath 88

Juicy Couture
Juicy Couture 156

Jupiter
Komfort Kruiser 115

Kangaroo Korner
Adjustable Fleece Pouch 120

Keds
Keds 74

Kelly's Kids
Kelly's Kids 70

Kelty
Diaper Daypack 135
Kangaroo 125
Speedster Deluxe 255
Speedster Deuce 261
Wallaby 127

Kiehl's
Baby Gentle Foaming Hair & Body Wash 84
Nurturing Cream for Face and Body 91

Kolcraft
Baby Sit & Step 2-in-1 Activity Center 55
Perfect Height Swing With Mini Maestro 63
Travelin' Tot 4-in-1 Activity Gym . 203
Universal Car Seat Carrier 242

Kumi KooKoon
Silk Baby Throw 193

Lamaze
Drop & Pop Activity Gym 45

Lambs & Ivy
Lambs & Ivy 192

Land of Nod
Land of Nod 192

Land's End
Do-It-All Diaper Bag 136
Little Tripper Diaper Bag 137
Triple Compartment Diaper Pack 141

Lands End
Lands End 156, 192

Le Top
Le Top 71

LeapFrog
Learn & Groove Activity Station 57
Magic Moments Learning Seat 52

Little Forest
Baby Barrier Cream 145

Little Me
Little Me 71

Little Miss Liberty Round Crib Company
Little Miss Liberty Round Crib Company 197

Little Tykes
5-in-1 Adjustable Gym 44

Liz Lange
Liz Lange 156

Loom
Marsupial Diaper Bag 138

Lubriderm
Unscented Moisture 92

Maclaren
Global Buggy 228
Quest 229
Rally Twin 260
Rocker 52
Techno Classic 231
Techno XT 231
Triumph 232
Twin Traveller 262
Volo 233

Mamas & Papas
Splash Barnacle Activity Playmat ... 47

Mamma's Milk
Double Layer Slings 123

Maya Wrap
Baby Sling 122

Me Too!
Hook On High Chair 176

Medela
Harmony Breast Pump 213
Medela 156
Pump In Style Advanced Breastpump 214
Single & Double Deluxe Breastpumps 214
Symphony 215

Michael Stars Maternity
Michael Stars Maternity 156

Million Dollar Baby/DaVinci
Million Dollar Baby/DaVinci 198

Mimi Maternity
Mimi Maternity 156

Mobi Technologies
MobiCam Baby Monitor 185

Moby Wrap
Moby Wrap 125

Morigeau-Lépine
Morigeau-Lépine 198

index: by manufacturer

Motherhood Maternity
Motherhood Maternity 156

Mountain Buggy
Breeze 246
Terrain Single 249
Urban Double 263
Urban Single 250

Mum
Messenger Diaper Bag 139

Munchkin
Angled Tri-Flow Bottle System 207
My First Cup 218
Safety Duck Tub 81

Munchskins Skin Care
Bum Bum Balm 147

Mustela
2 in 1 Hair and Body Wash 83
Baby Vitamin Barrier Cream 146
Bebe Cold Cream 89
Facial Cleansing Cloths 90
Foam Shampoo For Newborns 87
Sunblock Lotion SPF50 94

Naissance On Melrose
Naissance On Melrose 157

Natart
Natart 198

Naturino
Naturino 74

Nava's Designs
Nava's Designs 192

NettoCollection
NettoCollection 198

New Basics, The
Cohen, Michel MD 162

New Native Baby
Baby Carrier 121

No-Cry Sleep Solution, The
Pantley, Elizabeth 162

NoJo
NoJo 193
Original Babysling 125

Nurseryworks
Nurseryworks 193

Nursing Mother's Companion, The (5th Ed)
Huggins, Kathleen et al 162

Oeuf
Baby Lounger 48
Oeuf 198

OFFI & Co
OFFI & Co 199

Oi Oi
Back Pack Diaper Bag 132
Messenger Bag 138

Oilily
Oilily 71

Old Navy
Old Navy 157, 71

Olian Maternity
Olian Maternity 157

One Step Ahead
Ultra EZ Baby Carrier 127

Orajel
Baby Tooth And Gum Cleanser 95

OshKosh B'Gosh
OshKosh B'Gosh 71

Pali
Pali 199

Payless Shoes
Payless Shoes 75

Pedipeds
Pedipeds 75

Peg Perego
A3 234
Aria 235
Aria Twin 256
Culla 236
Dondolino 169
Duette 258
Pliko P3 MT 238
Prima Pappa Rocker 173
Primo Viaggio 104
Venezia 243

Petit Bateau
Petit Bateau 72

Petunia Pickle Bottom
Boxy Backpack 133
Shoulder Bag 140

Phil & Ted's
e3 Explorer 247, 260

Pine Creek
Pine Creek 193

Platy Paws
Platy Paws 75

Playtex
Baby Magic Calming Milk Bath 84
Baby Magic Gentle Hair & Body Wash 85
Big Sipster Spill-Proof Cup 216
Diaper Genie 151

First Sipster Spill-Proof Cup.........217
Insulator Spill-Proof Cup.........217
Insulator Sport Straw Cup.........218
Premium Eazy Feed Nurser..........210
VentAire Bubble Free Bottle........211

Playtex Baby Magic
Gentle Baby Lotion......................91

Polo Ralph Lauren
Polo Ralph Lauren 72

Pottery Barn Kids
Pottery Barn Kids.......................193

Preemie-Yums
Preemie-Yums 72

Pregnancy Journal, The
Harris, Christine.........................163

Preschoolians
Preschoolians 75

Primo
Euro Bath Tub 80
Folding Potty Seat 222
Infant Bath Seat 80

Rachel Ashwell
Rachel Ashwell...........................193

Ragazzi
Ragazzi 199

RashMist
Diaper Rash Spray 148

Regal Lager
Diaper Dekor Plus Diaper
  Disposal System.....................151

Regalo
Easy Diner..................................175

Robeez
Robeez..75

Safety 1st
3-In-1 Potty 'N Step Stool 222
Acella Alumilite 235
All-in-One Reclining Booster
  Seat 178
Bouncin' Baby Play Place............55
Deluxe 4-in-1 Bath Station............79
Designer 22 Infant Seat 103
Diaper Pail.................................151
Fold-up Tub 80
Grow With Me Portable Booster
  Seat 179
In Sight 184
Intera 108
Neat Diaper Disposal System.......152
Odorless Diaper Pail...................152
On-the-Go Fold-Up Booster Seat. 179
On-the-Go Monitor 185
One Step Trainer Seat.................223

Potty N Step Stool 224
Safe Glow 2 Receiver Monitor 185
Tubside Bath Seat 82
Vantage Point High Back Booster 117

Sally Spicer
Baby Bag 131

Sherpani
Emi Carrier................................123
Lena Diaper Bag.........................137

Shoo Shoos
Shoo Shoos..................................75

Sign With Your Baby
Garcia, Joseph............................163

Silver Cross
Camden 236
Micro Stroller 229
Mini Stroller 229
Towne 242

Skip Hop
Duo Diaper Bag..........................136

Sony
900 MHz BabyCall Monitor 183

Sorelle
Sorelle 200

Stokke
KinderZeat 171
Stokke 200
Xplory.......................................244

Storkcraft Baby
Storkcraft Baby 200

Stride Rite Shoes
Stride Rite Shoes 76

Strolex
Sit n Stroll 5-in-1 Travel System... 110

Sumersault
Sumersault.................................194

Summer Infant
Baby's Quiet Sounds Video
  Monitor 184

Summers Lab
Triple Paste Medicated Ointment
  For Diaper Rash 149

Super Baby Food
Yaron, Ruth 163

Sutemi Gear
Pack Baby Carrier 126

Svan of Sweden
Svan Chair 174

Sweet Potatoes
Sweet Potatoes 72
Talbots
Talbots 72
Teacollection
Teacollection................................... 72
The First Years
2.4 GHz Ultra-Range Monitor 182
4-Stage Feeding Seat 177
49 MHz Two Receiver Monitor ... 182
Clean & Simple Spill-Proof
  Sports Bottle 216
Comfort Care Gum &
  Toothbrush Set 96
Easy Comfort Double
  Electric/Battery Breast Pump ... 212
Easy Comfort Manual Breast
  Pump.. 212
Night & Day Bottle Warmer 210
On-The-Go Booster Seat............. 179
Soft Trainer Seat 224
Sure Comfort Newborn-to-
  Toddler Tub 81
Swing Tray Portable Booster 180
Take & Toss 219
Tub-to-Seat Bath Complete 81
Tigex
MultiFlow Bottle.......................... 209
Timi & Leslie
Diaper Bag.................................. 134
Tiny Love
Gymini 3-D Activity Gym 45
Gymni Super Deluxe Light And
  Music... 46
Tom's Of Maine
Baby Shampoo & Body Wash 86
Natural Anticavity Fluoride
  Toothpaste for Children 96
Touchpoints: Guide to the First Six Years of Life
Brazelton, T Berry....................... 164
Unisar
Angelcare Movement Sensor
  with Sound Monitor 183

Valco Baby
Runabout 249
Vera Bradley
Baby Bag 132
VIPP
Diaper Pail 152
Weleda
Calendula Baby Cream............... 147
Children's Tooth Gel 96
Wendy Bellissimo
Wendy Bellissimo 194
What To Expect The First Year (2nd Ed)
Eisenberg, Arlene et al 164
Eisenberg, Arlene et al 164
Whisper Wear
Hands-Free Breast Pump 213
Womanly Art of Breastfeeding (7th Ed), The
Gotsch, Gwen et al.................... 165
Wry Baby
Wry Baby...................................... 73
Your Pregnancy Week by Week (5th Ed)
Curtis, Glade et al 165
Zolowear
Cotton Sling 122
Zooper
Boogie.. 245
Jazz.. 248
Peas & Carrots Highchair........... 172
Rhumba...................................... 240
Swing.. 241
Tango.. 261
Waltz 243
Zydeco 251
Zutano
Zutano 73

Notes

Your recommendations make the lilaguide better!
please share your notes with us at www.lilaguide.com

Notes

Your recommendations make the lilaguide better!
please share your notes with us at www.lilaguide.com

Notes

Your recommendations make the lilaguide better!
please share your notes with us at www.lilaguide.com

Notes

Your recommendations make the lilaguide better!
please share your notes with us at www.lilaguide.com

Notes

Your recommendations make the lilaguide better!
please share your notes with us at www.lilaguide.com

Notes

Your recommendations make the lilaguide better!
please share your notes with us at www.lilaguide.com

Notes

Your recommendations make the lilaguide better!
please share your notes with us at www.lilaguide.com

Notes

Your recommendations make the lilaguide better!
please share your notes with us at www.lilaguide.com

Notes

Your recommendations make the lilaguide better!
please share your notes with us at www.lilaguide.com

Notes

Your recommendations make the lilaguide better!
please share your notes with us at www.lilaguide.com